Test Your Money-Smarts

Warm up your parental reflexes with these 20 kids-and-money situations—common experiences, at least in principle, for most parents. Once you've identified your level of parental agility and authority, read on; you'll find plenty of Dr. Tightwad's strategies and ideas for teaching your kids the value of a dollar. Remember, raising money-smart kids starts with you.

1. Your 7-year-old daughter loses the $5 she got for her birthday from her Aunt Mary. You:
a. Ask Aunt Mary to send another $5
b. Tell your child she should have put the money in the bank
c. Let her do chores to make up the $5
d. Tell your child she should have been more careful ✔

2. Your 14-year-old son has been saving half of his allowance and money earned from neighborhood jobs. Now he wants to use the money to buy a $200 compact-disc player. You:
a. Allow him to buy it ✔
b. Offer him your old turntable instead
c. Tell him there's no way he can touch his savings
d. Buy it for him

3. Your daughter has mowed your lawn since she was 12. Now 14, she wants to make money by mowing neighbors' lawns. She also wants to be paid to do your lawn. You:
a. Say "Okay, and go ahead and use our mower and gas"
b. Hire a neighbor's kid to do your lawn
c. Tell her to forget it because mowing your lawn is her job
d. Say "Use our mower and pay for the gas you use. We'll pay you half of what you charge neighbors" ✔

4. You usually pay $40 for your son's sneakers. Now he wants a pair of $200 inflatable high-tops. You:
a. Chip in the $40, and let your child come up with the balance ✔
b. Say "I'll buy a $40 pair, or you can still wear your old ones"
c. Buy them, because "everyone else has them"
d. Buy yourself a pair, too (everyone else has them!)

5. Your 15-year-old daughter gets an allowance for which she is expected to help out around the house. She has ceased to help. You:
a. Hire a neighbor's kid to help clean the house
b. Stop the allowance altogether
c. Continue to pay until the child turns 18
d. Tie the amount and payment of the allowance more closely to chores accomplished ✔

Test Your Money-Smarts (cont'd.)

6. You're trying to teach your 16-year-old about the stock market. She invests her own money in a stock you selected. It loses money. You:

a. Make up the loss

b. Hire a neighbor's kid to make future stock picks

c. Say "That's how the market works. Too bad"

d. Share the loss with her, and help her figure out what to do with the remaining stock

7. Your son is getting his driver's license, which means that your insurance will go up. You:

a. Sell your car and buy bicycles for the entire family

b. Pay the increased premium—he is part of the family, after all

c. Make him pay the increase

d. Split the increase and make him pay for his own gas

8. You finally allow your daughter to shop for her own school clothes. She comes home with the ugliest clothes you ever saw. You:

a. Let her keep the clothes, but have a discussion about buying clothes that suit her and will last

b. Grin and bear it, because at least she likes the clothes—and bought them on sale!

c. Say "I knew I couldn't trust you with that much money"

d. Make her return the clothes—with you in tow

9. Your 10-year-old took on a paper route to earn money but is getting lazy. He's in danger of getting fired. You:

a. Hire the neighbor's kid to help him out

b. Tell him to do the job right or not at all

c. Pick up the slack by getting up early to help him deliver papers and collect fees

d. Warn him that he's likely to lose his job and income, and then allow him to do so

10. You're standing in a toy store and your son is insisting that he needs a $60 video game. You:

a. Fork over the cash to avoid a scene

b. Fork over the cash but tell him next time he'll have to pay part of the bill

c. Don't fork over the cash, and otherwise proceed as in step b

d. Proceed as in c, and suggest that he try the game over at the neighbor's to see if he really likes it before he buys it

11. After telling your children that they absolutely, positively cannot have Super Nintendo, their doting Auntie Mame arrives and presents them with one. You:
a. Tell Auntie Mame that the kids can't accept the gift
b. Grit your teeth and accept the gift
c. Sit down and start playing
d. Thank Auntie Mame for the gift, and at a later date, ask her to consult with you before purchasing expensive gifts for the kids

12. Your daughter receives a $20 birthday check in the mail from her grandparents. You:
a. Let her spend it as she wants—it's a gift
b. Deposit the check in the bank for your daughter
c. Tell your daughter to save $5 and let her spend the rest
d. Call Grandma and tell her $20 doesn't buy much nowadays

13. You bought your 16-year-old a car on the condition that he not leave the school grounds during lunch hour. He does, and totals the car. You:
a. Tell him to get his bicycle tuned up
b. Ground him for a month and limit him to using the family car at your discretion, provided he pays for his gas and part of the insurance bill
c. Buy him another car
d. You'd never be in this predicament, because you'd never buy a 16-year-old a car in the first place

14. Your son is on his way out the door for a date when he casually asks for $20. You:
a. Tell him you didn't know he had a date, and ask him where he thinks he's going anyway
b. Give it to him, plus an extra $10 for gas
c. Tell him that date and gas money come out of his allowance, as previously agreed
d. Give him $10 for gas

15. It's your preschooler's birthday, and he gets so many presents from family members that he quickly gets bored and toddles off to play. You:
a. Give the remaining gifts to the neighbor's kid
b. Put the gifts away to open another time
c. Proceed as in b, and determine that you will set up a college fund for your child and ask relatives for contributions in lieu of gifts
d. Open the rest of the presents yourself

Answer Key

Add up the point values of your answers to get a sense of where you stand.

1. a. 0, b. 1, c. 2, d. *3*
2. a. *3*, b. 0, c. 2, d. 1
3. a. 2, b. 0, c. 1, d. *3*
4. a. *3*, b. 2, c. 1, d. 0
5. a. 0, b. 2, c. 1, d. *3*
6. a. 1, b. 0, c. 3, d. *2*
7. a. 0, b. 1, c. 2, d. *3*
8. a. 3, b. *2*, c. 0, d. 1
9. a. 0, b. 2, c. 1, d. *3*
10. a. 0, b. 1, c. 2, d. *3*
11. a. 1, b. 2, c. 0, d. *3*
12. a. 3, b. 1, c. *2*, d. 0
13. a. 1, b. 2, c. 0, d. *3*
14. a. 0, b. 1, c. *3*, d. 2
15. a. 0, b. *2*, c. 3, d. 1
16. a. 0, b. 2, c. 1, d. *3*
17. a. 2, b. 1, c. 0, d. *3*
18. a. 0, b. 1, c. 2, d. *3*
19. a. *3*, b. 0, c. 1, d. 2
20. a. 0, b. *2*, c. 1, d. 3

Summary

0-10 *Either you should adopt the neighbor's kid or you just like taking tests.*

11-29 *Keep this up and your kids will still be living at home when they're 30.*

30-49 *You're on the right track, but you could use a consultation with Dr. Tightwad.*

50-60 *You and your kids are well on the way to being money-smart. Compare notes with Dr. Tightwad to learn how you can fine-tune your approach.*

Test Your Money-Smarts (cont'd.)

16. Your 17-year-old works three nights a week and weekends, and his grades have dropped significantly. You:
a. Hire the neighbor's kid to do the homework
b. Make him quit the job
c. Don't do anything; he's almost an adult, and his grades are his responsibility
d. Tell him to pull up the grades and consider cutting back on hours, or face quitting altogether ✓

17. Your 5-year-old wants everything in sight when you go to the supermarket. He begins to make a scene when you say no. You:
a. Wear ear plugs and let him scream his little lungs out
b. Leave him home from now on
c. Buy him what he wants
d. Let him choose one item ✓

18. Your son is heading for college in the fall and will need spending money. You:
a. Tell him that if he stays in his room and studies, he won't need spending money
b. Agree to send a weekly allowance
c. Tell him to get a summer job
d. Discuss his needs, see what he has available from jobs and savings, and agree to supplement that with an appropriate allowance ✓

19. Your 22-year-old son quit his first post-college job and has moved home "temporarily." You:
a. Agree on a combination of chores and a contribution to household expenses, and mutually set the date by which he will move out on his own
b. Tell him that he's an adult now and he has one week to get his act together and leave
c. Give up your home office so he can have his old bedroom back
d. Ask him to do some chores around the house

20. Your kids, 6 and 8 years old, ask you what would happen if you died: where would they live, who would take care of them? You:
a. Tell them you aren't going to die and there's no need to discuss it
b. Ask them if they would like to live with Uncle Eddie (as your will currently specifies)
c. Tell them that they would probably go to live with Uncle Eddie and his family (but you don't have a will and haven't discussed it with Uncle Eddie)
d. Proceed as in b, and take the opportunity to write a letter to Uncle Eddie outlining how you would like the kids raised in your absence

KIPLINGER'S
MONEY-SMART

KIDS

BY JANET BODNAR

KIPLINGER BOOKS, Washington, D.C.

KIPLINGER
BOOKS

Published by
The Kiplinger Washington Editors, Inc.
1729 H Street, N.W.
Washington, D.C. 20006

Library of Congress Cataloging-in-Publication Data

Bodnar, Janet, 1949-
Kiplinger's money-smart kids (and parents, too) / by Janet Bodnar.
— 1st ed., 1st print.
p. cm.
Includes index.
ISBN 0-938721-27-5 : $12.95
1. Children—Finance, Personal. 2. Saving and thrift. I. Title:
Money-Smart kids (and parents, too).
HG179.B567 1993
332.024—dc20

93-30251
CIP

This publication is intended to provide guidance in regard to the subject matter covered. It is sold with the understanding that the author and publisher are not herein engaged in rendering legal, accounting, tax or other professional services. If such services are required, professional assistance should be sought.

First edition, fourth printing. Revised March 1995. Printed in the United States of America.

Book designed by S. Laird Jenkins Corp.
Cover illustration by James Mitchell

Acknowledgements

"**F**amily values" has become a catch-phrase in the '90s, as parents of the baby boomlet grapple with all the problems inherent in rearing children—not the least of which is passing along to their kids a healthy attitude toward money and the ability to manage it. In this book, I've tried to make their lives easier by giving parents sound advice on how to accomplish that goal, and how to meet some of the financial challenges they face as parents. I've also tried to express some of the frustration and, yes, the humor, that goes along with teaching kids that they will not die if they don't get a chartreuse leather coat.

As a parent I'm indebted in that effort to my children, John, Claire and Peter, who provided both inspiration and information. Thanks, too, to all the other children and parents who contributed questions and answers; a special nod to the parents and children of St. Camillus School in Silver Spring, Md.

As a journalist I'm indebted to all the sources who shared their time and thoughts with me, and to the staff members of *Kiplinger's Personal Finance Magazine*, without whose research and expertise I never would have been able to meet my deadline: Knight Kiplinger and Ted Miller, Jane Clark, Kris Davis, Bill Giese, Nancy Henderson, Jeff Kosnett, Kevin McCormally, Dan Moreau, Susan Province, Ronnie Roha, Manny Schiffres and Melynda Wilcox.

Thanks also to Pat Mertz Esswein, the editor of this book, who did what all good editors do by taking the manuscript and making it better; David Harrison and Jennifer Robinson for their ideas and encouragement; Jenny Cliff O'Donnell and Karmela Lejarde, who meticulously double-checked the facts (and even had some fun testing games and software); and to copy editor Jennifer Lorenzo and proofreader Dianne Olsufka.

Most of all, thanks to my husband, John, who put up with the clacking of computer keys far into the night. Last but not least, my hat is off to Dr. Tightwad, the *real* champion of family values.

Janet Bodnar

MONEY-SMART

KIDS

Contents

CONTENTS

MONEY-SMART

KIDS

Introduction

By Knight A. Kiplinger
Editor in Chief
Kiplinger's Personal Finance Magazine

More than 45 years ago, the Kiplinger organization started the first magazine devoted to teaching Americans how to handle their money. Over the years since, many of our readers have shared with us stories of their experiences with money—their successes, foibles and valuable lessons they learned the hard way.

It became clear to us that the seeds of sensible —and irresponsible—money management are sown early in life. And it's hard to break bad habits embedded in childhood. That's why we're publishing this new guide for parents who want help in teaching their kids about money.

For better or worse, children learn by observing and imitating the people they care about, especially their parents. That's a scary thought for us parents, because it means our behavior is a stronger teacher than all our carefully chosen words of wisdom. This applies to everything in the family—the way we eat, spend our leisure time, treat each other. And it applies to handling money, too. If we are impulsive shoppers and haphazard savers, that's the model we're setting for our children. If we use money as a means of punishment or a substitute for emotional sustenance, our children are more likely to do the same when they grow up.

Decades ago, it was easier to raise children as responsible money managers than it is today. The linkage between work and earnings was tangible when families toiled together on farms, in small businesses at or near their homes, or in factories located in their neighborhoods. When young people worked for pay, they typically contributed most of their earnings to the family kitty, to help make ends meet. People bought on credit out of necessity, not to indulge themselves, and they saved for large purchases. In the days before television, especially sponsor-driven programs targeted at children and teens, kids might have coveted their neighbors' neat things, but the sphere of emulation was smaller—and less expensive.

My, how times have changed. Many of today's kids don't have a clear idea of just what their parents do for a living. Some seem to think the money coming out of the ATM is a gift from the bank, not a withdrawal of Mom's or Dad's earnings. There's been a major change in the motivation for teenage employment, too. Today many teens work after school or on weekends not to help support their family or save for college, but purely for their own discretionary purchases of entertainment, trendy clothes or a car. Ironically, most of them have more control over their earnings as teenagers than they will ever have as adults, when they will finally be responsible for boring obligations like food, shelter and insurance.

If you've sensed by now that many of the problems of youthful money handling are rooted in our culture of affluence, you're right. The challenge for *any* parent is to teach restraint and responsibility in a society that doesn't put much value on those traits.

This book can help. Janet Bodnar, senior editor of our magazine, has written a guide that is as warm and witty as it is wise and practical. Through all the discussion of allowances, shopping and after-school jobs, one theme keeps recurring—the importance of communication. Healthy families talk openly about *every* important subject. They include the kids in discussions and solicit their ideas, even if the parents make the final decision. This is the way kids learn to weigh alternatives and make the tough choices.

As parents of three children, ages 12, 10 and 8, my wife and I know firsthand how tricky this is. My best wishes to you, and may *your* children turn out to be the most "money-smart" kids on the block!

Knight Kiplinger

Washington, D.C.

Money Really Does Grow on Trees

Q. *Dear Dr. Tightwad: My children want to buy everything they see. Do they think money grows on trees?*

A. Actually, they think it pops out of bank machines.

A book about kids and money? That should be easy. After all, any parent knows that if you've got kids, you don't *have* any money.

That's all the more reason for giving kids a grasp of the subject before it slips through their fingers, and yours. But if you're like most parents, you've probably resorted at one time or another to flinging platitudes at your kids: "Don't you know the value of a dollar?" (Of course they don't.) "When I was your age, the tooth fairy only brought a dime." (For which, remember, you could buy two full-size candy bars, ten chewing-gum balls or a single-scoop ice cream cone, with three cents to spare.)

With all the other demands on your time, teaching your kids about money has all the allure of cleaning out the basement: You know you should do it, but you just never get around to it.

"Setting limits in this day and age is not only possible, it's necessary."

Dr. T. Berry Brazelton

And time isn't the only factor. Money is one of the last great taboos; nowadays, parents may find it easier to talk to their kids about sex and drugs than to tell them how much money they make. To complicate things even further, money matters can't always be reduced to a common cents discussion. Within a family, parents can wield money as a weapon, flaunt it as a symbol of power or use it as a stand-in for love. And looking at how you manage money can reveal things about your own personality that you'd rather not face. If you're an unreformed shopaholic, you may feel understandably ambivalent about urging your teens to stay within a clothing budget. And so, like the basement, you leave it for another day.

But kids, like time and tide, wait for no parent. What you don't teach them, their peers—and the media—will. And what an education it will be: that clothes make the woman and sneakers the man, that video games and MTV are their birthright, that credit cards will satisfy every need and gratify every wish. They will learn, in short, that money really does grow on trees.

Your Kids' Financial Reality

You can't blame kids for buying into that myth when they're buying so much else these days. Children between the ages of 4 and 12 have annual income of more than $14.4 billion, of which they spend around $8.8 billion and save almost $6 billion, according to James McNeal, marketing professor at Texas A&M University and an expert on children and their finances. Less than half of their income comes from allowances, 20% from working around the house and 16% from their parents as gifts. They get 10% of their money from work they do outside the home and 8% as gifts from relatives or friends.

The two-thirds of their income that is spent breaks down like this, according to the latest figures available:

- $2 billion on candy, soft drinks, frozen desserts, fruit and other snacks, such as chips and popcorn;

- $1.9 billion on toys, games and crafts;

- $700 million on clothing;

- $600 million on movies, spectator sports and live entertainment;

- $486 million on video-arcade games;

- $264 million on "other" expenditures: stereos and telephones, fragrances and cosmetics, cassettes and compact discs.

"Kids who have everything they want soon lose respect for money and for their parents."
Ann Landers

Parents are totally in charge of their kids' purchases only up to about age 3; after that, children are given choices—what kind of beverages to drink, ice cream to eat, toys to play with. At age 3, about two-thirds of the kids begin asking for things on their own, either because they've seen them in the store or on TV. From that point on, children are a recognized consumer force. By the age 4½ kids are selecting the things they want and watching their parents buy them (typically cereal, toys and snacks, in that order); by 5½ the kids are making the purchases (toys, snacks and gifts for others) and the parents are watching. By age 8 children make independent (unassisted) purchases while shopping with their parents.

For the most part, kids are doing all this consuming with their parents' blessing. Children are getting more money at a younger age than they did in the past, and letting them make purchase decisions is seen as a way of teaching them to be self-reliant. That's also a big help to frazzled moms and dads, many of whom are single parents or part of a dual-earner household. So it's not surprising that in addition to the money children spend directly, they have an enormous impact on what their parents buy. McNeal estimates that children between the ages of 4 and 12 influence adult purchases to the tune of $132 billion a year in 62 product categories—everything from canned pasta (60% of sales influenced by children) to bicycles (40%) and athletic shoes (20%).

Teenagers are spending an average of $62 a week of their own and their parents' money, according to

Electronic Youth

• •

A recent nationwide survey of 2,017 teens, ages 12 to 19, revealed that during a recent year:

- 14% bought a home stereo
- 13% bought a portable radio
- 11% bought a CD player
- 11% bought a small personal stereo with headphones
- 7% bought a home video game system
- 5% bought a portable CD player
- 5% bought a personal computer

Source: Teenage Research Unlimited, 1992

Teenage Research Unlimited in Northbrook, Ill.; that's $93 billion coming out of the pockets of 12- to 19-year-olds. Boys spend $42 of their own money and $22 in family money; for girls, the figures are $39 and $21. As they have for generations, teens are buying clothes, cosmetics, snack foods and movie tickets. What's different today is that they're spending more on electronic gear and other big-ticket items. In addition, slightly more than half of the girls, and a third of the boys do some grocery shopping every week to help out those frazzled moms and dads.

An Advertiser's Dream

That kind of buying power is simply too tantalizing for advertisers to ignore. Increasingly, they're bypassing parents and making their pitch directly to children. "Kids enjoy new things and they aren't set in their ways, so they're an ideal target," says Irma Zandl, who heads the Zandl Group, a New York City research firm that studies the youth market. If sneakers had been sold as an adult product, says Zandl, they never would have gotten to be a multi-billion-dollar business.

Besides the legendary Reebok Pump sport shoe, the list of products that owe their success to kids is long and varied: string cheese and individually wrapped cheese slices; Looney Tunes Meals and other frozen dinners for kids; Gap clothing stores; and My First Sony electronic products. After Jolly Rancher candy repositioned itself to appeal to the "tweens" market (kids around ages 9 to 12), it became a hit with an age group that craves its super-fruity flavor. Kids have helped make

Snickers the most popular candy bar on the market; they appreciate the combination of flavors and refer to Snickers as a "candy sandwich." Boys have a taste for chewy snack foods, such as Doritos. Girls have a nose for intense fragrances, such as Electric Youth. *Batman* and *Terminator II* owe their megahit status to repeat business from young viewers, some of whom saw *Dirty Dancing* eight or nine times.

While adults might be health- or price-conscious, that kind of appeal won't work with kids. Advertisers have to be careful not to offend parents, who are still, after all, the biggest spenders in the house and the ones who ultimately make most purchase decisions. But advertisers' main goal is to hit kids where they live: sports, music, an overwhelming desire to be cool and fit in. And they're getting through. As part of his research, McNeal asked a group of 112 second, third and fourth graders to "draw what comes to your mind when you think about going shopping." From their response, it was clear that to shop means to buy, not just to look; 82% of the children depicted themselves reaching for products. The children drew themselves buying 38 different categories of goods and named a specific brand in 20 of those 38 categories. All the food brands and 90% of the nonfood brands drawn by the children were also marketed to them. One third-grader misspelled the words *shirts* and *skirts,* but correctly spelled the brand name *Esprit,* including its distinctively designed open *E.*

Nike athletic shoes offer another "brilliant" example of marketing to teens, according to Zandl. Teenage boys are preoccupied with performance; when asked

PEANUTS reprinted by permission of UFS, Inc.

> *"Differences between the sexes as shown in market research aren't going to change. Sex differences are there from birth and it's absurd to think we can erase them."*
>
> Dr. T. Berry Brazelton

who they'd like to meet, they tend to cite people who are outstanding in their fields. So Nike used celebrity endorsers like Michael Jordan and stuck with them for years, to the extent that the company "totally meshed itself and the celebrity in the eyes of young consumers," says Zandl. So powerful was Nike's image as a performance shoe that many kids thought Reebok's Pump was made by Nike.

The Difference Between the Sexes

Boys like Nike, but girls like Keds. That illustrates another truism about advertising to kids: Sexism sells. When researchers at the Zandl Group conducted a study of how young people between the ages of 13 and 24 spend their money, they sent out thousands of questionnaires. In reading the anonymous responses, "you'd never for a minute confuse male and female," says Zandl.

Girls liked diet sodas and flavored seltzer water; boys liked root beer and Mountain Dew. Girls watched *Beverly Hills 90210*, boys watched *Cheers*. Boys used no-nonsense toiletries like Head & Shoulders, girls preferred the luxurious feel and fruity scent of Salon Selectives. Asked to name their favorite supermarket department, girls chose health and beauty aids, boys, frozen foods.

In another study by the Kaplan Educational Center, a national test-prepping company, high school girls picked *Seventeen* as their favorite magazine, while boys chose *Sports Illustrated*. If they had to choose, most boys said they'd rather be rich than smart, followed by athletic. Girls, on the other hand, choose to be smart, wealthy and pretty. So it's little wonder that boys respond to ads that are sports-oriented and aggressive; girls respond to ads that are, well, cute. One of their favorites was a carpet commercial featuring a baby zooming around in a walker. Despite the growing interest in sports among girls, "Cindy Crawford will be a more powerful spokesperson than Monica Seles," says Zandl.

Are Kids Savvy Shoppers?

If kids are tempted to consume conspicuously, indulging their wants as never before, advertising isn't totally to blame. As McNeal observes, advertisers may be pulling children but parents are pushing them simply by making so much money available. The real question is, how well equipped are kids to handle the pressure at both ends?

It would be possible to make the case that America's schoolchildren not only can't read, write and do their sums, but they can't count their change either. When Consumer Federation of America and American Express sponsored a nationwide test of the consumer knowledge of high school seniors, the students scored an average of just 42%. For example, only 18% knew that the annual percentage rate is the best indicator of the cost of a loan; 22% knew that ingredients on food labels are listed by weight, from most to least, and 18% that auto-insurance rates offered by different companies to people in the same area with similar driving histories can vary by 100% or more. A 1992 survey of high school students, college students and the general public by the National Council on Economic Education turned up big gaps in knowledge of the economy as well; 64% of those surveyed couldn't even define what a profit is.

Children themselves confess to sometimes being naive and even gullible shoppers. In *Zillions,* the consumer magazine for children, a group of kids recite their worst "buying blunders": Maggie plunked down

Zillions for Kids

• •

You can help your kids develop smart consumer habits early with a subscription to *Zillions: Consumer Reports for Kids.* A recent issue of this lively magazine, published by the consumer adviser whose name it bears, offered comparison-test results for hamburgers, milkshakes and bubblegum; gave advice on surviving a haircut and getting respect from store clerks; and featured an exposé of sneakers. *Zillions* should appeal to the late grade school and junior high crowd (six issues per year, $16; Subscription Dept., P.O. Box 51777, Boulder, CO 80321; 800-234-1645).

$20 for a board game that looked exciting in TV ads but turned out to be boring; Jonathan handed over big bucks for hightops that didn't help him improve his basketball game; Becky bought a shirt at one store and later saw it at another store for half the price; Theresa bought a cheap squirt gun that broke the first time she used it.

But let's look on the brighter side. Even adults were hard pressed to do well on the Consumers Union test; they scored an average of 16 points higher when they were asked similar questions. Only 37% of the grown-ups knew about annual percentage rates, 21% about auto insurance premiums and 36% about food labels.

The Good News

Look around the country and you'll see that where kids are given the incentive and opportunity to learn about money, they're catching on quickly:

- At Young Americans Bank in Denver, where all the customers are under age 22 and come from all 50 states, the average loan customer is 17 years old and has borrowed an average of $1,700 to buy anything from a car to hay for a herd of goats. In more than four years the bank only had to repossess two cars (and no goats). Kids may not understand APR, but somewhere along the line they've picked up the notion that it's a good idea to repay a loan. (For more on Young Americans Bank, see Chapter 6.)

Calvin and Hobbes © 1987 Watterson. Reprinted with permission of Universal Press Syndicate. All rights reserved.

- In a class on economics, fourth-graders in Wilmington, Del., rattle off terms like "market clearing price," "factors of production" and "opportunity costs" as they discuss marketing strategies for the new products they have cooked up: the "super-duper spaghetti scooper" and other gizmos for making it easier to eat spaghetti (see Chapter 9).

- In a discussion about money with a third-grade class in Silver Spring, Md., kids want to talk about collectibles, currency exchange rates and the Great Depression.

- Despite their reputation as yuppie puppies, schoolchildren around the country socked away $11 million in three years as part of Save for America, a reincarnation of the old school saving program (see Chapter 6).

James McNeal concedes that most college kids would be hard-pressed to figure out the unit price of a six-pack of beer. But his observation is that, overall, children "manage to spend and understand money and the marketplace system reasonably well." Even the kids in the *Zillions* article learned some valuable lessons: Maggie tries out a new board game at a friend's house before springing for it herself, Theresa took back her broken water pistol and got a refund, Becky looks around for bargains instead of buying something at the first place she stops and Jonathan is practicing harder.

A Game Plan for Parents

Parents, take heart. Even in this age of consuming passion you can still teach your kids to be savvy shoppers, super savers and cautious users of credit. You just need to find a successful strategy, and the time to use it.

Of course, what works for you won't necessarily work for your neighbor. Your family values and financial circumstances, as well as the personality traits of your children, may be quite different. But

"I think it's easier today to teach kids about money, because there are so many more opportunities for a child to earn and learn."
John Templeton, mutual fund pioneer

there is a common theme in how you should teach your kids about money: Be candid, be consistent and use your own good common sense.

The Lesser of Two Evils
• •

Q. *Dear Dr. Tightwad: We've always tried to be forthright in teaching our children that money doesn't grow on trees. But our strategy seems to have backfired, because our kids think we're poor and cheap. What should we do?*

A. Keep up the good work. Better for them to think you're poor and cheap than rich and extravagant. Discussing money matters with your kids can be tricky, and it's possible for them to get the wrong impression. But it sounds as if you're moving in the right direction, and it's important to keep on going. Explain to your children that watching where your money goes doesn't mean you're poor; it just means you have to parcel out your income to cover lots of different expenses. Shopping for the best price doesn't mean you're cheap, just that you want to make your money go as far as it can.

Your children could probably benefit from more hands-on experience in spending money. The next time you have to shop for their clothes, tell the kids in advance how much you have to spend. Then let them have a hand in choosing the items they want without busting the budget.

Beyond those general guidelines, this book can help you fill in the particulars. Within it you'll find suggested solutions to the problems that plague parents: how to cure a case of the gimmies, set up a workable allowance plan, cultivate the savings habit. And you'll see how you can do it with a minimum of time and effort—for example, by turning everyday encounters with cash machines into mini lessons on money management.

You'll also find guidance on how to help your kids cope with the economy at large by holding down a job or starting a business of their own. You'll hear from the people who study kids and money, as well as the real experts out there in the trenches—parents and kids themselves. You'll get answers to adult concerns about kids and money—where to find enough of it to pay for college, how to provide for your children if you die, how to launch your kids on their own and what to do if they boomerang back. As the aforementioned frazzled parents, you're likely to feel overwhelmed by the task of turning your children into financial whiz kids. But the job is a lot more manageable if you forget about raising a future Peter Lynch, Sam Walton or Bill Gates or setting up an elaborate allowance system. Instead, focus on *your* top priority, whether it's encouraging your kids to give to charity or standing firm on not buying what everyone else has. You're the parent; that's your job. You're in charge, and if you set the tone in even one area, it will echo throughout your child's life.

When you've finished, you probably still won't be able to resist trying out a few money cliches on your kids—only this time they'll know what you're talking about.

Careful, the Kids Are Watching

Q. *Dear Dr. Tightwad: When I was growing up, my parents didn't have much money and I knew I couldn't have everything I wanted. But nowadays there seems to be lots more money around and kids expect more. How can I raise my children with the right kind of values?*

A. Even today it needn't be as difficult as you think if you remember one timeless rule: What you say to your children isn't nearly as important as what you do.

When James McNeal of Texas A&M does his research on children and money, he limits his studies to kids between the ages of 6 and 12. That's because at 12, he says, children's behavior changes dramatically. A child who grew up drinking Pepsi, for example, will suddenly switch to Dr Pepper because that's what all his friends are drinking. McNeal finds that children do a good job of taking guidance from their parents until about age 10, then they start looking to their peers.

That means you have about ten years to develop money-wise kids who won't pick up the bad habits of their friends, both teenagers and adults, as they get older. Even if you never sit your kids at your knee and teach them the birds and bees of financial life, they'll get an education just by watching and listening to you.

Do you scold your spouse for spending too much money—and are you chided in return for being too stingy? Within your family, do you talk freely about money or are you secretive? Is money a lightning rod for emotional as well as financial tensions? As noted in the previous chapter, parents can wield money as a weapon, as in the case of the breadwinner with the higher salary who metes out the crumbs to other family members to keep everyone in line. They can flaunt it as a symbol of power—as do the Joneses with whom everyone is always trying to keep up. Or they can use it as a stand-in for love by substituting presents for their presence.

Your children's attitude toward money will be shaped by nature—what they inherit from you—and nurture—what they pick up along the way. Despite the heavy influence of their peers, it's likely they'll end up the spitting image of you. So before you try to mold them, have a go at picturing yourself as they see you.

Despite the heavy influence of their peers, it's likely your kids will end up the spitting image of you.

The Apple Doesn't Fall Far From the Tree

Olivia Mellan is a Washington, D.C., psychotherapist who specializes in trying to resolve money conflicts. On one occasion when she was featured on a radio talk show, Mellan received a call from a man who recounted an experience from his youth. When he was a boy, he worked for his mother in the family restaurant. She always worried about being on the edge of bankruptcy, and he developed a nervous stammer as a result. When he became an adult, his mother began reminiscing once about the good old days, when the son was young and they had made a lot of money in the business. That came as a shock to the son, who started screaming at his mother—and lost his stammer. "It was instant catharsis, every therapist's dream," says Mellan.

Kids & Money

Parents who grew up during the Great Depression spent a lifetime trying to teach a new generation of children what it was like to have to save coffee grounds. Wealthy families with mixed feelings about their money often overemphasize the virtue of not having any. The self-made man, on the other hand, sometimes insists that his children follow his example. Because circumstances can't be duplicated, expectations like those are unrealistic. Yet they had their effect on you, even if it was precisely the opposite of what your parents intended. Take the case of the woman whose father worried constantly about money and made her account for every penny of her allowance. She promised herself never to take money that seriously or to let her financial affairs be controlled by someone else. As a result, she turned into a spendthrift who bristled when her husband so much as tried to balance their joint checking account.

You're likely to return to your roots eventually, however, even if you feel inclined to play the prodigal in between. A more typical example is the woman who never received an allowance as a child, relying instead on her parents to give her money when she needed it. Further, her parents didn't want her to earn money of her own until she was graduated from high school; they felt that she had time enough as an adult to join the working world. A sure prescription for a spoiled brat? On the contrary. One reason she didn't get an allowance was that her parents didn't make a lot of money, and that remains her most vivid image. Even though she didn't have an outside job, she was responsible for doing much of the housework while her mother worked to supplement the family's income. Now a middle-aged professional, she's better off than her parents were and can afford to spend more freely. But she's also cautious in her buying habits and has built a savings cushion. "By not giving me an allowance or making me work, they probably broke all the rules about teaching me money management, but it was the atmosphere that counted most," she says.

Gender Differences in Managing Money

Whether by nature or nurture, your sex is likely to have an influence on your attitudes toward money. It starts slowly but shows itself early. Among children between the ages of 4 and 12, McNeal's studies show, girls have lower weekly income than boys ($7.66 vs. $8.87), mainly because they get lower allowances. They also spend less than boys (around $4.10 vs. $5.50) and save more (43% of their income vs. 38%), even though they're in stores more often.

On the whole, though, McNeal doesn't find significant differences in the consumer behavior of young girls and boys. "There's a kid culture before there's a gender culture or even a national culture," he says. It's a culture that values play above all else, and the more outrageous the plaything the better. Parents might be attracted to toy kitchens or cars—scaled-down versions of adult products—but kids are enamored of green slime and talking teenage turtles, which have no counterpart in the adult world.

In adolescence, however, boys and girls show definite, and traditional, preferences in the things they buy (see Chapter 1). Irma Zandl of the Zandl Group, which researches the youth market, thinks human nature makes them favor what they do just as it accounts for other differences. "If you ask kids between 13 and 15 about their favorite times in history, over 30% of the boys list periods of war. Girls just don't do that," says Zandl. But culture, and peer pressure, may have something to do with it as well. If girls have a natural inclination to wear tight jeans and paint their faces, TV and print images of Cindy Crawford certainly encourage it.

By the time they're young adults, both sexes are showing more fundamental differences in their attitudes. In a study of upper-level college students, most of them in their twenties, Charlotte Churaman of the University of Maryland found that women are more

There's a kid culture before there's a gender culture or even a national culture. It values play above all else, and the more outrageous the plaything the better.

likely than men to believe that getting rich isn't a realistic investment goal. They're also more likely to consider investing in stocks too big a gamble, to be unwilling to go for broke and to seek help with their finances.

Men are more likely to read financial journals, believe they have adequate financial resources and prefer selecting their own investments. They also have more confidence in their knowledge about money and their ability to manage it.

Even after marriage, differences persist. A nationwide survey of 2,000 people by Oppenheimer Management Corp. showed that while women play a leading role in day-to-day management of household finances, they're less involved with longer-term financial planning issues such as taxes, insurance or investments, and their knowledge of investments is low relative to that of men. For example, 62% of women said they don't understand how a mutual fund works, compared with 50% of men.

Because formal school training in financial affairs was sketchy, the role models for most of today's adult women were their own mothers, who tended not to get involved in financial matters, observes Oppenheimer president Bridget Macaskill. She doesn't see much change in domestic roles today. Says Macaskill, "Women do the shopping, arrange for the sitter and are constantly trying to get through a huge list of jobs. So when the man says, 'I'll do the tax return,' you say, 'Good, that's one less thing I have to worry about.'"

Calvin and Hobbes © 1989 Watterson. Reprinted with permission of Universal Press Syndicate. All rights reserved.

There's evidence that things are changing. Maryland's Churaman says differences between the sexes have been narrowing as more women make business decisions in jobs outside the home. In Churaman's study, there was some common ground. Men and women were similar, for example, in their priorities: "Being in control" and "knowing where I stand" ranked first, followed by "working for an improved standard of living" and "saving regularly." In the Oppenheimer study, 88% of women would be confident of their ability to invest a $10,000 windfall and 89% of the married men were confident of their wives' ability to invest $10,000.

Still, family squabbles about money are all but guaranteed. Disputes about money (along with sex and children) are among the leading causes of divorce in the U.S.

Disputes about money (along with sex and children) are among the leading causes of divorce in the U.S.

Your Money Profile

Overshadowing even your sex in determining your attitude toward money is your basic money personality. See if you recognize yourself in the following portraits.

- **The Accountant.** You keep your checkbook balanced, and one of your greatest thrills is watching your savings account grow. You blanch when your spouse spends impulsively on a piece of furniture or a set of golf clubs. You're a downer to live with, but you'll never be broke. For you, money means security.

- **The Social Worker.** You regard money as filthy lucre, and the quicker you wash your hands of it the better. You are, however, willing to spend it on the people, and causes, you love. You're the one who gets suckered into hosting the family dinner every Thanksgiving, and you probably have a "Save the Whales" bumper sticker on your car. For you, money means affection.

Show me a couple that doesn't fight about money, goes the old one-liner, and I'll show you a couple on the way to their wedding.

• **The CEO.** You own a BMW and a Mercedes, live in a house you can't afford and are planning to remodel the kitchen with your next bonus. When your kids bring home a good report card, you write them a check. Your motto is, the one with the most toys wins. For you, money means success.

• **The Entertainer.** Every Friday afternoon you have a couple of drinks with the gang from the office and you pick up the tab. Every Saturday night you go out to dinner with the neighbors and you pick up the tab. You never balance your checkbook and can't be bothered saving receipts. You drive your accountant spouse crazy but your neighbors and co-workers love you. For you, money means esteem.

You can probably place yourself and your spouse in one of these four broad categories but not necessarily in the same one. Show me a couple that doesn't fight about money, goes the old one-liner, and I'll show you a couple on the way to their wedding. Olivia Mellan further breaks down money personalities into eight types that are polar opposites:

• **Hoarders,** who find it difficult to spend money, versus *spenders,* who can't seem to hang on to it. A subspecies is the *binger,* a combination of hoarder and spender who saves up pennies only to blow them all at once.

• **Money monks,** who feel anxious when they have too much money, versus *money-amassers,* who feel anxious when they don't have enough.

• **Money-worriers,** who balance their checkbook over and over and finish their taxes in January, versus *money-avoiders,* who ignore the checkbook and can usually be found licking the stamp on April 14.

• **Risk-takers,** who relish gambling on the stock market and even more exotic investments, versus *risk-*

avoiders, who are reluctant to venture forth from the security of bank certificates of deposit.

Even if you and your spouse are similar, one of you will tend to take on the role of foil. In a family of hoarders, for example, someone has to spring for living-room furniture and clothes for the kids. If you're both spendthrifts, one of you will feel the need to play guardian of the checkbook. Either way, some conflict is certain, and your children are bound to pick up on it. In extreme cases, children may take the side of the preferred parent, choose the position that will win them the most affection or simply leave the field altogether and refuse to have anything to do with money.

Kenneth Doyle, a financial psychologist at the University of Minnesota who deals with such problems, recalls a poignant personal experience. After he and his wife divorced, he took his then-10-year-old daughter to a fair. While they were strolling through the booths, she suddenly realized that she had forgotten to bring her own money to spend—and worried that her father didn't have any. "She had picked up my stress and was hoarding her cash to take care of dad," says Doyle. "So we worked on convincing her that I was all right, and that she should keep her money and learn to spend and enjoy it."

Ways to Meet Each Other Halfway

None of the money personalities described above is necessarily bad; all have their good points. In fact, your spendthrift spouse probably secretly admires your self-discipline. What you need to do is keep from getting too far out of balance. The key to resolving potentially tense situations is to know what makes your spouse crazy and resolve to, if not completely change your ways, at least meet your partner halfway.

In her guide *Ten Days to Money Harmony,* Mellan recommends a series of weekly exercises in role rever-

Even if you and your spouse are similar, one of you will tend to take on the role of foil.

The spender isn't necessarily the one who is at fault here. Sometimes the sober half of this duo is simply afraid to part with money.

sal, or practicing behavior that's out of character for you. For example, in the case of a money monk married to a money-amasser, the monk should try splurging on something that he or she would otherwise consider selfish or decadent, while the amasser sets aside a day on which he or she doesn't spend, save, invest or deal with money at all. They write down their feelings and reactions, give themselves a reward, and continue the exercise for several weeks—long enough, ideally, for it to make a permanent difference in their behavior or for them to at least appreciate one another's position.

Does This Sound Familiar?

Here's a look at some other key flashpoints guaranteed to ignite financial fireworks in a marriage, with suggestions on how to defuse them.

He: *"You're always spending money we don't have."*
She: *"You're so tightfisted we never have any fun."*

Try shock therapy. Present the spendthrift with your paychecks and your bills and let him or her do the budget. For cases in which spending has gotten seriously out of control, you may have to consult an organization such as Consumer Credit Counseling or Debtors Anonymous (see the accompanying box), or seek professional help.

Remember, though, that the spender isn't necessarily the one who is at fault here. Sometimes the sober half of this duo is simply afraid to part with money. When that's the case, it might help to lay out your financial goals—retirement, children's education, a major vacation—to see whether you're on track toward achieving them. Once you see where you stand in dollars and cents, one spouse may be convinced that you need to spend less or the other might feel more comfortable about spending more.

This kind of exercise can be invaluable for kids, too. One reason they seem to think money grows on trees is that they have no experience in setting goals and making choices. They don't understand why they can't have everything they want when they want it. It helps them to hear that you're holding off on buying the new car because the house needs painting or forgoing dinners out to help pay for your vacation at the beach.

"It's important for them to hook into your chain of logic," says Kathleen Hoover-Dempsey, an associate dean at Vanderbilt University. Hoover-Dempsey recalls the day her 12-year-old son announced that he wanted to play lacrosse and presented her with a list of equipment adding up to more than $200. She told him she didn't think lacrosse was in the cards, and she told him why: He had never played before, and it seemed like a lot of money to spend on something he wasn't sure he'd stick with. He ended up agreeing. "It was important for him to hear me say what I was thinking and not just, 'we can't afford it,'" says Hoover-Dempsey.

She: *"Our money's just sitting in the bank. We ought to invest."*

He: "Yeah? You want to end up like Charlie, who lost his shirt in the market?"

Help With Debt

If you need help coping with spending and debt, one of the following organizations may help:

- **Bankcard Holders of America** (524 Branch Drive, Salem, VA 24153; 703-389-5449) is dedicated to consumer credit education and advocacy. It provides a credit and financial referral service and information about low-interest, no-annual fee and secured credit cards. For a list of BHA's publications, write the address above.

- **Consumer Credit Counseling Service** (National Foundation for Consumer Credit, 8611 Second Ave., Suite 100, Silver Spring, MD 20910; 301-589-5600) provides free or low-cost, professional financial guidance and counseling to consumers at more than 850 offices nationwide. To locate the CCCS office in your area call 800-388-2227 or the telephone number above.

- **Debtors Anonymous** (General Service Board, Inc., Box 400, Grand Central Station, New York, NY 10163-0400; 212-642-8220) has a 12-step program for those struggling with overspending or debt.

The ticklish problem of different tolerances for risk can be easily resolved if you both realize you don't have to commit to all or nothing. If one of you must take risks, do it with 10% of your assets instead of the whole nut. If you're reluctant to move beyond the safety of a bank, take it one step at a time by investing in a relatively safe utility stock or blue-chip company instead of an aggressive-growth mutual fund. If you each have your own IRA or 401(k) tax-favored retirement plan, each of you can decide how to invest the money.

If you still can't reach an amicable agreement, you might seek help from a neutral third party, such as a financial planner, who can recommend investments and act as a buffer to absorb some of the worry (and the blame).

He: *"How can I balance the checkbook when you can't even hold on to an ATM receipt?"*
She: *"I've got more important things to think about."*

Whip the disorganized spouse into shape by starting small: Get him or her at least to toss receipts into a shoebox. Move on to assigning specific tasks—who's going to balance the checkbook, who's going to monitor credit card charges so you don't use up your credit line. Set aside one day a month to talk about family finances. Then switch bill-paying responsibilities every six months.

If all else fails (and it just might), be prepared to go it alone. One couple settled their squabbling when the wife officially hired her husband to be her bookkeeper. Now that they've made it a business arrangement, she takes their finances more seriously and he's less resentful.

If you're the one who's stuck with keeping the books and the very word budget sets your teeth on edge, make it easy on yourself. As long as you're meeting your savings goal, you probably don't need to fiddle with a budget at all. If you aren't, you don't have to keep track of every nickel and dime. Instead, make a guess about what your expenditures are and then compare your estimates with the bills as they come in. That will show you where your spending is out of line and you can focus only on those areas where you want to cut back.

She: *"Your kids are already costing us a bundle in child support. Why do you have to spend so much on them when they come to visit?"*
He: *"They're my kids, and I'll spend as much as I want."*

Court-ordered child support is one thing, but what often rankles a new spouse is unanticipated demands on the noncustodial parent's pocketbook. One solution is to set aside a certain amount for extra child-related expenses. But money may not always be the problem. The new spouse may simply want reassurance that he or she is top priority, and you may get better results by expending a little extra time and attention rather than cash.

Kids and money are often at the center of other prickly problems involving divorce and remarriage. "Whatever money means to you and your spouse will be magnified if you go through a divorce," says Doyle. (For a more extensive discussion of some of the problems and solutions, see Chapter 11).

He: *"You spent $120 on a pair of sneakers for Johnny? You're spoiling those kids rotten."*
She: *"I'm only buying them what the other kids have. Besides, we can afford it."*

It's the sociological phenomenon of our time: Love equals stuff. The more stuff our kids have, the more we must love them—and the better parents we must be. It's exacerbated by parental guilt about not being around more and by the very natural desire for our kids to fit in.

The solution is both breathtakingly simple and excruciatingly difficult: Just say no. Your kids will still love you in spite of your refusal to gratify their every wish (or perhaps because of it). Someone has to be the adult in the house and it might as well be you. It

"If you worry that your child doesn't have as much stuff as other kids in the neighborhood, the problem isn't your child, it's you."
Ann Landers

doesn't pay to say no all the time, but choose the battles that are important to you and fight them to the end.

Take the case of those $120 sneakers. If you think they're an outrageous purchase, put your foot down. Tell your son they don't fit into your budget. If you're inclined to compromise, tell him how much your budget does allow for sneakers and let him make up the difference. With his own cash on the line, he may think twice about buying those shoes—if not right away, then perhaps six months down the road, when he has outgrown the shoes and he's $60 poorer. You can only hope.

Use the same strategy even when you can afford the shoes and it's the principle, not the cash, that is at stake. Never lie to your children and tell them you can't afford something when you can. Be honest and tell them why you don't choose to buy it or why you'd prefer to spend your money on something else.

Dr. David Lustig, a child psychologist in Florida and co-author (with Dr. Marvin Silverman) of *Parent Survival Training* (Wilshire Book Co.), tells about watching one couple argue with their 12-year-old, who had saved up for a pair of expensive sneakers. The bone of contention was whether he would wear them all the time. The parents wanted him to wear the shoes to school but not for play, so they'd last six months instead of two. The child refused, saying he wouldn't be caught dead in anything else. "The kid was obsessed with brand labels, and the parents needed to take a stand," says Lustig. So the parents flatly refused to buy the shoes at all.

Calvin and Hobbes © 1987 Watterson. Reprinted with permission of Universal Press Syndicate. All rights reserved.

At the other extreme were the well-to-do parents who had given their teenage son a car, with the understanding that he not use it to leave school at lunch time. Sure enough, the son flouted the rule and smashed up the car to boot. His father's response was to buy him another one. That father, says Lustig, taught his son a lesson that would "damage his perception of money for the rest of his life."

She: *"Every time I tell the kids they can't have something, they go to you, and you say they can. You're undercutting my authority."*

He: "Ease up; you're too uptight."

Sounds like a classic confrontation between an *accountant* and an *entertainer*. If spending money is part of your spouse's personality, it would be counterproductive to accuse him or her of being a bad parent. Instead try a positive approach. In private, tell your spouse that the two of you need to work as a team and be consistent in your behavior so the kids don't play one of you against the other. Failing that, explain to your children that you have your way and dad has his, and both are okay. "I have a streak in me that likes flash," says Doyle. "I tell my daughter that people use money in different ways. I like to be impulsive, and her mom is more careful."

To Tell or Not to Tell

Q. *Dear Dr. Tightwad: Lately my 10-year-old daughter has been asking questions about how much money we make. I've always tried to be honest with her, but....*

A. Then don't tell her. Being honest doesn't have to mean telling all, especially when your daughter probably won't be able to process the information anyway. Whether you make $30,000 or $130,000, it will sound like big bucks to her—certainly big enough to buy that doll or video game or bicycle.

But don't avoid the issue. Your daughter is old enough to hear an honest appraisal of your family's finances if not the numbers themselves. If you're on a tight budget, she'll understand why she isn't going to get the new bicycle. If you're comfortably well off but choose not to buy certain items, she'll get a lesson in family values. If you're like most people, cutting back on dinners out to pay for the summer vacation, say, she'll get a glimpse into real life. Later, when she's in high school, you can use your own circumstances to teach her about balancing checkbooks and paying bills. But don't feel obliged to share every detail.

The kids will still tend to go to the spouse who's easier, but at least everyone will know what's going on and the two of you can stop fighting about it and maybe meet each other halfway.

Mistakes to Avoid

You probably won't be able to change your attitude toward money. The ideal is to reach a happy medium, or at least be aware of and honest about your shortcomings. If you have a tendency to pinch pennies, let your kids in on the secret and tell them why you consider it a good—or bad—trait. If you're a shopaholic, tell them you're not the world's greatest authority on budgeting. They'll appreciate your candor and learn from your experience. Recall the anecdote at the beginning of this chapter about the man who, as a boy, developed a nervous stammer because of his mother's persistent (but apparently groundless) worries about being on the brink of financial disaster. "She could simply have told her son, 'I'm a worrier but we're doing fine,'" says Olivia Mellan. "That would have been much healthier."

In talking to your kids about money, follow these other golden rules:

Don't Duck the Issue

Whether they're pressed for time or just reluctant to bring it up, parents often give the subject short shrift. But children do think about money and sometimes get some cockeyed notions about it. One woman recalls that when she was in elementary school she wanted more than anything to take an after-school class in horseback riding, which cost $80 at the time. Her middle-class parents could probably have afforded the lessons, but she didn't dare ask for them. "It sounded to me like $80 would plunge the family into poverty...like it was the end of the world," she recalls.

Another woman recalls that when she was in the second grade she was "overwhelmed by the abundance of crayons, stars, paper and pencils in my teacher's supply cabinet. I couldn't imagine that my parents could ever afford to buy me those kinds of things, so I stole a bunch." Her parents, of course, made her return them and 'fess up.

You don't necessarily have to tell your children how much money you make. In fact, you probably shouldn't, at least until they're in high school. Younger kids have no context for a number as large as $30,000 or $50,000 or $100,000. It will only make you seem as rich as Croesus— or even Donald Trump. And you can probably think of a few other perfectly valid reasons for not being too frank. Money has traditionally been a private matter, and you may be understandably leery of having your kids broadcast your salary to the whole neighborhood. Or you may simply feel that kids are too young to be burdened with adult concerns about money.

But you still need to be honest and reassuring when your kids raise the issue. "Kids need to know they won't be destitute," says Harold Moe, who has chronicled his experiences with his own children in *Teach Your Child the Value of Money*

Handling Bad News

Q. *Dear Dr. Tightwad: My company is laying off workers and I expect to get a pink slip. We'll have to cut back on spending, but I'm afraid my kids won't understand. How much should I tell them?*

A. Enough to be straight with them but not so much that you burden them with problems they can't handle. They're almost certain to know that something is up. Even if you say nothing, you're bound to be more worried or tense, and they'll pick up on your cues. Better to be honest than to have them imagine things are worse than they are.

Besides, kids are surprisingly adaptable to economic circumstances. A recent survey by the American Board of Family Practice showed that, to help their families through a financial crunch, a healthy majority of teens are willing to get jobs, buy fewer clothes and give up some allowance.

For children of elementary-school age, a couple of good books that deal with the subject of a father losing his job are *Tight Times,* by Barbara Shook Hazen (Puffin Books), and *Ramona and Her Father,* by Beverly Cleary (Avon Camelot).

(Harsand Press). Before you speak, try to imagine what you'd say to a neighbor's child. Moe observes that "we tend to treat the neighbor kids a little more kindly than we do our own, and we're not as abrupt."

Be Consistent

If you've decided to give your kids an allowance and you've made a "no advances" rule, don't waffle—standing firm one week and handing over extra money the next. Your child will never learn the discipline of living within a budget if you keep expanding the limits. Today she's getting an advance on her allowance, tomorrow she'll be using one credit card to pay off the balance on another.

Repeat the following sentence ten times: "I will never tell my children, by word or example, to do as I say and not as I do." Your lecture on the wastefulness of scrapping a perfectly good video game system just to get the latest model will be in vain if you regularly trade in a perfectly good car just to get a new one with the latest bells and whistles.

Don't Play the Cynic

For adults it's de rigueur to complain about their jobs and criticize their bosses as a way of releasing tension. After venting their spleen, they usually go back to work and forget about the incident. But for kids who witness the outburst, the memory can linger, with destructive consequences, according to Peter Spevak, director of the Center for Applied Motivation, a psychology practice in Rockville, Md., that counsels underachieving teens. In his work, Spevak says, he encounters many 17- and 18-year-olds who have become "incredibly cynical" about the working world because they have been exposed too early to a negative attitude instead of the enthusiasm and inner satisfaction they need to see. Kids also need to start learning, by word and example, how much things cost, as well as how to use money, earn it, save it and keep it in perspective. The following chapters will give you ideas on how to tackle that task with kids of different ages.

Preschoolers: Taking in the Big Picture

Q. *Dear Dr. Tightwad: Whenever I take my preschoolers to the store, they come down with a bad case of the gimmies and I'm embarrassed. How can I cure them and make my shopping trips more pleasant?*

A. Try a little preventive medicine. Make clear before you go which treats you will and won't buy. With the ground rules set in advance, you have a leg to stand on if your kids start to play the gimme game. If you're willing to buy a candy bar, for example, they can spend their time trying to decide which one they want instead of bugging you for something else. If that doesn't work, leave the kids at home if you can.

You can start teaching your children about money as soon as they know enough not to try eating it. Chances are you already have, but with mixed success. In a survey conducted by Oppenheimer Management Corp., parents of children between the ages of 4 and 15 said they spend, on average, a little over an hour and a half each week discussing money with their children. But only 51% rated themselves as doing an excellent or very good job; 46% graded their efforts as fair or poor.

The survey didn't say whether the parents felt they needed more time or a more effective teaching strategy. But it's likely that they could have improved the quality of their efforts without significantly increasing the quantity of time they put in. Dealing with money is such a natural part of life that you don't necessarily have to set aside extra time to talk about it. Instead you can take advantage of situations in day-to-day life. When your child begs to press the buttons on the automated teller machine, use the opportunity to tell her how the money got there in the first place. Dragging your children to the supermarket becomes more pleasant for all of you if you keep them busy scouting out the best deals. A visit to your office opens the door to a discussion of where the money comes from to pay the household bills.

Your ultimate aim is to turn out independent adults who know how to manage money and have a healthy regard for what it can and can't buy. But with preschoolers you'll have to start with a less lofty goal—like how to tell the difference between a penny, a nickel and a dime.

Show 3-year-olds those three coins and they'll almost invariably choose the nickel. That about sums up the state of a young child's mind when it comes to money: Big is best, and who cares about the rest. Abstract concepts are beyond the ken of most preschoolers. Focus on concrete issues instead—what coins look like and how they can be exchanged for other things.

Not that preschoolers aren't capable of some surprisingly sophisticated behavior. Laurie Fratangelo was floored when her son, Jake, then 4½, announced that he was going to open a business selling lollipops—and save his profits to buy a car. Fratangelo operates her own home-based business selling children's clothing,

©1992, Washington Post Writers Group. Reprinted with permission.

"The technique that works best is for children and parents to...select specific shows to watch, and those are the only ones you watch. Only by watching with your kids can you understand what they're being exposed to."
Shari Lewis

and Jake had observed with more interest than his mother realized. He began asking his mom's customers to buy lollipops and eventually got his grandfather to build him a plywood stand from which he could conduct his business. Then he decided he wanted to expand into selling juice as well.

Of course, there were a few snags in the operation. At first Jake wanted to sell the lollipops for $14 each, until he was talked down to 3 cents. And his mother says it took him a while to grasp the concept of paying his supplier.

At the Grocery Store

Most children get their first look at the world from the seat of a shopping cart. So learn to make the most of the opportunity, and avoid some nasty scenes. To forestall a bad case of the gimmies, for example, present your children ahead of time with several coins (adding up to 50 cents, $1 or whatever you deem appropriate) and tell them they can choose one treat (with your guidance) and pay for it themselves. To keep them from wanting everything they see, offer choices. If they have their eye on both the chocolate-chip cookie and the container of juice, tell them to pick one.

As you cruise the aisles, let the children toss your items into the cart and count them as they go in. Keep the children busy hunting for the brand of soup or crackers that you buy, or let them choose between two different kinds of cereal. If they decide to buy something from a vending machine, let them put in the coins and scoop out the change.

Watching Television

If your kids spend part of Saturday morning in front of the television, make it a point to join them. James McNeal, kids' spending expert and marketing professor at Texas A&M, advises that you "intervene between advertisers and kids when the kids are 3 or 4 years old and you still have influence." Preschoolers can't always tell when the television show ends and the ad begins. They need you to explain to them that when they hear the voice saying, "We'll be right back after these brief messages," they're about to hear a sales pitch for something you may not want them to have.

Arthur Pober, director of the Children's Advertising Review Unit (CARU) of the Council of Better Business Bureaus, suggests that parents show their kids this demonstration of how to be a "TV star": Take three apples that look similar. Then "dress up" one of them by sticking raisins or marshmallows into it, putting it into a colorful box or shining a flashlight on it. Ask your children which they'd be inclined to buy. If they choose the spiffed-up apple, have them take a bite out of each one. Does the "star" actually taste any better? (See the accompanying box.)

Don't be surprised if despite your best efforts your preschoolers still want it all. Don't panic, either. At that age, it's natural for them to ask for everything they see—and promptly forget about it. They'll be happy with whatever you get them. Enjoy it while you can; they won't always be so easily satisfied.

Seeing Through the Hype

The **Children's Advertising Review Unit** (CARU) was established by the advertising industry to promote responsible children's advertising and to respond to public concerns. CARU publishes *A Parent's Guide; Advertising and Your Child*, which discusses how you can monitor and explain advertising to your children, and for advertisers, *Self-Regulatory Guidelines for Children's Advertising*. To order, contact CARU (845 Third Ave., New York, NY 10022; 212-705-0124).

Lending a Hand

Children this age are old enough to pick up toys, put away clothes or help make the bed. They probably won't do any of those things, of course, unless you make the demands manageable, stick to them and give your kids a hand. For kids, chores become less work and more play if they're doing them with mom or dad. Settle on one chore a day and let your children help choose which one it will be. Present it as a privilege that your children enjoy now that they're growing up (they're still young enough to buy that).

Of course, you can offer a little incentive as well. It can be as simple as a chart showing the chores to be done and the days of the week. Each time a job is completed, your daughter gets to stick a star on the chart. Seven stars and you might buy her a small treat—an ice cream cone or a drink at the corner store. Think of it as a reward—positive reinforcement for doing something good—rather than a bribe—a payoff for not doing something bad. (For more on rewards and when to give them, see Chapter 5.)

Whiling Away a Rainy Afternoon

You have to figure out something to occupy the kids' time anyway, so you might as well kill two birds with one coin. There are, of course, the old standbys, like playing store. If you're looking for new ideas, Bonnie Drew offers lots of them in her book *Moneyskills, 101 Activities to Teach Your Child About Money* (Career Press). Here's a selection of games from Drew's book that are appropriate for getting preschoolers used to handling coins. They're also manageable, short and fun.

Story time

Let your children handle a penny, a nickel, a dime and a quarter. Show them the pictures on each coin and tell a story about each one. (Remember, it's Lincoln and the Lincoln Memorial on the penny, Jefferson and Monticello on the nickel, Franklin D. Roosevelt and the torch and olive branch on the dime, and Washington and the American eagle on the quarter.) Then let them make impressions of the coins in modeling clay.

Treasure hunt

Fill a box or dishpan with sand, rice, beans or packing peanuts, hide five pennies in it and ask your children to dig for the "treasure." Have them count out the coins. You can add other coins later and ask the kids to sort them into groups.

Heads up

Start with five nickels and five pennies. Explain that the side of the coin with the man's head is called "heads" and the other side "tails." Show your children how to spin and roll each coin and ask them to guess which side will be showing when it lands, heads or tails. Have them balance a nickel on the tip of a finger and see how far they can walk across the room. When the coin falls, let them call heads or tails.

Animal crackers

Place five pennies and a nickel on the table and explain that five pennies are worth the same as one nickel. Then break out a box of animal crackers and let the children "buy" them for one cent per cracker; let them buy five crackers at once with the nickel. Pour a small cup of juice and pretend that it costs five cents. Let your children choose to buy the juice with either five pennies or one nickel. Then eat and drink up.

What You Can Expect

You'll be surprised at how fast preschoolers catch on. It didn't take long for Jake Fratangelo, the lollipop tycoon, to figure out that there are five nickels in a quarter and four quarters in a dollar. And at this age, that's about as much as you can hope for.

Don't be upset when your 4-year-old tears open birthday cards, shakes them to see if there's money inside and immediately asks to be taken to the store to spend it. You're not raising a greedy little kid, just a normal one. Four-year-olds think in concrete terms, and spending is more concrete than saving. If your child knows that money can be exchanged for things, you're off to a good start that you can build on.

Money Fun

No peeking now, whose images are on the following coins?

- *Penny*
- *Nickel*
- *Dime*
- *Quarter*
- *Half-dollar*

Answers: Starting with the penny: Abraham Lincoln, Thomas Jefferson, Franklin Roosevelt, George Washington, John Kennedy

The Middle Years: Curiouser and Curiouser

Q. *Dear Dr. Tightwad: Our kids are constantly telling us that unless they have a certain brand of sneakers or a certain kind of toy their friends will think they're dorks. We want them to fit in, but sometimes we can't afford what they want or we just don't choose to buy it.*

A. Don't feel obliged to. When you were a kid you probably used the same line on your parents (read drip for dork). Yet you survived somehow, and so will your kids.

By second grade, kids no longer prefer a nickel over a dime, and they can even make a stab at counting change. But they still have trouble grasping abstract ideas about money. Bonnie Meszaros, associate director of the Delaware Center for Economic Education, has learned a lesson or two from her own daughter, Morgan. When Morgan was 8 years old, her mom convinced her to put a $10 birthday gift into the bank by reminding her that she could draw it out again if she wanted to buy something. Would the bank give her the same $10 bill, Morgan wanted to know. Her mother explained that she would get a $10 bill but not the same one because the bank had already used that to lend to other people. Morgan was appalled. In her mind, the purpose of a bank was to keep her money on a shelf until she was ready to take it out.

Despite their misconceptions, children this age are eager to learn—from you—so take advantage of the influence you still have. Amy Dacyczyn, the self-described "frugal zealot" from Leeds, Maine, who publishes the newsletter *Tightwad Gazette,* a compendium of money-saving tips, noticed "spendthrift rumblings" in her daughter Jamie when she was about 7. So Amy began to take Jamie with her on her regular canvasses of yard sales. "It was a real eye-opener for her to see that she could get My Little Pony for 25 cents at a yard sale instead of $7 at a store," says Amy.

Children this age are eager to learn—from you—so take advantage of the influence you still have.

How to Spend a Buck

They're too big to sit in the shopping cart, and having them tag along grumpily behind you is like trying to shop with a ball and chain attached to each leg. So get rid of them, but nicely:

- **Send them to the cereal aisle** with instructions to find a box of cereal that will be popular with your family, doesn't list sugar among its top ingredients and costs less than, say, $4. Tell them they can pocket the difference between your price limit and the actual price of the cereal. To challenge older children, show them how to look for the lowest unit price instead of the lowest price per package.

- **Have them choose three kinds of soft drinks** (or some other product): A big-selling national brand, a less-popular national brand and the store brand. Note the prices per package and the unit prices. When you get home, pour the soft drinks into three unmarked glasses and try your own taste test. Which soft drink tastes best? Which is the best value?

- **While you're making your shopping list, let your children plan a special lunch** for themselves and one or two of their friends. Have them stick to a budget—say, $10—and encourage them to use the weekly food advertising supplement as an aid. Then, while you do your shopping, send them off to do theirs and see if they can beat the budget without having to modify the menu.

- **Have your children help you clip grocery coupons and then track down the items** at the store. Offer to match any savings you realize and let the kids put the money into their savings accounts.

The bottom line: The kids learn valuable lessons in how to use a unit price tag, how to read ingredient labels, how to compare different brands, how to evaluate product advertising and how to stay within a budget. And you get your shopping done in peace.

Once they've absorbed the basics at the local market, you can branch out. When his two sons, Craig and Lyle, were in elementary school back in the '70s, Ed Henry of Silver Spring, Md., gave them the responsibility of being "dad for a day." The Henrys lived in the New York City area at the time and the kids were always begging to be taken to an amusement park. So Ed would give the "designated dad" a budget and make him responsible for planning a family outing to the park of his choice. The kids would be up at dawn to push their red wagon to the ice house around the corner and buy ice for the cooler. In the car the designated dad would

Calvin and Hobbes © 1989 Watterson. Reprinted with permission of Universal Press Syndicate. All rights reserved.

sit behind the driver and hand over the money at toll booths. At the park the kids would haggle over whether to eat or ride (Craig always wanted to splurge on french fries, while Lyle hoarded his pennies for an extra turn on the coaster.) The kids were required to hold enough in reserve to pay the tolls on the way home but "once their money was spent, that was it," says Ed. With Craig in charge the day sometimes ended early, but Lyle often came home with money in his pocket, which he was allowed to keep.

Did the lessons stick? Craig now directs music videos and still doesn't have much of a head for numbers. Lyle got his college degree in finance and works in the mortgage department of a commercial real estate firm.

Watching Television With a Critical Eye

By this age, kids are sophisticated enough to figure out when a commercial doesn't ring true in practice. When the oldest of my three children was 8, I took them to McDonald's to sample Mighty Wings, spicy chicken wings that McDonald's had been trumpeting in an advertising blitz. The 8-year-old observed that the real wings weren't nearly as juicy-looking as the televised version and the hot sauce wasn't as thick.

But ultimately you want to help them spot the hype before they're disappointed in a purchase. When your children see a commercial showing kids whooshing by on in-line skates or guiding a remote-control car around hairpin turns, ask them if they could do the same without practice. Kids naturally expect a toy to work exactly as they saw it perform on TV so it's important to teach them that they may need to be patient and learn to master a skill.

Before you spring for a much-wanted toy, take your children to the store and have them look at the coveted item in its box, where it isn't surrounded by a glitzy TV background and special effects.

"When our kids were young we set limits on TV viewing, and the kids said they'd go next door and watch it. We said go ahead, but you're not doing it here. If they did, at least they'd be socializing. But they didn't go next door."
Dr. T. Berry Brazelton

Instead of rushing to be the first one on the block to have a new toy, encourage your children to be patient and let someone else be the guinea pig. After your kids have had a crack at playing with the toy, they may find they can live without it after all. One youthful reader told *Zillions,* the consumer magazine for kids, about the dumbest purchase he had ever made: an expensive remote-control car that wound up eating batteries. If only he had waited, he discovered, he could have gotten the next generation car, with rechargeable battery packs.

Kids this age are old enough to understand the difference between fact and opinion, and you can use this as a talking point when you watch a commercial on TV. The next time you and your kids see Michael Jordan quaffing a cold drink, ask the kids why they think Michael has chosen that particular drink:

- Is it because that's the absolute best-tasting drink on the market, or because Michael happens to like it?

- Did the soft-drink company pay him to do the commercial?

- Why would an advertiser pick a TV or sports star to pitch its product?

- Would your kids buy the drink on the strength of Michael Jordan's say-so?

- Is it possible that Michael Jordan can't stand the taste of the stuff?

Children this age can also detect hype; by this time, they've probably bought or received as a gift something that didn't measure up to its TV image. When *Zillions* publishes its annual ZAP awards (for "ZAP it off the air, please!") it is deluged with nominees. Among the recent winners, chosen by a panel of 12 readers: The G.I. Joe Battle 'Copter, which was portrayed in the ad as able to fly high and engage in combat but didn't do those things; L'il Miss Singing Mermaid, who sang underwater in the ads but in reality could only sing out of water and not always very well;

and Oxy 10, which in the ads seemed to make pimples disappear—poof—by magic. In *Consumer Reports'* video *Buy Me That Too* (see the accompanying box), kids were annoyed with some of the kids' clubs being promoted by fast-food restaurants, TV stations and others. They felt they didn't get much in return for their membership and, most disappointing, they didn't get the names of other club members.

Tricks With Allowances

By this time, your kids are old enough to get an allowance (more, much more, on that subject in Chapter 5). If you give one, dole out a variety of small-denomination coins and bills. If the allowance is $2, for example, you might give a one-dollar bill and four quarters. This helps teach children money equivalents and also makes it easier for them to set aside money for specific purposes, such as saving or charitable giving.

And don't forget taxes. Neale Godfrey, author of *The Kids' Money Book* (Checkerboard Press), takes issue with parents who raise their kids to think that taxes are bad. You might disagree with the amount or allocation of your tax dollars, but they do pay for needed public services, such as police and fire departments and schools. For her own two children, Godfrey explains what a tax bracket is, sets out a tax jar and has the kids

---

It May Look Yummy...

The next time you see a commercial for a big, juicy, fast-food burger, ask your kids how the picture stacks up against the real McCoy. Then share with them a few fun facts about food commercials. For example, those juicy burgers are mostly raw, just seared for a few seconds on each side; the grill marks are added by hand, the sesame seeds are glued onto the bun one by one, and a piece of cardboard is slipped into the bun to keep it from getting soggy.

Other tricks of the food stylist's trade: Shortening, sugar and food coloring make ice cream that doesn't melt, liquid school glue makes cereal milk that looks creamy, and dishwashing liquid makes hot chocolate that looks bubbly (the marshmallows are styrofoam balls).

These and other behind-the-scenes glimpses into advertising aimed at children are included in a series of three half-hour videotapes created by *Consumer Reports: Buy Me That, Buy Me That Too* and *Buy Me That 3*. First shown on cable TV's HBO, *Buy Me That* and *Buy Me That 3* are available from Public Media Inc. (800-343-4312) for $49 each. *Buy Me That Too* is available from Ambrose Video (800-526-4663) for $69.95.

kick in 15% of their allowance. They learn the difference between gross and net income while providing for the common good: The kitty goes for something the whole family can enjoy, such as a night at the movies.

Be on the lookout for unexpected openings to slip in a lesson that otherwise might fall on deaf ears—what author and parent Harold Moe calls "hot buttons." Moe recalls his own frustration in trying to get his son, Rolf, who was around 8 years old at the time, to save money. Then Rolf saw the movie *Star Wars* and was hooked; he voluntarily saved his money to join the official fan club and was determined to become a Jedi knight. Moe saw his chance and leaped. "We talked about how Jedis have to save money for college, and the next day Rolf put on his Jedi robe and opened a savings account." Now, years later, Moe observes with satisfaction that Rolf has several thousand dollars in the bank that otherwise wouldn't be there "just because we talked about the need for Jedi knights to go to college."

Brand-itis Sets In

● ●

Q. *Dear Dr. Tightwad: My fifth-grade daughter has started noticing clothing labels. Last week she came home and announced that where you buy your clothes is as important as what you're wearing. I can't afford to buy all her clothes from a "name" store—and I wouldn't want to if I could—but how do I tell her that?*

A. Just the way you told Dr. T. It's best to be honest with kids from the start about what your pocketbook, and your conscience, will allow. That way you don't set up any false expectations.

You're walking a fine line here because you want to maintain your own family's standards without making your daughter feel too left out. If your conscience and your wallet allow, strike a deal. Tell her you're willing to buy an item or two from the "name" store each season (preferably when they go on sale). So, she might choose the baggy shirt that all the kids are wearing—but wear hers over standard-issue jeans.

Rainy-Day Perk-ups

Nothing tops games like Monopoly or The Game of Life for teaching kids how to handle money. If Monopoly seems daunting for younger kids, don't be afraid to bend the rules a bit to let players build houses and hotels even if they don't own all the properties of a single color. Or try Monopoly Junior, which older kids (and adults) will like, too, because you can play an entire game in about 45 minutes.

Other money-oriented board games, such as the following, are more specialized and less widely distributed.

- **The Allowance Game** (Lakeshore Learning Materials; 2695 E. Dominguez St., Carson, CA 90749; 800-421-5354; $14.95, plus $4.25 for shipping and handling). As they travel around the board, players encounter various kid situations in which they earn or spend their allowance, such as mowing the lawn, walking the dog, paying a library fine, or playing video games. The first player to save $20 wins. (for primary level)

- **Roup** (Porter Planet-3 Games; P.O. Box 773, Smethport, PA. 16749; 800-828-4525; $28.50, plus $5 for shipping). Players bid in rubles for 39 properties, such as the Kremlin, Red Square, the Lenin Mausoleum and KGB headquarters. The game ends when all money has been transferred from the Old Communist Bank to the New Democracy Bank and all properties have been sold to private owners. (late primary and up)

- **Stocks & Bonds** (Avalon Hill; 4517 Harford Rd., Baltimore, MD 21214; 800-999-3222, credit card orders only; $25, plus $4 for shipping and handling). Billed as a game for "investors of all ages," this challenging stock-market game requires equal measures of luck and skill and the ability to get through lengthy instructions. It may be one to play

Calvin and Hobbes © 1988 Watterson. Reprinted with permission of Universal Press Syndicate. All rights reserved.

with your teenagers.

Then again, you don't need to buy a board game just to play around with money:

- **All those catalogs cluttering your den** are freebies just waiting to impart a lesson or two. Give your children an imaginary budget of, say, $250 or $300 and let them choose an entire winter or summer wardrobe.

- **If you decide to order take-out food**, make it your

Fun Money Reading and Software

Take advantage of rainy days and bedtime to slip your children some broccoli with their milk and cookies. Dozens of books and software programs teach kids about money and economic concepts in the context of fun. Here's a sampling:

Books for Younger Kids

- *Alexander, Who Used To Be Rich Last Sunday,* by Judith Viorst (Aladdin Books), about a boy whose money burns a hole in his pocket. (primary)

- *Arthur's Funny Money,* by Lillian Hoban (Harper and Row), in which Arthur sets up a bike-washing business to earn money for a T-shirt. (primary)

- *The Berenstain Bears Get the Gimmies,* by Stan and Jan Berenstain (Random House), in which Brother and Sister Bear come down with a case of the "galloping, greedy gimmies." Other money-oriented books in this popular series include *Trouble with Money, Mama's New Job, Meet Santa Bear.* (primary)

- *Every Kid's Guide to Intelligent Spending,* by Joy Berry (Living Skills Press), teaches children about advertising, impulse spending and how to be a thoughtful consumer. Berry has also written *Every Kid's Guide to Making and Managing Money.* (primary)

- *Eyewitness Books: Money,* by Joe Cribb (Alfred A. Knopf). An encyclopedic history of money, foreign currency and trading. (primary or intermediate)

- *From Gold to Money,* by Ali Mitgutsch (Carolrhoda Books). Defines bartering, counterfeiting, minting and earning money. (primary)

- *Freckle Juice,* by Judy Blume (Dell), in which Andrew uses five whole weeks of allowance to buy a secret freckle recipe and learns some valuable consumer lessons as a result. (primary or intermediate)

- *The Go-Around Dollar,* by Barbara Johnston Adams (Four Winds Press), in which a dollar bill travels from person to person. The book also explains where and how money is made. (primary)

children's responsibility. Present them with the menu, a price limit and instructions to plan a meal that satisfies the whole family and doesn't bust the budget.

Facing Down Peer Pressure

As your children approach their "tween" years—ages 9 through 12—they'll be influenced more by their peers and their peers' possessions. Now you'll

- *How Do Octopi Eat Pizza Pie?* (Pizza Math, part of I Love Math series; Time-Life for Children), in which colorful characters introduce everyday math concepts and problem solving. (primary)

- *If You Made a Million,* by David M. Schwartz (Lothrop, Lee & Shepard), in which Marvelosissimo the Mathematical Magician shows the reader what money looks like and demonstrates the concept of a million dollars. (primary)

- *The Kids' Money Book,* by Neale S. Godfrey (Checkerboard Press). Answers such questions as: What is a checking account? Where did piggy banks get their name? And, how do banks earn money? (primary or intermediate)

- *Money,* by Benjamin Elkin (Children's Press). Explains why we use money and what we can do with it. (primary).

- *The Money Book: A Budget Book for Children,* by Diana J. Olden and Vicki Smith (Smith & Daniel). Mostly budget sheets for ages 8 to 11. (primary)

- *The Money Book: A Smart Kid's Guide to Savvy Saving and Spending,* by Elaine Wyatt and Stan Hinden (Tambourine Books). Tips and hints about earning, banking, budgeting and saving money. (primary)

- *The Monster Money Book,* by Loreen Leedy (Holiday House), in which members of the Monster Club discuss money, how to manage and spend their dues and how to be a smart shopper. (primary)

Software for Younger Kids

All software programs listed here are available for Macintosh and IBM-compatible computers.

- *The Coin Changer* (Heartsoft). Money-counting and time skills are taught using realistic graphics. (primary)

- *Money and Time Adventures of the Lollipop Dragon* (Society for Visual Education), in which the Lollipop Dragon leads kids through their paces to learn basic money-counting and time skills. (early primary)

hear the plaintive wail that death is the only imaginable alternative if they don't get those $120 sneakers or $80 jeans. Steel yourself. It doesn't hurt to give in on small things, or even on a few big ones that are really important to your kids. But every family has its line in the sand, whether it's a Super Nintendo or a private phone, and it's worth digging in your heels.

Kids need to understand which things your family can afford and which things it values. If something they

Fun Money Reading and Software (cont'd.)

- *Money Works* (MECC). Helps kids learn to recognize values of different coins, buy things, count correct change and see how international exchange rates affect their money's value in other currency systems. (primary)

- *Treasure MathStorm* (The Learning Company). A computer game designed to teach math, time and money skills. Players try to collect treasures, catch elves and melt the ice kingdom. (primary)

- *What's Your Strategy?* (Wings for Learning). Teaches math concepts such as recognizing geometric shapes and sizing up spatial relationships and skills such as counting coins. (late primary)

Books for Older Kids

- *All the Money in the World,* by Bill Brittain (Harper Collins Children's Books), in which a boy gets his wish for just that, with disastrous consequences. (intermediate)

- *Coping with Money,* by Richard S. and Mary Price Lee (The Rosen Publishing Group). Offers advice on coping with

allowances, designing a budget, investing and saving for college. (teens)

- *Henry and the Paper Route,* by Beverly Cleary (Dell), in which Henry Huggins faces the obstacles to starting a business. (intermediate)

- *Henry Reed's Babysitting Service,* by Keith Robertson (Dell), a classic in which Henry and partner Midge Glass start a babysitting service and are challenged by market surveys, advertising and costs, not to mention the antics of their young charges. (intermediate)

- *Making Cents: Every Kid's Guide to Money,* by Elizabeth Wilkinson (Little, Brown). Offers detailed money-making ideas for older kids. (intermediate)

- *Night of a Thousand Pizzas,* by Ann Hodgman (Berkley Publishing), in which the kids at Hollis Elementary try to figure out a way to eliminate a surplus of 1,000 pizzas. (intermediate)

- *Smart Spending: A Young Consumer's Guide,* by Lois Schmitt (Charles Scribner's Sons). Explores budgeting,

want costs too much, or if you just don't choose to buy it, explain your rationale. In fact, it may be more important for you to listen to their wishes than to satisfy them. "Nobody ever died from not getting a Betsy Wetsy," says Eda LeShan, author of *What Makes You So Special?* (Dial Books), which counsels kids on how to deal with peer pressure.

What does hurt is to make children feel they have to be like others in order to be worthwhile. Sympathize with

misleading advertising, consumer fraud, warranties and consumer complaints. (teens)

- *Your 1st Book of Wealth,* by A. David Silver (The Career Press). A beginner's guide to collecting, investing and starting your own business. (teens)

- *The Money-Book Store* catalog (National Center for Financial Education; P.O. Box 34070, San Diego, CA 92163; 619-232-8811) lists other financial games and books and is available for $1.

Software for Older Kids

All software programs listed here are available for Macintosh and IBM-compatible computers.

- *A-Train* (Maxis). Fledgling empire-builders create a railroad, then a city, and strive to show a profit. They can build more capital by playing the stock market, borrowing from the bank, and selling and leasing their properties. By the creators of *SimCity* and *SimEarth,* this sophisticated game is for the patient and computer-smart. (teens)

- *DinoPark Tycoon* (MECC). Children learn how to operate their own business as they build a dinosaur theme park (sound familiar?). Players buy dinosaurs and real estate, set up concession stands and hire and fire staff. (primary to adult)

- *Hot Dog Stand* (Sunburst Communications). Players manage money and run a business while operating a hot dog stand at eight computerized football games. This program is part of the Survival Math series, which also includes *Travel Agent Contest, Smart Shopper Marathon* and *Foreman's Assistant.* (intermediate and teens)

- *The Oregon Trail* (MECC). Adventurers travel by covered wagon from Independence, Mo., to Oregon. Along the way, they learn how to shop for and buy the supplies they need and make their money last the trip. (late primary to adult)

- *Whatsit Corp.* (Sunburst Communications). Would-be entrepreneurs run a small, one-product (whats-its) business for six months, making all the same decisions that any business owner must make. (late primary to adult)

their desire to fit in, and maybe even meet them halfway, but emphasize that it's okay, even desirable, to be different. Kids who don't learn to buck the crowd when they're young will have trouble saying no when they're teens.

Remember that the choices you make with regard to such things as where you live and where you send your children to school can make a big difference in the amount of peer pressure on your kids, and in their, and your, ability to resist. Sending your kids to an expensive private school can end up costing far more than the tuition if you're constantly being pressured to keep up with the Jones kids' winter ski trips and summer camps. The easiest way to deal with such influences is to avoid them altogether by not sending your kids to the expensive private school in the first place.

Whatever lifestyle decisions you make, at some point you'll probably have to fight the battle of the latest fad in $60 jeans. But if you've been talking to your kids about money-related issues all along and are willing to keep talking, you won't have to relinquish the field to their friends. Kids can accept differences among families if they understand their own family's philosophy and financial circumstances and if they feel they're getting a fair hearing.

Allowances: All You Need to Know

Q. *Dear Dr. Tightwad: My 7-year-old daughter wants to have an allowance, but I think that she's too young. Should I give her one?*

A. Swallow hard and hand it over. Nothing beats an allowance for hands-on experience in managing money. And by the age of 6 or 7, children generally can be counted on to handle money without losing it or being tricked out of it.

Ever wonder whether the hands-on experience of a steady allowance will let your kids get their hands on too much of a good thing? Never fear, the kids will probably get at least as much in dribs and drabs if they're on the parental dole. One mother of two teenage daughters offered to give both girls a clothing allowance, but they turned her down flat. "They probably figure they're making out better with me buying," she says ruefully.

Kids who don't receive allowances get access to about as much money as kids who do, according to a survey of children around the country conducted by *Zillions,* the consumer magazine for kids. But the children with allowances are happier with the amount they receive, and they feel better off because they have more control over their money. Kids who get allowances are

"Kids should be raised with the idea that money is not the most important thing in the world, but if you want the better things in life you have to buy them."
Ann Landers

also more likely to save money. (The survey didn't ask, but their parents probably feel better off, too, because they're not slowly being nickeled and dimed to death.)

The rest of this chapter addresses the most common questions that parents—and kids—have about allowances.

How Much is Enough?

Q. *How much of an allowance should I give?*

A. Enough so that your children can squander it, but not so much that you'll be upset when they do. Sit down with your children and decide what expenses their allowance will have to cover. You might expect an 11-year-old to budget lunch money for an entire week, but that's probably too much to ask of a 7-year-old.

Don't underestimate a kid's cost of living. Take a lesson from Lamb Chop, the puppet on the PBS show starring Shari Lewis and her animal friends. In one episode, the lovable lamb was negotiating for a raise in her penny-a-week allowance. "Do you buy anything?" asked Shari. Retorted Lamb Chop, "If I save it for 12 weeks, I can blow it on a pack of gum." Shari and Lamb Chop eventually settled on 7 cents a week, but if you're going to leave room for a pack of gum your children will need at least a quarter, not the nickel of your youth.

The latest *Zillions* survey showed that allowances haven't gone up much over the last five years. Kids' total income has risen because they're getting extra money for doing jobs. But the magazine concludes that after you factor in inflation, kids 12 and under can buy about the same amount of stuff today as kids the same age could buy five years ago.

When you and your children settle on an allowance, be open and realistic about what you expect the money to cover. Besides school lunches, you might want your 11-year-old to pick up the cost of snack foods and games at the video arcade but figure that basic expenses for clothing and school supplies are your responsibility. By the time your child is 15, however, it's reasonable to expect him or her to be kicking in for clothes, movie tickets and the French Club ski trip. It's a help to ask other parents how much they're giving. Ultimately, though, you can't let an "expert" or your neighbor down the street make your decision for you; you'll have to go with your own instincts and values.

Q. *But it would help if I knew how much other parents were giving. What's the scoop?*

A. Point taken. See the box at right for a reference point. According to a study of ninth graders in St. Paul conducted by Jeylan Mortimer, Katherine Dennehy and Chaimun Lee of the University of Minnesota, children from a higher-income background are more likely to get an allowance, but they don't get more money. In fact, the study showed that family income has no bearing on the amount of allowance children receive. Kids from different economic backgrounds had access to about the same amount of money from all sources: allowances, gifts, special jobs and paid work outside the home. Regardless of their income, parents with higher education levels were more likely to give their children an allowance, and the parents' education level also had a positive effect on how much their kids saved.

Overall, about three-fourths of the students reported ever having received an allowance, and more than half had started to get one before the age of 10. White and minority students were equally likely to have received an allowance, although white students started receiving theirs earlier and had more in savings. Children in single-parent families were more likely to receive an allowance than children of two-parent families.

Your Kid's Perspective

Q. *Help! I need a raise in my allowance but my parents don't want to hear about it. They still think things cost as*

Allowances

Here are average weekly allowances nationwide in 1993, according to a survey by Youth Monitor, a syndicated service of Nickelodeon and Yankelovich Clancy Shulman:

Age	Amount
6 - 8	$1.99
9 - 11	4.17
12 - 13	5.82
14 - 15	9.68
16 - 17	10.80

much as they did when they were kids. How can I get them out of the dark ages?

A. You'll never win your parents over by telling them they have no idea how much things cost today. Remember, they're paying the household bills, so they *know* how expensive things are. Maybe that's why they're reluctant to give you a raise or can't afford to.

Whatever you do, don't whine. Instead, make a list of your income and expenses (use the work sheet on pages 54 and 55). If you find that your savings are zilch and you're squandering all your money on snacks and entertainment, you're not going to win sympathy—or extra cash—from your folks. Instead, try the following needs-versus-wants exercise, which may help you cut back on the unimportant stuff and save for the important things you want. Your parents may be so impressed by your initiative that they'll give you a token raise anyway.

If you have bigger expenses—lunches, transportation, clothes—and are having trouble making ends meet, talk with your parents, or maybe take them on a shopping excursion to scope out the situation. Don't expect them to spring for the latest—and most expensive—wardrobe. You may have to compromise on less-expensive shoes if you really must have the latest in jeans. Maybe your parents will increase your clothing allowance if you're willing to accept more responsibility for buying your clothes.

Calvin and Hobbes © 1989 Watterson. Reprinted with permission of Universal Press Syndicate. All rights reserved.

Needs vs. Wants

Q. *My child is supposed to use his allowance to buy his school lunch, but he keeps running out of money in the middle of the week and then doesn't eat. What should I do?*

A. Rethink the plan. Your son is obviously having trouble handling the responsibility, which means he probably isn't ready for it. Give him his lunch money every day instead of expecting him to budget a week's worth at a time. Or see if you can arrange to pay the school directly for your son's lunch, perhaps a week or a month at a time. If he insists on spending his lunch money for other things, let him—but teach him to make his own sandwich at home and brown-bag it to school.

Q. *So what should I do if my kids blow the whole wad on candy, baseball cards and arcade games?*

A. Bite your tongue and keep a firm grip on your wallet. You, of course, have the right to veto any purchase that's unhealthy, unsafe or in violation of your family's principles. Outside of that, though, you have to expect your kids to go a little wild, at least at first. You can only hope that they'll calm down once they realize that no more money is forthcoming to bail them out.

They may surprise you with just how tight-fisted they can be. Child psychologist David Lustig relates the experience of one of his partners in practice, who was

A Money Record for Kids

Use this work sheet to keep track of your money. At the beginning of the month, start writing down the money you receive and the money you spend. At the end of the month, you'll see whether you came out even (you spent as much as you received), ahead (you spent less than you received and have money left over to add to your savings) or behind (you spent more than you received and might have had to borrow money from Mom and Dad to pay for something). You can do this for a whole year by making 12 copies of the work sheet (record the cost of using the copier at the library under Odds and Ends, below).

The work sheet may help you decide that you want to spend your money differently next month. Maybe you want to increase your income by asking for more odd jobs around the house. Perhaps you will spend less on snacks so you can save up for a new pair of skates.

But remember, just because something is listed on this work sheet doesn't mean you have to buy it—or that your parents will let you. Besides, they may expect you to use part of your allowance to buy school lunches. They may expect you to save some of your money and to give some of it to help other people or your place of worship. It's a good idea to write down those amounts first thing each month so you'll set them aside and not spend them on something else.

Month _____

Where My Money Comes From

My allowance	$	_____
Odd jobs		_____
Babysitting, paper route, and so on		_____
Gifts		_____
Money borrowed from my parent(s) (or someone else)		_____
My Total Income	$	_____

What I Spend My Money On

Money I owe my parent(s) (or someone else)	_____
My savings (savings account or piggy bank)	_____

My church or other charity (like Unicef) _____

Gifts for my family and friends _____

Lunch money _____

Clothing I help pay for _____

School supplies and fees
   (class parties, science projects, and so on) _____

Snacks (sodas, chips, candy, gum) _____

Fun stuff I pay for
   Books, magazines and comics _____
   Toys _____
   Things I collect _____
   Special stuff for my room
     (posters and so on) _____
   Entrance fees
     (for the skating rink, rec center, and so on) _____
   Club dues & uniforms
     (Girls Scouts, 4-H) _____
   Art and craft supplies
     (including taking pictures) _____
   Holiday costumes (Halloween) _____
   CDs, tapes and records _____
   Video and computer games _____
   Videotapes (bought or rented) _____
   Movies _____
   Other outings (amusement parks,
     museums, zoos and so on) _____
   Souvenirs and postcards _____
Odds and ends _____

My Total Expenses $ _____

My Total Income $ _____
Minus My Total Expenses   - _____
Money Left Over $ _____

accompanied to the store by his 8-year-old son. As they were leaving, the boy picked up a plastic toy and put it on the checkout counter. If he wanted it, he was told, he'd have to pay for it himself. Replied the boy: "You don't think I'd spend my money on that junk, do you?"

Once in a while—but only once in a while—you may get a legitimate request for an advance on your kids' allowance. Whether you give in depends on the circumstances, how responsible your children have proved to be in the past and how often they make such a request. If you do decide to hand over the money, set up a fixed repayment schedule. With older children you might consider charging at least a nominal rate of interest. Or to save yourself the bookkeeping hassle you might work out a deal: You advance them the money; they pay you back within, say, one month—and owe you a free lawn-mowing as "interest."

Linda Jessup is the founder of the Parent Encouragement Program, a parent-support group that teaches a practical approach to child-rearing. She and her husband David also developed a cradle-to-college system for teaching their own seven children how to manage money. A cornerstone of their plan was to stand firm and let the kids get out of their own tight corners. Imagine, for example, a situa-

What About Losing Stuff?

• •

Q. *Dear Dr. Tightwad: My kids are always losing things, and I end up paying to replace it all. What can I do to make them more careful?*

A. Stop covering their losses.

- **Make 'em stew.** You bought little Johnny a $20 wristwatch for Christmas, and by Easter the watch is history. If you're willing to replace it, at least make Johnny wait till next Christmas—and next time, buy a cheaper watch.
- **Make 'em sweat.** Your child comes home with a note from school telling you she owes $10 for a lost library book. Tell her to come up with the money from the stash in her dresser drawer. She doesn't have a stash? Have her do extra jobs around the house to earn the $10, and then take it to school.
- **Make 'em pay.** Your son tries out for the football team but quits, leaving his uniform in his locker instead of turning it in. A month later you get a $150 bill for a lost uniform. Your son doesn't have $150, and it would take too long to work off the debt. Do what one dad did: Pay the $150, but deduct $5 a week from your son's allowance until the debt is repaid.

tion in which a child is invited to a birthday party but has run through his allowance and doesn't have enough to buy a present (one of the expenses the allowance is supposed to cover). "We tend not to give loans," explains Linda, "so we would discuss his choices and the advantages and disadvantages of each." He could, for example, not go because he doesn't have a gift. Or he could give something of his own that his friend likes. Or he could make a card and enclose a promise to buy the gift next week. He could give a gift of service and offer to help his friend clean his room or let him ride his bike. "We have also allowed kids to be socially ungrateful and go without a gift," says Linda. "But that problem has tended to correct itself."

Q. *I'm trying—unsuccessfully—to get my kids to manage a monthly allowance. They blow the money on stuff like compact discs and then run out of lunch money. Do you have any suggestions, or should I just bag the whole idea?*

A. Don't give up without a fight. Even though they seem like irresponsible spendthrifts, your kids may simply be having trouble budgeting. It's often tough for kids (and grown-ups) to tell the difference between things they need and things they want and to set priorities. Here's an exercise that will help:

1. On a sheet of paper, have your kids write down their total monthly (or weekly) income from all sources— allowance, jobs, gifts. Then have them write down

---

The High Cost of Movies

Q. *Dear Dr. Tightwad: With summer here and so many good "kid" movies out, I'm spending a fortune on theater tickets and overpriced soft drinks. Hey, I like the films, too, and it's a cool way to keep the kids occupied on hot summer days. But how can I control the cost short of smuggling in contraband treats?*

A. Dr. T assumes that you're already taking advantage of cheaper seats at matinee or late afternoon performances, so it's tough to cut ticket prices further unless you're willing to wait for the movie to come to your local video store.

Banning all treats would make a big dent in the cost. But if you and the kids *like* munching on cheese nachos, overpriced though they are, strike a deal: You buy the tickets and the kids buy their own treats. When they see that buttered popcorn can eat up a week's allowance, they may decide to buy one order and share—or do without. In any case, you won't be left holding the bag.

what they're *expected* to buy with their money and what they'd *like* to buy. Give them free rein to include everything from pencils to a Porsche.

2. A week or so later, pull out their paper again. Have the kids break the big list into two smaller ones: the boring stuff they have to buy—such as school supplies and lunches, toiletries and whatever else you've agreed on—and the fun stuff they want. Tot up expenses in the have-to-buy column, compare it with total monthly income and see how much is left.

3. In another week or so, go back to the list. Now that your kids know they have, say, $10 a week to spend on the fun stuff, they can see that if they use the money to buy a CD every couple of weeks, they won't be able to afford the new jeans. If they must have the jeans, CDs will have to wait.

Seeing all this in writing and over the course of a few weeks somehow makes it easier to categorize the items on a wish list as must-have, can-wait or in-your-dreams. It may suggest other possibilities as well—a part-time job for your kids or even a bigger allowance. If none of this works, maybe your kids *are* irresponsible spendthrifts. Cut them back to a weekly allowance until they're more mature.

Q. *My 14-year-old daughter wants a clothing allowance so she can buy her own clothes. Should I trust her?*

Francie reprinted by permission of UFS, Inc.

A. Should you trust her not to buy a black leather jacket with lug nuts dangling from the collar? Probably not. Should you trust her to spot a bargain and buy the jacket on sale? Probably so, provided you've given her some training along the way. By the time children reach their early teens, they ought to be on their own to buy birthday gifts or an occasional article of clothing for themselves. If they've been getting an allowance, it may be time to see whether they can handle the money on a monthly basis, rather than weekly. You can gradually expand their financial responsibilities; by the time they're juniors or seniors in high school, it's not unreasonable to expect them to manage a quarterly clothing budget.

But they can't do it alone. When the Jessup children were in elementary school, their mother would take them on shopping expeditions for back-to-school clothes and point out what was well made and what would shrink in the wash, what was faddish and what would still be stylish a year later. When they were 11, the children began to get a quarterly clothing allowance of $100 (since raised to $150), which was supposed to cover everything except shoes and coats. "One year my daughter didn't buy new socks or underwear, and hers eventually disintegrated," says Linda Jessup. "She gained a whole new sense of respect for things that only you know you're wearing."

If you cringe at the prospect of your child wearing an expensive leather jacket and torn underwear, take the gradual approach. Help your kids monitor their expenses for several months so that you each have a good idea of how much they'll need. Then set a monthly allowance, but hand it out in weekly installments until you're confident they're able to make it last. Or keep control of some purchases—coats, shoes, underwear—yourself.

Even with a gradual approach, not every child is ready for a clothing allowance at age 11. When April Allmond allowed her 12-year-old daughter, Jennifer, to go off by herself at the shopping mall, she "wandered

Kids & Money

In a Childreach survey of 10- to 14-year-olds, conducted by Louis Harris, 61% of the kids said they would give up some of their pocket money to help feed kids in poverty-stricken countries, 50% would go without some presents at Christmas and 37% would give up money for summer vacations, but only 27% would sacrifice their back-to-school clothing allowance.

If saving and giving are important values you want to teach your kids, don't be afraid to force their hand.

around for two hours and then came back and said, 'I need help,'" recounts April. At 14, however, Jennifer set off with a gift certificate and a money-off coupon and came back with "a really attractive wardrobe."

Doing Good

Q. *Should I force my children to save their money or give a portion to charity, or should I let them do it on their own?*

A. It would be ideal if they were to do it on their own with a little encouragement from you. But if saving and giving are important values you want to teach your kids, don't be afraid to force their hand. You could use the three-jar allowance system: a portion for saving, a portion for spending, a portion for giving. In the Jessup household, each child was expected to tithe 10% and put at least twice that amount into savings, just as their parents strove to.

The Rhyne family of Seattle requires their children to contribute 10% each to savings and to a charity of their choice. One year the kids decided to "adopt" a mother and her four children who had been deserted by their husband and father. "At Christmas, the gift-giving was awesome; they used more than their allotted charity money to buy things for the family," says Craig Rhyne. "On my son's Christmas card to us, he wrote that this year he had learned it was better to give than to receive."

Work for Pay

Q. *If I give my kids an allowance, should I expect them to do chores in return?*

A. Do you want the professional view or the parental one? Child-development experts generally recommend that you not tie your children's allowance to chores. "If kids get the idea that the only reason they do what they're supposed to do at home is to get paid for it, you're going to develop a bunch of little mercenaries," says Martin Ford, a developmental psychologist and professor of education at George Mason University. "They won't develop the sense that they do things as part of their responsibility to the family."

Many parents apparently don't buy that reasoning. Perhaps the idea of simply handing money over to their children sounds too much like a free lunch. Or perhaps they can't figure out any other way to get little Billy to make his bed. In any case, surveys consistently show that most kids who get allowances have to do chores in return. When *Zillions* asked 45 kids whose allowances were tied to chores how many jobs they were expected to do each week, the list ranged from two to 11, with three or four about average. James McNeal of Texas A&M says his studies of children and their money show that basic allowances are decreasing while income from chores at home (and outside jobs) is on the rise.

But linking allowances and chores can present practical problems for parents. If little Billy makes his bed on only four days out of seven, do you give him his weekly dole? If his income is dependent on work completed, you'll have to go to the trouble of coming up with a pay scale per chore and monitor which ones actually get done. And what if one week little Billy decides that he doesn't need any money, so he doesn't do any work?

Consider Your Goals

To help you find a workable solution to the allowance-for-chores quandary, Dr. T offers this set of guidelines:

- **If your main goal is to teach your kids to manage money,** go ahead and give them an allowance with no strings attached (but with an appropriate lecture on why you're being so generous). It's the easiest system for all concerned and will serve your purpose of getting money into their hands. To avoid giving your

Surveys consistently show that most kids who get allowances have to do chores in return.

To avoid turning your children into money-grubbers, expect them to do a couple of basic chores—gratis.

kids the impression that they're entitled to handouts, don't go overboard. You might give them a small base allowance that isn't linked to chores and let them earn extra money for bigger jobs such as raking leaves, washing the car or cleaning the garage.

- **If your main goal is to teach your kids that they don't get something for nothing,** make chores the quid pro quo for their allowance and don't feel guilty about it. To make the bookkeeping easier, and to make the connection between work and pay, you might even pay them as soon as a job is done to your satisfaction instead of waiting for a designated payday. To avoid turning your children into little money-grubbers who refuse to do anything without being paid, expect them to do a couple of basic chores—making their beds, cleaning their rooms—gratis.

Two Families' Systems

Brent Neiser, executive director of the Institute of Certified Financial Planners, has always used a strict fee-for-service system with his two children. The Neisers didn't pay for certain "family" chores, such as doing the dishes or keeping one's room clean, but they put a price tag on jobs that a maid or a neighborhood teenager might be hired to do: emptying the wastebaskets, cleaning the bathroom, raking the leaves, washing the car. It was the children's responsibility to keep a record of what they had done and present their parents with an itemized bill by 9:30 each Sunday morning; then they could immediately deduct 10% for their weekly tithe. The idea, says Neiser, was to give the children, both of whom were adopted at the ages of 8 and 6 from difficult backgrounds, a sense of family structure. But it had unexpected benefits. When little brother was old enough to take over the job of emptying wastebaskets, "he felt great," recalls Neiser. "He was getting to do something his big sister had done."

The Rhyne family adopted another system. When the Rhyne children were 12, 10 and 7, they and their parents signed an agreement in which mom and dad promised to pay a hefty monthly allowance that would cover clothing (except for "Sunday clothes" and basics such as winter gear and underwear), gifts, savings, charitable donations and spending money. The 10-year-old got $50 a month, the 11-year-old, $60. In return, the kids agreed that each day they would do certain personal jobs, such as making beds and clearing their own dishes after meals, and at least one family job, such as vacuuming the rug or feeding the dog. To earn extra money, the kids can do extra jobs, such as planting the garden or cleaning the garage.

Allowances aren't strictly tied to work, but on payday job performance is reviewed. "We aren't drill sergeants," says dad Craig Rhyne. But if a child has done a chronically sloppy job, a fine is deducted from his or her next allowance. If mom and dad ended up doing the chore, they keep the money. But if a sibling did the job, the sibling gets the extra cash. "Can you imagine—some of brother's allowance going to his little sister," says Rhyne. "Do you think he learns fast?"

The Rhynes have packaged their experience into *Monthly Money,* an allowance system that comes with a parents' manual and a folder with separate compart-

Ideas on Work for Pay

Q. *Dear Dr. Tightwad: I don't like the idea of just handing over an allowance to my kids, and I'd like to link the money with chores. Any suggestions on how to do this successfully?*

A. Keep it simple. Try one of these strategies.

- **Choose-a-chore.** Attach a value to household jobs and let your kids select the ones they want to do. This plan works best with kids who need or want money. If they don't, the work may not get done.

- **Point system.** Invest in a big calendar or bulletin board and have your kids tally a point each time they do something helpful around the house. At the end of the week you can award, say, 10 cents a point. This plan works best for younger children who do fairly simple tasks that are roughly equal in value, such as making beds or setting the table.

- **Negative option.** Put your kids' allowance—say, $5 a week—in quarters in a glass jar (or use dimes for a smaller amount). Each time your children don't respond to your request for help, take out a quarter. At the end of the week, they get to keep what's left.

ments for each item on the kids' budget ($19.95 for the "economy" version, plus $5 for shipping and handling; 800-547-4848).

Q. *If I don't pay my kids, how do I get them to do chores?*

A. There's the rub. You could simply try asking, especially if your kids are still young. Many parents anticipate doing battle on the chore front, but unless you and your kids are barely on speaking terms, they should respond to your request. After all, you're the parent.

"If you project self-confidence in your relationship with your children, you won't have to rely that often on techniques to get them to do what you want," says John Rosemond, family psychologist and author. "Put your cards on the table, and walk away and let your child come to grips with the hand." Rosemond recalls an incident that occurred when his own daughter was a teenager and he asked her to wash the dinner dishes. She protested that she had too much homework, and he replied that she could fit in both. Again she refused. "I got up, looked at her and said, 'You know and I know that you're going to do the dishes, so there's no point in wasting any more time.' I walked out and she did the dishes."

Even if you're not a trained professional, this bears trying at home. If it doesn't work, deal yourself a new hand. You might, for example, let your children have a say in choosing the jobs they'll do. That cuts down on the complaining and gives them a vested interest in doing the job right.

It's also an opportunity for you and your kids to move beyond bedmaking and taking out the trash. Author and family counselor Eda LeShan recalls talking to a group of kids who complained that all they got to do were the "dumb" jobs. "They're given 'dumb' things to do because their parents don't trust them," says LeShan. She tells of a friend who had to be out of town for a few days and put her 10-year-old in charge of taking telephone messages. "That's pretty sophisticated for a 10-year-old, but the child was very proud of being trusted to do it."

Children also feel more comfortable with what's expected of them when it's part of a daily routine. Chances are you already have a schedule for getting your kids to do their homework or get ready for bed, so Plan C is to make chores part of the drill. Making beds goes with brushing teeth in the morning, and clearing the table goes with doing homework at night.

Martin Ford of George Mason University is the father of two young sons. When older son Jason turned 5, he received, along with gifts, one chore to do; another is added on each birthday. By age 7, he was responsible for making his bed, setting the table for dinner and doing his homework. "It's a mark of maturity," says Ford, "and we make it a matter-of-fact expectation that he does the job." Ford figures it's just like the real world: "Some managers think you can't get workers to do anything unless you pay them," he says, but setting high standards and expecting them to be met works, too.

I Won't Do It

If your children flatly refuse, much as they might refuse to eat their peas at dinner, their behavior could be a symptom of a power struggle that you may be able to defuse by talking things out. (For example, you might say: "Just as everyone in the family is expected to sample at least three bites of all the food that's on the table, everyone is expected to pitch in and do his or her share of work.") If not, you may have to fall back on those few well-chosen words: "Because I said so and I'm the Mommy/Daddy." That strategy works better with younger children than with adolescents, who may require more drastic measures—the "no peas, no dessert" approach. Simply tell them that until they make the beds/vacuum the floor/give the dog a bath, you will not take them to the soccer game/movies/shopping mall. Then stand firm. It shouldn't take more than one or two missed matinees for them to get the message.

"We made our kids budget for [an allowance] by figuring out what their expenses were and how much they needed. With my kids the impulse was to hold it down rather than pump it up because they didn't want to tell me how much money they were blowing."
Jane Bryant Quinn

Or, like the Jessups, you may be able to think of a more creative solution. By age 11, all of the Jessup children were expected to be jacks of all trades, able to do the laundry for the family, prepare a simple, well-balanced meal and do the marketing. Starting at age 5, each child was given a weekly job, which the child had a hand in choosing. For example, a child might go "into training" to learn how to vacuum, cook or make lunches. If the child chose vacuuming, "I'd ask what days I could count on having it taken care of, and I'd expect it to be done at that time," says Linda. If it wasn't, "I'd point out to the child that he or she chose the job and ask what the problem was." Sometimes the solution was as simple as a gentle reminder—one kid hung a sign from his own bedroom doorway to remind himself—or trading jobs with someone else.

"I need some short-term economic stimulus."

But sometimes Mom had to take matters into her own hands. Once, when Linda was dissatisfied with the performance of her kitchen and trash crew, she prepared a sign, complete with vicious-looking flies, announcing that the kitchen was closed by order of the Jessup Health Department. When the kids arrived home after school, ravenous for snacks, Linda told them the kitchen was unsanitary and she wasn't willing to cook there. Finally, four of the kids put together a team-cleaning effort and the kitchen was reopened.

One final piece of advice about chores: Things should get better. When your kids are 6 they'll leave their wet towels crumpled on the bathroom floor. When they're 13 they'll leave them crumpled in the closet. But by the time they're in college, they should have the presence of mind to hang them neatly—over the doorknob.

Never Underestimate the Power of a Kid

Q. *I'm sick of hearing my kids argue about whose turn it is to empty the dishwasher and take out the trash. I've tried paying them to do chores, I've tried making up schedules, but I can't find a system that works. Any suggestions?*

A. Don't change the system, change the chores. Your purpose in requiring your children to do household jobs is to teach them responsibility and get help with some of the things you don't have time to do. So why settle for mundane tasks that don't take much time anyway? Give them bigger jobs that are potentially more interesting—and more likely to get done:

- **Santa's helpers.** Even 8-year-olds can wrap a stack of gifts or trim a tree. So what if the paper is torn and the ribbon is cockeyed? Grandma and Aunt Sis will love it. So what if one branch is sagging under the weight of 20 ornaments? You can always move them after the kids are in bed.

- **Kitchen aides.** Put your kids in charge of planning and preparing dinner once a week or breakfast on Sundays. The next time you have to come up with four dozen chocolate chip cookies for the class Halloween party, let your children do the baking.

- **Water babies.** Put them in charge of watering the garden, washing the car or the (low) windows, hosing the deck—any outside job that requires water (preferably from a hose or sprinkler), especially when it's hot outside.

- **Wardrobe masters.** Make your kids responsible for at least sorting and putting away (and possibly even washing) their own clothes. Trust them to pack their own suitcases for family trips. (Just check to make sure they've brought underwear.)

- **Party planners.** Anticipation is half the fun, so let them write the invitations, plan the games, put the treats in the goodie bags, make the poster for pin-the-nose-on-the-witch and help serve the food.

The point is to raise your parental expectations. One mother agreed to let her 11-year-old son take money from her purse for a comic book, only to find it was a special issue that cost $40. She kept the book until he worked off the debt—by helping her install drywall in his bedroom.

Good Grades, Good Pay

Q. *When my children behave particularly well or get good grades, I reward them with extra cash. Is that appropriate?*

A. Like the issue of linking allowances with chores, there's apparently a difference of professional and public opinion on whether money should be used as a reward. The pros say no. Better to reward children with a hug, words of encouragement or some nonmonetary treat like stickers or a later bedtime to let them know you're proud of them. That way, the virtue of doing their homework or getting good grades becomes its own reward, and they learn the personal satisfaction that comes with a job well done. In the Minnesota study, students who got an allowance were less likely to get internal satisfaction from working than students who didn't get an allowance.

But money can be too powerful a motivator for parents to resist. Frustrated by the lack of response when she asked her two new stepsons what was going on in school, one woman offered to pay the boys 25 cents, up to 50 cents a day, every time they reported something new they had learned. "That encouraged them to think back over their day; it got them using their minds," she says. When the boys kept forgetting to put on their seatbelts, she started a game: first one buckled up gets a quarter. "Boy, what a turnaround," she laughs.

Using money as an incentive can be appropriate if you give small amounts under the right circumstances.

For example, reward your kids after the fact for behaving well at the supermarket instead of promising them money ahead of time if they don't throw a tantrum. It may seem like splitting hairs, but the former is more of a reward, while the latter is an out-and-out bribe.

Payment for grades is a particularly touchy issue. Some parents are appalled by the idea, but others are quite willing to fork over the cash, on the theory that school is a child's primary employment and he or she ought to be rewarded for doing good work (especially if that child is forgoing a part-time job in favor of full-time studying). Brent Neiser pays his children not only for good grades but also for improvement in grades, with bonuses for a positive attitude or unexpected quality. "I want to let them know they can be paid not just for manual labor but for intellectual efforts as well," says Neiser. One mother compromised by agreeing to pay her son $5 for each *A* on his report card, on condition that the money be put into his college savings account.

Eventually, however, relying too much on financial incentives can impoverish you and won't do much to enrich your kids, either. You want to wean them from money, just as you weaned them from treats when they learned to go to the potty by themselves. "Money shouldn't be used as a reward beyond

Cents as Incentives

Q. *Dear Dr. Tightwad: My husband is always slipping our kids a couple of dollars to get them to practice their music lessons or sports. I don't like the idea, but he says it's not a lot of money and it will give them an incentive to work harder.*

A. Your husband is probably wasting his money. If your kids like what they're doing, they don't need any other reward. If they don't like what they're doing, maybe they should be playing a different musical instrument or sport.

If you can't get your husband to change his tune, try getting him to change his system. Instead of simply paying off the kids in cash, suggest that he reward them with "music money": For every 15 minutes spent practicing, they earn, say, one dollar in music money. When they've accumulated 20 music dollars, they're entitled to a new CD or a trip to the movies.

Young sports enthusiasts often have their eye on a new tennis racket, soccer bag or baseball glove. In this case try "sports cents": For every 15 minutes of practice, you credit your athletes with 100 sports cents. Once they've accumulated enough cents to pay for the coveted piece of equipment, you agree to spring for it.

"My kids didn't have a strong interest in money, so it wasn't much of a motivator as a punishment. They didn't care if I took away their allowance."
Jane Bryant Quinn

the age of 11 or 12," says Peter Spevak of the Center for Applied Motivation. By that time, rewards should be internal; if your daughter does a good job of cleaning up her room, make it a point to compliment her effort and comment on the satisfaction she must feel.

Let's face it, though: No one is ever too old for the occasional blowout. A spontaneous family dinner out to celebrate good report cards is a sure-fire morale booster.

The Parent Giveth, the Parent Taketh Away

Q. *What about fining my kids if they misbehave?*

A. Far better to make the discipline fit the deed. If the children are fighting about which show to watch on TV, they don't watch any. If they dawdle in doing their homework or getting ready for bed, they don't play Nintendo.

Still, monetary disincentives have been known to do the trick if you use them strategically. (Translation: Hit 'em where it hurts, but not too often.) When the Durney family moved to a new house with a laundry chute, the children got it into their heads that cleaning up their rooms meant tossing all items of clothing into the chute. Tired of fishing her kids' clean clothes out of the laundry bin, Peggy Durney told them each item of clean clothing would cost them 10 cents. That did the trick.

It would also be appropriate to make your kids pay if their carelessness causes damage that money can fix. When Lucas and Kendra Durney got into a friendly tussle while they were wearing their church clothes, Kendra's tights were snagged and ruined—and Lucas was responsible for replacing them. If the damage is more extensive—for example, your kids break a neighbor's window after being warned repeatedly not to play ball so close to the house—it's their responsibility to apologize and to offer to pay for at least part of the repair costs.

To discipline your children, you're best off using some of the same strategies you'd use to get them to do chores, chief of which is the force of your own authority. If your children pay attention to you in general and want your approval, just telling them what you expect of them—and indicating that you'll be disappointed in them if they don't deliver—can get them to do what you want.

That doesn't mean you should wield dictatorial power. Kids are more inclined to cooperate with you if you're open to them when they have a problem or complaint. But deep down parents know that their children are only as disciplined as they themselves are and that kids will push as far as they can. When parents draw the line, kids are stopped; when parents slide, so do kids. It's too exhausting to draw the line all the time, so you have to pick and choose your confrontations. To gain leverage, you may have to resort once in a while to techniques like time-out or grounding or the "if...then" gambit: "If you do x, then I'll be forced to respond by doing y."

Whatever you do, do it sparingly. Even good, effective tactics can lose their impact if they're overused. If you're basically insecure, your kids will sense that. Like the boy who cried wolf, you'll find that your attempts at taking charge will eventually lose their effect, and you could be forced into buying your kids' cooperation. As one parent lamented of her teenage son, "the only way I can control him is with money."

When parents draw the line, kids are stopped; when parents slide, so do kids.

And Now, for Your Regularly Scheduled Allowance

Q. *Sometimes I lose track of when I've given my kids their allowance, and when they remind me of it I always get the feeling they're trying to slip in an extra week. How can I keep from being rolled?*

A. Pay on a regular schedule, preferably a quiet weekday—maybe even your own payday—instead of the hectic weekend. Same goes for giving kids a raise in their allowance. Agreeing in advance on an annual allowance review to take place on the child's birthday or the first day of school will save your child the trouble of nagging you, and save you the pain of having to listen.

To schedule allowances for his youngest daughter, Cristi, when she was 11, Bill Corbett of Pocatello, Idaho, came up with a novel system of home banking. Corbett designed check vouchers and registers, then multiplied Cristi's weekly allowance of $6.50 by 52 and gave her a yearly allowance credit of $338. When she needed money, she wrote out a "check," entered the amount in her register, subtracted it from her balance and handed it over to Dad, who promptly cashed it. Cristi was allowed to withdraw up to three weeks of allowance at one time, but she could get the full amount of birthday money or money she had earned by doing a job.

Corbett's strategy effectively quashed plaintive cries of "You forgot my allowance," and it had other pluses. Cristi learned how to write checks and keep a register. Knowing that she had to husband her resources until the end of the year, she became adept at managing money. In two of the first five years that she used the system, she ended up with surpluses of around $100 each. Her dad wrote a real check for the amount of the surplus and deposited it in her college fund.

In a similar vein, Bill Todd of San Antonio started ParentBanc ($14.95, plus $4.95 for shipping and handling; 800-375-2262) with his two youngest children. Each boy gets a monthly allowance credit—$10 for the 9-year-old, $100 for the 17-year-old. Todd says the system has made both boys avid savers. The older son opened a real checking account with $1,000 when he turned 16; the younger son has saved $250 in three years. "They like to see it grow to the next $100 level," says Dad.

Q. *Systems like those sound great, but whenever I try to start one I don't seem to be disciplined enough to make it stick and after awhile we go back to our old slipshod ways.*

A. Don't be so hard on yourself. You don't have to duplicate all those wonderfully organized systems. Just pick and choose the tips that will work best in your household. Despite the emphasis on giving children an allowance as early as age 6 or 7, John Rosemond didn't bother with one until his own kids were teenagers. Then, says Rosemond, "we used the allowance to represent the fact that we were going to give the kids expanded autonomy over their lives."

Financial rewards for good behavior are frowned on by child-development experts. But used judiciously, they can work. One family created an inventive system to encourage their daughter to practice the piano. For every half hour of toil, she earns one "piano dollar," funny money with Beethoven's visage subbed for George Washington's. When she accumulates 20 piano dollars, she's treated to a meal at the fast-food restaurant of her choice.

If you don't have the time or the discipline to construct an elaborate system, concentrate on whatever is most important to you, whether it's teaching your kids to manage an allowance, do chores or contribute to charity. If you do nothing else, at least talk to your children about money when the opportunity presents itself, such as when you're withdrawing cash from the bank machine or paying bills. Brent Neiser has walked his kids through their tax returns, taken them to rental property he owns and discussed the responsibilities of landlords and tenants, shown them his credit report, and talked about the virtues of prepaying a mortgage. Says Neiser, "I can't think of anything I wouldn't share with them."

If you don't have the time or the discipline to construct an elaborate system, concentrate on whatever is most important to you.

Get Your Kids Hooked on Saving

Q. *Dear Dr. Tightwad: My kids seem to spend all their money on candy, movies and tapes. Is there some way to get them to save for important things like college?*

A. In your dreams. Unless kids are teenagers, college is a vague concept in the faraway future. To encourage younger kids to save, you need to make it worth their while by giving them a more manageable goal.

When Greg Gonzalez was 7 years old, he signed up for a school saving program and started squirreling away $10 to $20 a week—money he got from doing jobs around the house and practicing the piano. By the time he was 10, he had more than $1,000. Not satisfied with the rate of interest he was earning in the bank, Greg withdrew most of the money and began diversifying into a mutual fund and stocks, even as he continued to replenish the money in his bank account. While some kids his age were frittering away their allowances on Big Macs and Mickey Mouse T-shirts, Greg was buying shares in McDonald's and the Walt Disney Co. While other kids were paying to see basketball games, he bought a piece of the Boston Celtics.

Despite their reputation as yuppie-puppies, today's kids, especially younger ones, aren't all unregenerate spendthrifts. Kids under 12 actually save around 30% of their income, about half in banks and half stashed away in drawers. That's the highest rate recorded for children in two decades and more than double what it was in the mid '80s, according to research by James McNeal of Texas A&M. The latest figures show that 4-year-olds, who save over half their income, take top honors. The rate declines rapidly, to 37% at age 5, 27% at age 6 and a low of 17% at age 7. But then the rate begins moving up again and levels out at around 30% for children ages 9 to 12.

"It's the Tooth Fairy. She says if I FedEx her my tooth, she'll electronically transfer money into my bank account."

McNeal says the big jump in savings could simply reflect that parents are providing their kids with more money, or that parents are encouraging their kids to take more responsibility for managing money at an earlier age. But why speculate when we can ask an expert: Greg Gonzalez, what makes you save? "I get excited about what the money will grow into and what I'll be able to do with it when I grow up." How would he advise parents to get their kids hooked on savings? "Make them excited about it too."

To raise a generation of super savers, give them a reason to save. To keep them interested, reward them for their efforts. To guarantee their success, devise a system that makes saving easy.

Eyes on the Prize

Kids today have more reasons to save than their predecessors did a generation ago: big-ticket items, such as designer clothing or video equipment and games, that their parents are reluctant to buy. If you're feeling in a generous mood the next time your son simply must have a pair of $120 sneakers, offer to pay a portion of the price if he picks up the rest of the tab. Such a deal is a win-win situation: You save money and get the psychological satisfaction of saying no to what you probably consider a ridiculous request; he learns to save money and gets the psychological benefit of hearing you say that two-letter word.

The younger the child, the smaller and more immediate the goal should be; it ought to be something—a toy car, a set of paints, an action figure—that the child can reach within a few weeks. To make the task seem manageable, Jean Ross Peterson, author of *It Doesn't Grow on Trees* (Betterway), suggests attaching a picture of the coveted item to your child's bulletin board, along with a calendar and a plastic bag to hold accumulated savings. When the weeks are crossed off and the bag is full, let your child relish his reward.

Saving Ideas for Kids

Q. *Dear Dr. Tightwad: I'm a 9-year-old who gets an allowance and I'd like to save more of it, but every week it's gone. How can I keep it longer?*

A. Recognizing a problem is always the first step toward solving it, so Dr. T predicts you'll have a nice fat bank account some day. For now:

- Have your parents hang onto part of your allowance so you won't be tempted to spend it all.

- Don't carry money with you when you hit the stores; just browse. You can always come back if you want to buy (but often you won't).

- Divide your allowance among envelopes for saving, spending, or giving to charity. Only blow the spending envelope.

- Set your sights on something you really want. That will give you an incentive to save.

One Family's Savings Goal

Older children can move on to bigger, more expensive goals. You can even make saving a family project. For the Coogans of Michigan (not their real name), the catalyst that got them into the thrifty frame of mind was a first-ever family vacation to Florida. Ray Coogan is disabled by a chronic illness. His wife, Trudy, is a hairdresser. Of the five Coogan children still living at home, four are teenagers with part-time jobs. They all decided to pool their money for the trip south to visit another Coogan child.

As organizer and chief cheerleader, Ray Coogan set a relatively low initial goal of $2,500. He figured meeting it would be such a morale booster that everyone would be encouraged to aim even higher and extend their stay in Florida. All working family members were given a savings goal and offered a bonus: For meeting their goal quickly or making an extra effort (by requesting extra work hours, for example), they would be rewarded with an additional $25 in spending money for the trip.

Ray organized weekly family meetings to track their progress. "It wouldn't have worked if we hadn't had him to spearhead the whole thing and light a fire under everyone," says Trudy. Within three months the Coogans had saved $4,000 and were on their way in a rented van. Next year, maybe they'll head west.

What's a Parent to Do?

Q. *Dear Dr. Tightwad: My kids fritter away all their money and I'd like to teach them good savings habits, but I don't know how far it's appropriate for a parent to go.*

A. As far as it takes to get your point across. For example, Dr. T thinks its just fine for you to require your child to save a certain percentage of his allowance.

Also, because young kids have a tough time with abstract concepts like saving for college, encourage them to save for smaller, more manageable goals that they can reach within a reasonable amount of time. One big incentive is to offer to match what they save dollar for dollar.

Don't ignore teens, who are in most need of a reality check, and on whom you can have the biggest impact psychologically and financially. They're probably earning a part-time income, so don't be reluctant to make them save part of it for college or other post-high school plans.

Play Numbers Games

If you really want to get older kids excited about saving, dazzle 'em with numbers—in particular, the magic of compound interest. (Interest, of course, is the money a bank will pay you for letting it use your money; compounding means that you also earn interest on the interest paid, which gives your savings an extra boost.) Kids are turned on by the idea that over time their

"Compound interest is marvelous in the long run."

John Templeton, mutual fund pioneer

money can grow. In a money-management course for high school students prepared by the College for Financial Planning, the most popular chart in the workbook is the one that shows how fast an IRA will grow. To wit, if you put in $2,000 a year for nine years starting at age 22 and earn 9% on your money, your $18,000 will grow to $579,000 by the time you're 65. (By the way, 9% isn't an unreasonable rate of return. The Standard & Poor's 500-stock index has returned a tad over 10% annually, on average, since 1926).

For a dramatic illustration of the magic of compound interest, Harold Moe, co-author with wife Sandy

How Your Money Will Grow

You can use this table to figure how much to save or invest to accumulate a specific amount by some future date. Say you and your daughter are planning for her to save $5,000 by the time she starts college six years from now. Assuming that she could earn 8% on her savings and investments, how much should she put away monthly?

Find the place in the table where six years intersects with 8%. Divide that number—926—into your goal of $5,000. The result tells you that your goal is 5.4 times the total generated by $10 monthly deposits. Your daughter will have to set aside $54 each month to reach the goal on time, assuming an 8% return.

Year	5%	6%	7%	8%	9%	10%	11%	12%	13%	14%	15%
1	$123	$124	$125	$125	$126	$127	$127	$128	$129	$130	$130
2	253	256	258	261	264	267	270	272	275	278	281
3	389	395	402	408	415	421	428	435	442	449	457
4	532	544	555	567	580	592	605	618	632	646	660
5	683	701	720	740	760	781	802	825	848	872	897
6	841	868	897	926	957	989	1,023	1,058	1,094	1,132	1,171
7	1,008	1,046	1,086	1,129	1,173	1,220	1,268	1,320	1,374	1,430	1,490
8	1,182	1,234	1,289	1,348	1,409	1,474	1,543	1,615	1,692	1,773	1,859
9	1,366	1,435	1,507	1,585	1,667	1,755	1,849	1,948	2,054	2,168	2,288
10	1,559	1,647	1,741	1,842	1,950	2,066	2,190	2,323	2,467	2,621	2,787
15	2,684	2,923	3,188	3,483	3,812	4,179	4,589	5,046	5,557	6,129	6,769
20	4,128	4,644	5,240	5,929	6,729	7,657	8,736	9,991	11,455	13,163	15,160
25	5,980	6,965	8,148	9,574	11,295	13,379	15,906	18,976	22,714	27,273	32,841
30	8,357	10,095	12,271	15,003	18,445	22,793	28,302	35,299	44,206	55,571	70,098

Moe of *Teach Your Child the Value of Money,* performs the checkerboard trick, which is guaranteed to knock the socks off everyone from elementary-school kids to adults. It works like this: You raid the penny jar or make a trip to the bank and load up on pennies—say, $10 to $20 worth. Then you take out the family checkerboard and place one penny on the first square in the first row. Double the number of pennies in the second square, and continue doubling them until you reach the end of the first row, at which point you'll have 128 pennies. Then, with a flourish, point to the pile of pennies that remains and ask your audience to guess how many will be left after you've filled the entire checkerboard by doubling the amount of pennies on each square. After a suspenseful pause, announce triumphantly that there probably isn't enough money in the whole world to complete all 64 squares.

With older children, you can go on to more math legerdemain. The rule of 72, for example, states that dividing 72 by the interest rate you're earning tells you roughly how long it will take your money to double (and dividing 72 by the number of years in which you want to double your money will tell you how much interest you need to earn). If you're earning, say, 8%, your money will double in about nine years.

By the time your kids are in high school, they should be able to use the accompanying table, which shows how much a deposit of $10 a month will grow at various rates of interest over different periods of time. You can easily use the chart to calculate how quick you can get rich with any monthly deposit.

A Spoonful of Sugar

No less a light than John Templeton, the mutual-fund pioneer and advocate of long-term saving, observes that "learning to save is so important that parents should reward their kids for doing it." One of the most effective rewards you can offer is an incentive system in which you match all or part of your child's

Money Fun

How much is a million? A million dollars would be a stack of pennies 95 miles high, enough nickels to fill a school bus, or a whale's weight in quarters. A million one-dollar bills would weigh 2,500 pounds and stack up to 360 feet. We rack up $1 million in interest on the national debt every minute and 26.4 seconds.

savings. This tactic works well with children of all ages, but especially teenagers who might be saving for a big-ticket item such as a car.

Rewards themselves don't have to break the bank. Sometimes a pat on the back is all it takes to push a child in the right direction. Consider the enthusiastic students of Bay Terrace School, P.S. 169, in Bayside, Queens, which has a magnet program in business, finance and international trade. More than two-thirds of the school's students are savers in a program with Chemical Bank, says principal Joel Seigerman. They've saved just under $100,000 in assets in 450 accounts. They're children like:

- **Hillary Fingerhut:** "It's a cool thing to do," says Hillary, who advocates taking draconian measures if kids let their allowances burn a hole in their pockets. "Keep part of their allowance. When they ask for more money, don't give it to them."

- **Kenny Sokol:** "I never had a bank account before, and when I got the notice from school I said to my mom, 'Please let me have one.' Parents should tell their kids, 'What happens if your father loses his job and has to borrow money?'"

- **Rachel Nierenberg:** "Last year I thought I would like to save for college, so I started the banking program and I usually put in $2 every week," says Rachel. But she might raid her account for something special—like the Felicity doll from the Pleasant Company's American Girls Collection.

As in all other aspects of teaching kids about money, your attitude is critical. One of the biggest

---

Helping Kids Save

• •

In the schoolbased **Save for America** campaign, PTA volunteers collect the kids' coins at school once a week, record the deposits on a computer, then take the disk and the money to the sponsoring bank. Save for America, under way in 28 states, has garnered more than $11 million. If you'd like to get your school in on the action, phone 206-746-0331 for more information, or ask your local banks if they have similar savings programs for schools.

reasons kids don't participate in school savings programs is lack of interest on the part of parents. Sherrie Avery is marketing director at First National Bank of South Miami, which sponsors Twiglet, a school bank that's run by students at David Fairchild Elementary in South Miami. In Avery's experience, some children who are gung-ho about the program lose interest when their parents don't share their enthusiasm. "Either the kids don't get an allowance or the parents don't give them money to save," says Avery.

Still, school banking programs, which were ubiquitous a generation or two ago and then all but disappeared, are making a comeback (see the accompanying box).

Systems That Work

Key to the success of any saving regimen, whether for kids or adults, is getting into the habit of doing it regularly, and that means making it as painless as possible. Among younger children, banks often conjure up an image of a place that takes your money but doesn't give it back, so saving is best begun at home, where kids can keep an eye on their money and watch it grow. For the same reason, children will be frustrated to see their money swallowed up by a piggy bank that

" HI. MY NAME IS DENNIS MITCHELL, AND I DON'T HAVE A PENNY TO MY NAME."

Dennis the Menace ® used by permission of Hank Ketcham and © by North America Syndicate

can be opened only by a well-aimed hammer. Better to make the money more accessible—in a bank with a lock, a wallet, a jar or that old standby, the cigar box. One inventive 11-year-old kept each bill carefully displayed in a photo album (and even folded the bills around the edge of the page so that half appears on one page and half on the next—a convenient way to double your money).

If your children are disciplined enough to save a portion of their allowance on their own, congratulations! If not, don't be afraid to exert some parental pressure.

- As noted in Chapter 5, you can impose the *three-jar allowance system:* a portion for spending, a portion for saving and a portion for charitable giving.

- Slightly more strict is the *half-and-half plan,* in which your children are required to save half of all the money they get.

- Or you might choose the *spare-change* method, which lets your kids spend their bills but save their coins (which eventually can be put into rolls and taken to the bank).

Although they may grouse about it, your kids will appreciate the discipline. When he was in fourth grade and getting an allowance of $1.50 a week, Jonathan Levy actually preferred that his parents hang on to the money and give it to him once a month instead of every week. "When you get it in bigger amounts it seems like you get more, and you don't spend it all at once on things like baseball cards like you sometimes do if you get it in small amounts," says Jonathan. "It's much easier to save that way."

What really irks Jonathan (not to mention countless other kids) is mom and dad dipping into his stash to pay the pizza man, the babysitter or the paper girl and then never getting around to paying him back. To solve the problem, he has suggested that his parents contribute a few dollars each payday to a spare-change bank. He'd oversee it, of course, but the whole family

Gone With the Wind

• • • • • • • • • • • • • • • • • • • •

Q. *Dear Dr. Tightwad: My children are really careless with money. They'll get a $5 birthday gift, and I'll find it lying on the floor. I'm afraid they're going to lose it altogether.*

A. Let them. Assuming your children are at least in elementary school, hanging onto the money yourself or making them put it in the bank is too draconian. Especially if the amount is small, you might as well give them a low-risk lesson in managing money. Allowing them to recoup a lost $5 by doing extra chores is too generous. If they eat the loss, they'll be more inclined to take better care of their money next time.

could dip into it for a no-interest loan when they needed petty cash. His parents liked the idea, says Jonathan, but they hadn't gotten around to doing it.

How to Open a Bank Account

Eventually your kids will get old enough, or accumulate money enough, to be introduced to the fine points of a real bank account. Remember how it worked when you were a kid? You could walk up to the window, give the teller your deposit and have the amount stamped in your passbook, where it grew right before your eyes. Not anymore. Most banks have done away with passbooks, even for kids' accounts, and many have minimum-balance requirements or impose stiff service charges on small balances that can add up to more than you make in interest and eventually deplete the account.

> ## A Bank for Young Americans
> •
> **Young Americans Bank** (311 Steele St., Denver, Colo. 80206; 303-321-2265), which offers savings accounts, checking accounts, credit cards and loans, has mail-in customers from all 50 states and several foreign countries. The average savings customer is 9 years old and has a balance of $260. Write or call for more information.

Jane Clark found that out when she opened an account for her son, Bennett, with about $300 in savings and birthday money. When Bennett's first monthly statement arrived, his mom was shocked to see that a $5 service charge had wiped out all the interest he had earned and then some. After several phone calls a bank official finally told her that the usual service charge on a small account should have been waived on a minor's account. Make sure your bank has a similar practice.

Bank policy on accounts for children varies among states, banks and even branches, depending on state law and banks' own preferences. As long as kids can sign their name, some banks will allow them to own accounts and make both deposits and withdrawals. More commonly, however, you'll probably have to co-sign the account, and you control it; your child may not be able to make withdrawals without your signature.

One notable exception is Young Americans Bank in Denver, where all customers are under the age of 22 (see the box on the preceding page). For kids under 18, Young Americans sets up joint accounts in the name of both parent and child, with two signatures required for most transactions. Parents actually need their children's authorization to make a withdrawal. The bank will also let you sign a release allowing your kids to make withdrawals on their own. Other financial institutions sometimes offer a similar option, so ask about it if you want your children to have more control over their own money.

After your children open an account at a bank, they may need your help in getting the money there. You may have to volunteer to be their personal banker, making deposits during school hours. Another option for older children is to grab a stack of deposit slips and let them make deposits by mail. They can give their cash to you, and you can write a check that they can send in with the slip.

A Tax Tip for Co-signed Accounts

Make sure your child's social security number is used as the tax identification number on any account on which your name also appears as co-signer. That way, interest earned will be treated as your child's income for tax purposes.

Children can make up to $600 in investment income in 1993 without having to pay any taxes. Income between $600 and $1,200 will be taxed at the child's 15% rate. But if your child is under 14, income above $1,200 will be taxed to him or her at your rate, even though the child is the principal owner of the account. That's the so-called kiddie tax, and it's intended to keep parents from ducking taxes by shifting income to their children. After your children reach 14, however, their income is taxable at their rate.

No Withdrawals Allowed?

Once your children have put their money into the bank, should they be able to get it out—to buy those $120 sneakers, for example—or should they be required to keep it there for longer-term goals like that college education? That decision is up to you. For many children, being able to withdraw the money to pay for some short-term goal provides most of the impetus for saving in the first place. Just getting your kids to put money aside is a major victory, even if they end up spending it on something you personally wouldn't have bought. Or you may compromise by allowing your children to withdraw a certain portion of their savings.

But some families have a different philosophy. Linda and David Jessup believe their children shouldn't draw on savings for things like Christmas presents or sneakers. Instead, they might give their kids a stipend of $25 to buy Christmas gifts or require them to earn at least part of the money they need. When one of their daughters wanted to take over a paper route and needed a new bicycle, the family agreed to pay half the cost if she earned the rest. She did—and carted the papers around in a wagon in the meantime. "Savings aren't for whims or present expenses," explains Linda. "They're for your future."

When to Lend a Hand

Q. *Dear Dr. Tightwad: My daughter has been saving money to buy a new bike. She doesn't have quite enough yet, but the model she has her eye on is going on sale. Should I lend her the rest or tell her she'll just have to wait until she has enough money even if it means missing the sale?*

A. If you're expecting Dr. T to save you a few bucks by telling you to hang tough and make your daughter wait, you're in for a surprise. Go ahead and lend her the money she needs. Even Dr. T has a heart (and can't resist a bargain).

Investing: Raise a Wall St. Whiz Kid

Q. *Dear Dr. Tightwad: I'd like my kids to learn how to invest some of their savings in stocks, but I don't know much about the market myself. What should I do?*

A. Read this chapter.

By the age of 11 or 12, about 10% of children have advanced from savings accounts to stocks and mutual funds. By the time they're teenagers, a few of them are on their way to becoming Wall Street rocket scientists. Such a one is Jonathan Hagelstein of Weston, Conn. By the time he was 15 he was managing his own $10,000 portfolio, "more than his father and I had when we got married," says his mom, Ann. Jon built up a core of reliable blue-chip stocks, including AT&T, IBM and Bell Atlantic, and also owned some personal favorites, such as Topps and Reebok. He took a big flier on Euro Disneyland. "I knew it was risky," says Jon, "but I passed up Disney before and I didn't want to make the same mistake twice."

To support his investing habit, Jon earned $20 a week working at a health-food store and got an additional $5 to $10 in allowance and gift money. All of it was going into a bank account from which he could make his own withdrawals without his parents' co-signatures. Not that he makes many withdrawals for things other than investments. "Sometimes I go on a spree and buy something like a stereo, but I save 90% to 95% of what I get," says Jon. He even reinvests all his stock dividends in more shares.

All this started with ten shares of AT&T purchased for him by his father when Jon was 7. "This taught him how to make money by becoming the owner of a company," says his father, Robert. "He used to get angry at MCI commercials." For Jon, the real investment bug bit a little later, when he was 10 and wanted to collect Topps baseball card sets as an investment. "I told him he could invest in the cards or the company," says his dad. He chose the company. His shares split several times and turned out to be a "super investment."

Kids as Stock Pickers

Buying your children shares in a company is the best way to get them started in the market. Investing in only a few shares can be expensive as far as commissions go, although there are ways to minimize your costs (see the discussion beginning on page 99). But the lesson you're teaching is priceless and the options limitless. Instead of buying your kids computer software or a video game on their next birthday, present them with shares in a company like Electronic Arts, which produces games for Sega Genesis. Other kid-pleasing companies: Coca-Cola, PepsiCo, Disney, McDonald's, NIKE, Sony, Tyco, Hasbro, Wendy's, Score Board, Marvel—you get the picture.

The beauty of it is, you don't even have to be an expert stock picker; you can let your kids do the choosing. Jon's strategy: "Look at which clothes kids are wearing in school, find out what recording labels they're listening to, what kind of CD players they have. When I go to the mall, I go to the toy stores and shoe stores and ask what's selling fastest." Noticing that kids in his school were sporting a new

"I'm trying to introduce my kids slowly to the stock market, but they're not reading annual reports yet."
Peter Lynch, mutual fund guru and author

A Simple Strategy

Q. *Dear Dr. Tightwad: I'd like to interest my daughter and son, ages 12 and 11, in investing, but I'm afraid it will be too complicated for them.*

A. What's not to understand about getting a piece of the action? Play your cards right and investing will pique your kids' interest because it appeals to their acquisitiveness.

1. Start with a little book called *Ump's Fwat: An Annual Report for Young People* (available for $2 from the Academy for Economic Education, 125 NationsBank Center, Richmond, Va. 23219; video version, $24.95; $3 more for an Instructor's Guide). It's a fanciful look at Ump, the first caveman capitalist, that will help kids understand such terms as stockholder and dividend.

2. After your children grasp the basics, help them draw up a list of kid-pleasing companies, like Disney and McDonald's.

3. Take your kids to the library and ask to see the *Value Line Investment Survey*, which will give you an analyst's report on each company, along with reams of data on prices and dividends. You can find similar information in *Moody's Handbook of Common Stocks* or *S&P Reports.*

4. Once your kids have settled on a company, help them purchase a share or two by going through a discount broker (see page 101) to minimize commissions on small purchases.

5. Show your kids how to follow their company's stock price in the newspaper (see the illustration on page 93). They'll take it from there—guaranteed.

line of overalls, Jon scouted out the company that made them—Merry-Go-Round Enterprises. It was a new company selling for around $4 a share. He decided not to buy the stock, and later regretted it when it split several times and went to $20 a share. When his mom bought a stair-climber, he sensed another trend in the making. It turned out the machine was made by Reebok, a stock he already owned.

When young people like Jon Hagelstein speak, even old pros like Peter Lynch listen. Lynch, the star money manager whose expertise at the helm of Fidelity Magellan helped make it the largest and most successful mutual fund in the country, observed in his book *One Up on Wall Street* that "the best place to look for the tenbagger (a stock that appreciates tenfold) is close to home—if not in the backyard then down at the shopping mall." When Lynch's three daughters came home from the mall raving about the Body Shop, a British company that specializes in soaps, skin-care products and perfumes, Lynch did some checking and concluded that the company "would become a money machine" and bided his time to buy when the price was right.

A glance at your kids' Christmas lists over the last couple of years would have pointed you in the direction of any number of prospects: Ohio Art Co. of Bryan, Ohio, maker of the Etch-A-Sketch, a holiday classic; Hasbro, which scored a bull's-eye with its Nerf Bow and Arrow and also makes Playskool and Tonka toys and Milton Bradley board games; Rubbermaid, which has a reputation as an innovator in both the household products industry and the toy business, with its Little Tikes line of preschool toys and furniture. FYI: Nintendo is a Japanese company that's traded in the U.S. as an American depository receipt (ADR), a certificate traded that represents ownership of a specific number of shares of a foreign stock. Newspapers don't carry all ADR prices, so they can be hard to track.

How to Scout a Stock

Kids can be fickle customers, so there's no guarantee that the latest fad will be around long enough to make a success of the company that created it. If you're serious about getting your kids started in solid stocks with growth potential, you, and they, will have to do some research on the companies. And that's where many parents feel they are on shaky ground. 'Fess up—you may not even feel comfortable explaining to your kids what it means to invest in the stock market or helping them follow the price of a company's shares in the newspaper stock tables.

Relax. It isn't all that difficult, and you don't have to go it alone. This book can help, and so can a clever little volume called *Ump's Fwat, an Annual Report for Young People,* available through the Academy for Economic Education (for order information, see page 88). Ump, by the way, is a caveman, and the Reggie Jackson of his day in a primitive game called fwap that bears an uncanny resemblance to baseball. Fwappers toss rocks into the air and slug them with a club, or fwat.

'Fess up—you may not even feel comfortable explaining to your kids what it means to invest in the stock market.

Ump's fwat was much coveted by the other fwappers, so he had an idea: Why not start a company to make and sell fwats? Thus might the first capitalist have been born.

Cave dwellers interested in investing in Ump's Fwat Co. didn't have access to all the information that you do when it comes to researching prospective stock picks.

- **You can get annual reports and other information for free** by contacting the company directly.

- **A trip to your local library** will probably turn up the *Value Line Investment Survey* (or call 800-833-0046; $55 for a ten-week trial), which provides analyses of near-ly 2,000 individual companies; gives historical data on prices, earnings and dividends; and assigns each stock a rating for timeliness and risk. Similar information is available from *Moody's Handbook of Common Stocks* and *S&P Reports*. One or the other is likely to repose on your library's shelves.

Investor Perks for Kids

On Christmas morning, a share of stock just doesn't have the same kid appeal as finding a bow and arrow under the tree. Come to think of it, even lumps of coal probably sound like more fun. But what if your kids got battery-operated cars, chewing gum or tickets to amusement parks as holiday gifts? Those are a few of the kid-pleasing perks that some companies offer their shareholders, and we've listed more here.

An administrative note: All shareholders are eligible to receive such perks, but if your shares are held for you by your brokerage firm in a "street name" account, you may have to call the company's shareholder-services department to make sure you get them.

- **Tandy** gives shareholders a 10% discount on Radio Shack computers, toys and games. Stockholders can apply the discount to as many items as they wish, provided that the total value is $10,000 or less and the items are purchased at the same time.

- **William Wrigley Jr. Co.** each December sends stockholders a 100-stick box of gum, with the flavor assortment personally chosen by CEO William Wrigley.

- **Anheuser-Busch** makes the list not for its beer but for its amusement parks. Shareholders receive a welcome packet of goodies, including information about 15% discounts on admission to Busch Gardens and Sea World.

- **Financial publications** such as *Kiplinger's Personal Finance Magazine, Money, Smart Money, Forbes and Barron's* are invaluable and easy-to-use sources. Another resource is *Square One: The Newsletter for the Beginning Investor;* Amy T. Rauch-Bank, editor ($29.95 per year; 259 Peninsula Lake Dr., Highland, MI 48357).

- **You also have access to on-line databases for your home computer,** such as those available through Prodigy and CompuServe. But with these services you may have to pay extra for the kind of detailed financial information that you can get for free from your library's *Value Line.* You'll have to decide if you, and your kids, are serious enough about investing to warrant the extra cost (you're likely to be charged a monthly fee as well as fees for on-line time).

- **Disney's Magic Kingdom Club** offers shareholders the opportunity to purchase the Magic Kingdom Club Gold Card ($45), which offers a slew of discounts at Disney resorts and theme parks: 10% to 30% at selected Disney resorts and hotels as well as on accommodations at Euro Disney; discounts on some theme-park admissions; and price breaks on rental cars and cruise ships.

- **3M,** for a small charge, will deliver to recipients of your choice holiday gift boxes filled with an assortment of 3M products, such as tape, Post-Its and other household items. "My two kids (and even the third big kid, Dad) insist on a box of 3M products in their stocking each Christmas," reports one New York mom.

- **American Recreation Centers (ARC)** gives shareholders free games at its bowling centers in California, Kentucky, Oklahoma, Missouri, Wisconsin and Texas, plus a 20% discount on merchandise in its Right Start juvenile-products catalog. There is one catch. To qualify, you have to own at least 100 shares of ARC stock. But there's always next Christmas.

In Ump's day, shareholders might have tracked the ups and downs of Ump's Fwat Co. by scanning the stock tables in The Gnu Yerk Times or The Welp Strit Journal. So can you. Don't be intimidated by what at first looks like endless gibberish. The tables are easy to interpret—and are much admired by math teachers for the practice they give kids in using fractions, decimals and percentages. For a detailed look at how to read and interpret the stock tables, see the accompanying illustration.

Child's Play

When it comes to stocks, don't sell short your kids' ability to process all this information—or at least enough of it to understand what it means to own a piece of the company whose products they're using, eating, wearing, listening to or playing with. Listen to this stock market analysis from sixth-graders in teacher Debra Masnik's class at Keene Mill School in Springfield, Va.:

- **Matt Suskiewicz:** "We bought Blockbuster Entertainment just when it had taken over Erol's because we thought it was a good move. But the price didn't rise right away because it takes awhile for a takeover to settle down. If we had more time, we would have done okay."

- **Stefi Sylvester:** "We steered clear of short-selling because the prices were too bouncy."

- **Angel Thomas:** "Disney looked good because *Robin Hood* and *Beauty and the Beast* were coming out, and the stock price did go up for a few weeks. But then it tanked."

- **Mike Mihalik:** "We didn't buy Disney because we thought there was too much competition from other movies, like *Hook.*"

The kids are doing a post mortem on the Stock Market Game, a 10-week project in which teams of students vied to turn a $100,000 investment into a winning portfolio. The game is sponsored by the Securities

How to Read the Stock Listings

A A small "s" next to the listing means the stock was split or the company issued a stock dividend within the last year. This is your signal that the year's high and low prices have been adjusted to reflect the effect of the split.

B An "x" indicates that the stock has gone "ex-dividend." Investors who buy the stock now won't get the next dividend payment, which has been declared but not paid. Most listings stick the "x" next to the figure in the volume column.

C Sometimes a stock has been issued so recently that it doesn't have a full year's history on which to base its pricing. In such a case the 52-week high

and low prices date from the beginning of trading and the stock gets a little "n" to the left of the listing.

D The dividend listed is the latest annual dividend paid by that stock.

E The yield is the stock's latest annual dividend expressed as a percentage of that day's price.

F The price/earnings ratio is the price of the stock divided by the earnings reported by the company for the latest four quarters.

G Prices—and price changes—are reported in ⅛-point increments. An eighth of a dollar is 0.125 cent.

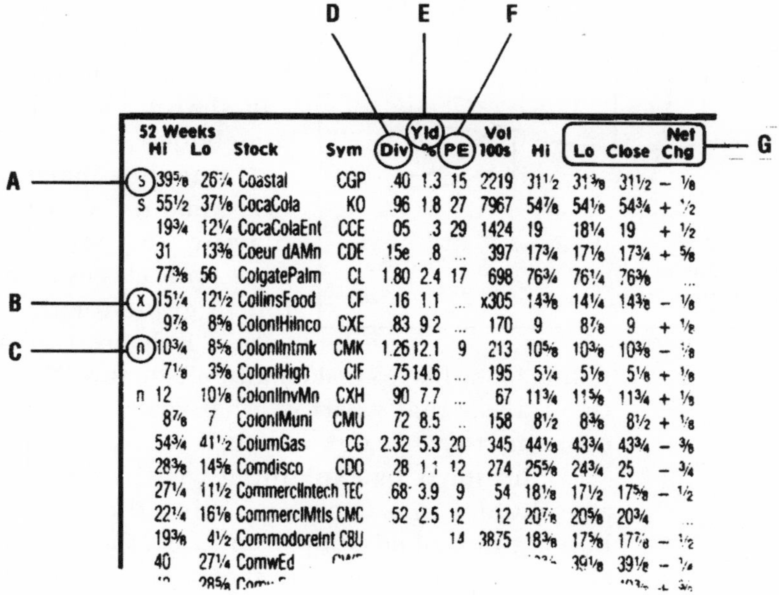

| 52 Weeks | | | | | | Vol | | | | Net |
Hi	Lo	Stock	Sym	Div	Yld %	PE	100s	Hi	Lo	Close	Chg
s 39⅝	26¼	Coastal	CGP	.40	1.3	15	2219	31½	31⅜	31½	– ⅛
s 55½	37⅛	CocaCola	KO	.96	1.8	27	7967	54⅞	54⅛	54¾	+ ½
19¾	12¼	CocaColaEnt	CCE	05	.3	29	1424	19	18¼	19	+ ½
31	13⅜	Coeur dAMn	CDE	15e	.8	...	397	17¾	17⅛	17¾	+ ⅝
77⅜	56	ColgatePalm	CL	1.80	2.4	17	698	76¾	76¼	76⅜	...
x 15¼	12½	CollinsFood	CF	.16	1.1	...	x305	14⅜	14¼	14⅜	– ⅛
9⅞	8⅝	ColonIHiInco	CXE	.83	9.2	...	170	9	8⅞	9	+ ½
n 10¾	8⅝	ColonIntmk	CMK	1.26	12.1	9	213	10⅝	10⅜	10⅜	– ⅛
7⅛	3⅝	ColonIHigh	CIF	.75	14.6	...	195	5¼	5⅛	5⅛	+ ⅛
n 12	10⅛	ColonIInvMn	CXH	90	7.7	...	67	11¾	11⅝	11¾	+ ⅛
8⅞	7	ColonIMuni	CMU	72	8.5	..	158	8½	8⅜	8½	+ ⅛
54¾	41½	ColumGas	CG	2.32	5.3	20	345	44⅛	43¾	43¾	– ⅜
28⅜	14⅝	Comdisco	CDO	28	1.1	12	274	25⅝	24¾	25	– ¾
27¼	11½	CommerclIntech	TEC	.68	3.9	9	54	18⅛	17½	17⅝	– ½
22¼	16⅛	CommerclMtls	CMC	52	2.5	12	12	20⅞	20⅝	20¾	...
19⅜	4½	Commodoreint	CBU			14	3875	18⅜	17⅝	17⅞	– ½
40	27¼	ComwEd							39⅛	39½	– ¼
	28⅝	Com									

Listing taken from the *Wall Street Journal*

Industry Foundation for Economic Education, in conjunction with the National Council on Economic Education, which has affiliates in each state. In the 1992–93 academic year, 500,000 sixth- through twelfth-graders in 44 states and the District of Columbia participated in the fall and spring competitions. (For information, call 212-608-1500, or write SIFEE, 120 Broadway, 35th Floor, New York, NY 10271.)

"General Electric 60—down ½;
General Motors 42—up one;
Gould Battery 30¼—up ½ . . ."

About 30 of them were in Masnik's class, where they split up into teams of about four students each. They were the youngest among several hundred teams from Northern Virginia schools, and they were green. "At first I knew absolutely nothing," admits Stefi Sylvester. "I thought the stock tables were just a bunch of numbers nobody ever read," adds Angel. "And I thought being a shareholder meant you shared your stock with somebody."

But they learn quickly, says Masnik, who has been playing the stock market game with classes as young as fourth grade for the last ten years. "Kids are capitalists by nature; they like to make money," she says. "If you show them a way that's part of what really goes on in the economy, they buy right into it."

She starts by explaining what it means to be a shareholder in a company (using the "Ump's Fwat" booklet described above) and asks the kids to name companies they know. She shows them a section of the stock market tables and asks them if they recognize any of the company symbols, then explains what the other symbols mean. They watch stock reports on television, and Masnik leads them in a discussion of how a stock might have come to trade at a certain price. They become as handy with the *S&P Corporation Stock Market Encyclopedia* as they are with a dictionary. They learn the tricks of the trade, like how to borrow on margin or short-sell a stock.

For kid purposes, short-selling is explained like this: Patrick borrowed a skateboard from Don. Patrick sold Don's skateboard to Billy for $60 and bought a new one for $40 when the price went down after Christmas. Patrick made $20 and returned the new skateboard to Don. "Sounds like Patrick made $20 on a ripped-off skateboard," says one kid. "Isn't that illegal?" asks another.

When the ten weeks are over, the kids are eager to share their strategies with a visitor. "Catherine [Rushworth] did the research for our team and high-lighted everything," says Nisha Jain. "We only looked at those companies that went up 1 ½ points a day." "We did better when we were just picking stocks at random," says Angel. "When we started to learn things, we went down." "We found U.S. Surgical on Prodigy, and that made us a lot of money," says Mike Macklin. "It was so fun—we got into lots of arguments," adds Mike Mihalik.

In the end, seven of Masnik's teams are among the top 20. Three of them have taken turns in first place, with one or another of them controlling the top spot for most of the ten weeks. And the winner, with a portfolio worth nearly $108,000, is the team of Matt Suskiewicz, Mike Macklin, Justin Tsuchida and Mike Cooke. They credit their success to some astute short-selling of Exxon and Boeing and that hot tip on U.S. Surgical. But they're restrained in their glee because they've learned a sobering lesson about the market. Says Matt, "If you had done nothing at all, you would have had $100,000 and ended up in fourth place."

"We did better when we were just picking stocks at random," says Angel. "When we started to learn things, we went down."

A Family Investment Club

At home, some parents, and grandparents, have made investing a family affair. Betty Taylor of Kansas City, Kan., started an investment club that includes four generations of her family, including her father, her three children and her nine grandchildren. "The youngest ones owned stock when they came into the world," says Taylor.

Each member of Taylor's club, grandkids included, can contribute a minimum of $5 a month to invest. Only those 18 or older get to vote on which stocks the family will buy and sell, but the younger children have considerable input, often based on their considerable intake of things like frozen yogurt. The family invested in TCBY when it was a fledgling firm, watched as the stock price rose with the popularity of frozen yogurt, and then bailed out when lots of other companies cut in on the craze and the stock price faltered. "It was a great way to teach the children that once a company has a niche, competitors come in," says Taylor.

She has also taught the children to invest in a few good stocks instead of spreading their money over a lot of companies (the family's portfolio generally includes eight to ten stocks) and how to handle a proxy vote: "We told them to vote for the management if they liked what the company was doing, and against it if they didn't." When kids are between 8 and 12 years old, says Taylor, they can learn to look up a stock in *Value Line* or color a chart tracking a company's earnings for the last ten years. She encourages teenagers to read a company's annual report, especially the report for the preceding year "so they can see what the president's

Start Your Own Club

• •

For information on starting an investment club, as well as basic information on investing in general, contact the **National Association of Investors Corp.** (711 W. 13-Mile Road, Madison Heights, MI 48071; 810-583-6242). The NAIC's $35 annual membership fee includes a subscription to *Better Investing* magazine; for an additional $89 a year ($125 for nonmembers), members can subscribe to the NAIC Advisory Service, which analyzes three individual stocks each month.

goals were and whether he met them." When one of her granddaughters returned from a school trip to Russia, Taylor debriefed her on which American companies had established a presence there.

Mutual Funds Made Easy

Besides shares of common stock, Jon Hagelstein owns shares in mutual funds (his favorites are the Janus Fund and Janus 20). Investing in a mutual fund isn't as direct as buying shares in an individual company, so the concept isn't as easily grasped, especially by younger children. And as a hands-on learning experience, it isn't as exciting as being part-owner of a specific company. But as an investment, it has certain advantages.

What you're doing is pooling your money with that of other investors. The fund's professional money managers take all that pooled cash and invest it in a portfolio of stocks (or bonds) that's designed to achieve a specific objective. Growth funds, for example, invest in companies that have the potential to grow (along with the price of their stock) but don't pay much in the way of dividends. Income funds concentrate more on bonds and other investments that pay interest, along with the stocks of companies that pay consistent dividends. Although growth funds are riskier than income funds, they're probably more appropriate for children, who have plenty of time to ride out the market's ups and downs.

Mutual funds can be ideal investments for small investors, and that includes kids, for these reasons:

- **You can find top-rated funds that have relatively low minimum initial investments**—for example, $250 for the Berger One Hundred fund (800-333-1001). Even better, many funds, like the Twentieth Century family of funds (with a couple of exceptions, including the Giftrust), will waive their minimum initial investment if you sign up for their automatic investment plans, described on page 103.

Money Fun

What are blue chips? *The term was introduced in 1904 to mean the stocks of the largest, most consistently profitable corporations. It comes from the blue chips used in poker—always the most valuable ones.*

- **Once you're in, you can buy additional shares in increments of $50 or less.**

- **You can buy funds through a broker, but you can also purchase no-load funds**—funds that charge no up-front sales fee—through the mail directly from the fund management company.

- **Your money buys instant diversification that isn't otherwise available to small investors** who don't have the money or the inclination to invest in a dozen or so individual stocks.

- **Best of all as far as your kids are concerned, there's plenty of time to ride out the ups and downs of the stock market.** Over time, investing in growth stocks or in a growth-stock mutual fund, will give them a better return than any other investment. Going back to 1926, large-company stocks have had an average total return (increase, or appreciation, of share price plus dividends) of around 10% a year; the total return on small-company stocks has averaged around 12%. That beats all other financial assets.

To make that point with her stepchildren (ages 19, 20 and 22), financial planner Anne Lieberman of San Rafael, Cal., opened a mutual fund account for each of them as a Christmas gift. Lieberman chose the Franklin Growth fund because it had a minimum initial investment of $100 and allowed her to invest additional money in increments of $25. The fund did so well that her youngest stepdaughter began to feel frustrated with the low yield she was earning on several thousand dollars she had in the bank. "We talked it over, and since she expected to need the money in the next few years, I told her to leave it in the bank and not risk it," says Lieberman. "But she understands the concept of investing, which most people don't get till they're 30 or older."

Lieberman's experience points out something else to remember about investing in the stock market—it's a risky business and you can lose big. But, again, kids have time on their side. If they choose a fund with a proven past or a bright future, they stand to win.

Keep Your Costs to a Minimum

Turning your kids on to stocks can be an expensive proposition. If you deal with a full-service broker, you'll have to pay a minimum commission to purchase a share or two of stock, which could be as much as $100 or more (well over the price of the shares). But there are ways to minimize your costs.

Scouting the Winners

To find winning funds among the thousands available, you can turn to several personal finance and investment magazines that provide regular coverage of mutual funds and rank their performance on an annual basis, and sometimes even monthly.

Among the most popular periodicals covering funds are *Kiplinger's Personal Finance Magazine, Money, Business Week, Forbes* and *Barron's.*

As with stocks, you can track daily price changes for mutual fund shares in the stock tables of your newspaper. The illustration on page 100 shows you what to look for.

Other publications, available in libraries and bookstores or directly from the publisher, provide comprehensive directories of funds. Among the most useful that also include performance information:

- *Donoghue's Mutual Funds Almanac,* with one-, five- and ten-year records for most funds, plus information on how to contact them. Updated annually ($42.95, includes shipping and handling; 290 Eliot St., Ashland, MA 01721-9104; 800-343-5413).

- *The Handbook for No-Load Fund Investors.* Excellent guidance on choosing a fund, plus performance data on about 1,700 funds. Updated annually ($49; P.O. Box 318, Irvington, NY 10533; 800-252-2042).

- *Individual Investor's Guide to Low-Load Mutual Funds.* Comprehensive information on about 500 no-load funds compiled by the American Association of Individual Investors; members get the book free. Includes risk ratings and portfolio holdings. Updated annually ($24.95; 625 N. Michigan Ave., Chicago, IL 60611; 312-280-0170).

- *Investor's Guide to Low-Cost Mutual Funds.* Published by the Association of No-Load Funds, it tracks more than 650 funds. Updated every January and July ($7; The Mutual Fund Education Alliance, 1900 Erie St., Suite 120, Kansas City, MO 64116).

- *Morningstar Mutual Funds.* Expert analyses of individual funds, updated every other week by Morningstar, Inc. (225 W. Wacker Drive, Chicago, IL 60606; 312-696-6000; $395 per year, so look for this one at your library). The same company publishes *Mutual Fund Sourcebook* ($225), a comprehensive directory of about 2,500 funds, ranked by various methods.

How to Read the Mutual Fund Listings

Most daily newspapers publish mutual fund tables in the business pages. Here's a guide to interpreting them.

N.A.V. is net asset value per share, what a share of the fund is worth.

Buy price is what you pay per share of the mutual fund.

Chg. is the change in the fund's NAV that day from a day earlier.

NL in the pricing column means you don't pay a sales commission when you buy shares of the mutual fund, that is, there is no up-front sales load.

p next to the fund's name means that it charges a yearly 12b-1 fee to cover the mutual fund company's cost of marketing, sometimes including commissions to brokers. Funds may be listed as NL, even if they charge this fee.

r means that the mutual fund may charge you a redemption fee (or back-end load) when you sell. These fees may be permanent or temporary, as with a contingent deferred sales fee, which may start as high as 6% and decline gradually the longer you keep your shares. A fund can have a redemption fee but still be called no-load.

t means that both p and r apply.

x **and/or e** stand respectively for ex-cash dividend and ex-capital gains distribution, meaning that the fund has just distributed income to current shareholders. That day's NAV will be reduced by the amount of the distribution per share.

Listing taken from the New York Times

A Custodial Account

If you already have your own account, your broker may be willing to cut you a deal if you're opening a custodial account for your children (to hold stocks or mutual funds, kids have to have a custodial arrangement with an adult). If you're buying a larger number of shares for yourself, ask if you can register some of them in the names of your children (you may have to pay a registration fee). Like banks, some brokerage firms set up a special fee schedule for custodial accounts. Another option is to buy the stock through a discount broker, such as Bidwell & Co. (800-547-6337); Kennedy, Cabot and Co. (800-252-0090); and Security Brokerage Services (800-421-8395). Some discounters, however, won't purchase single shares of stock, so ask for their terms.

Brokerless Alternatives

Or you may be able to make your initial purchase through one of these sources, which bypass brokers altogether:

- **The Low Cost Investment Plan of the National Association of Investors Corp.** (NAIC, 711 W. 13-Mile Road, Madison Heights, MI 48071; 810-583-6242). For a one-time fee of $5 per company, plus the price of the stock, NAIC members can buy shares in any of more than 110 firms participating in the plan. NAIC membership costs $35 a year.

- *Moneypaper* (800-388-9993). This monthly financial newsletter will buy initial shares of stock in more than 700 companies for subscribers. The cost per share, if that stock is mentioned in the current newsletter issue, is $15 plus the market price of the share. Otherwise it's $20 plus the market price. *Moneypaper* costs $72 a year.

- **First Share** (800-683-0743) takes a co-op approach to single-share purchases. The $15 membership fee entitles you to a handbook and gives you the right to purchase single shares of stock from other members.

Money Fun

Where did the dollar get its name? It originates from a silver coin called the Joachimsthaler minted in the 15th century in the valley (thal) of St. Joachim in Bohemia. Thalers flourished throughout Europe, and each country transformed the name slightly. In Holland it became daalder, in Scandinavia the daler, and in England, the dollar.

Once you join, each purchase costs $11.50, plus the market value of the stock.

Dividend Reinvestment Plans

If you or your kids still end up paying commissions that add to the purchase price of the stock, chalk it up as part of the cost of teaching your children about investing. Once you've purchased the shares, you may be able to recoup some of your expenses by signing your child up for the dividend reinvestment plan (DRP), if the company offers one. That way, dividends your child earns will go toward the purchase of more shares, but with no commission costs. Many companies allow DRP participants to kick in extra money in small increments, often as little as $10, to buy additional shares, also without any commission being charged.

Joining a DRP is one of the best ways for any small investor, adult or child, to buy stock. Around 800 companies offer DRPs; many of them are firms that would appeal to children: AT&T, McDonald's Coca-Cola, to name just a few. See the accompanying box for sources of DRP information.

Mutual Funds

Mutual funds also lend themselves to investing in small increments because you can arrange for the fund

For More DRP-y Information

You can get information on dividend reinvestment plans from a number of sources, including:

- *Buying Stocks Without a Broker* by Charles B. Carlson (McGraw-Hill; $16.95);

- *Directory of Companies Offering Dividend Reinvestment Plans* (Evergreen Enterprises, P.O. Box 763, Laurel, MD 20725; $28.95, plus $2 shipping);

- *DRIP Investor,* a monthly newsletter that comes with a free copy of *Buying Stocks Without a Broker* (7412 Calumet Ave., Hammond, IN 46324; $79 per year);

to automatically withdraw money from your bank account each month. That's what Jon Hagelstein does. He's investing $100 a month in the Janus Fund, but you can get by with even less. In the Twentieth Century family of funds, for example, you can set up an automatic investment plan for $25 a month.

A Word About Risk

Jon has some words of advice for would-be Wall Street tycoons: Leave your investments alone; if you buy and sell a lot, you'll be "murdered by commissions." And steel yourself to take a loss. "I am fully aware I can lose every single penny," he says.

Getting your kids to save at all is great; getting them to appreciate the risks and rewards of various kinds of investments is icing on the cake. Just like adults, they'll have different tolerances for risk and make different choices, depending on how much money they have and what they want to use it for. Here's a rundown on their options:

Garden-Variety Bank Savings Accounts

Still the best place to stash money earned from paper routes or babysitting. Your kids won't get rich fast on the interest they earn, but bank accounts are convenient and the money is safe as long as it's insured by the Federal Deposit Insurance Corporation (FDIC) or the National Credit Union Administration (for more on saving, see Chapter 6).

Bank Certificates of Deposit

These pay a higher rate than a regular savings account, but in return your kids will have to promise not to touch their money for a certain period—most commonly six months, one year, 2½ years or five years. Also, CDs usually require a minimum deposit of at least $500. They're insured by the FDIC up to $100,000.

Money-Market Mutual Funds

Instead of investing in stocks, these mutual funds invest in the "money market," which is a collective name that describes all the different ways in which governments, banks and corporations borrow and lend money for short periods. The interest rate changes every day, but it's generally higher than on regular bank accounts, especially when rates are rising. And, unlike a CD, your kids can get their money whenever they want it, although they (or you, on their behalf) will have to transact business by mail or phone. Money-market funds aren't insured; however, they're regarded as one of the safest uninsured investments around. Minimum balance requirements can be steep, but there are always exceptions that allow investors in for as little as $100 or waive minimums altogether. For older kids with money and savvy, money-market funds can be an alternative to a bank savings account.

Stocks and Stock Mutual Funds

Over time, they offer the greatest rewards and carry the greatest risks. When chosen well, they can be the best alternative for kids who are saving for a long-term goal, such as a college education.

"I don't know whether mortgage rates had gone up. Now may I continue?"

Drawing by Ed Arno; © 1980 The New Yorker Magazine, Inc.

Learning for Real

That's what the options look like on paper. How well can young people cope with them in real life? A few years ago, Victoria Felton-Collins, a financial planner in Irvine, Cal., and her husband, David Collins, decided to give the five teenagers in their combined families a real-world course in money management. They gave each child $4,000, with instructions to increase the value of their stake by saving or investing it. Each year their kids were to report on their progress, and at the end of the fourth year the one who had earned the best return would get the grand prize: a trip for two around the world using mom's and dad's frequent-flier miles.

Sisters Jennifer and Nicole pooled their money and entrusted it to a stockbroker friend who piled up hundreds of dollars in commissions and a stack of trade confirmation slips but lost all their money. Todd invested in stocks and mutual funds that went nowhere. Kim had big plans for her money, but ended up letting it sit in a money-market fund—and almost eked out a victory by default. The eventual winner, David Jr., showed up at family meetings with charts and graphs explaining his strategy of investing in growth mutual funds (but even he lost $500 on a hot stock tip from a friend).

In short, says Felton-Collins, "they did all the things adults do. But I'd rather have them blow the money now than blow the money for the down payment on the house later."

Money Fun

What's two bits? The Spanish silver coin called the piece of eight was worth eight reals. Brought to America, the coin became known as the Spanish dollar. Folks made change from it by cutting its soft metal into halves—four bits each—and quarters—two bits.

Collecting: Is There Money in All That Junk?

Q. *Dear Dr. Tightwad: My son's room is jammed with boxes of baseball cards, stacks of comic books and a closetful of old toys. Every time I tell him to clean up the mess he tells me all that stuff is going to be worth money some day. Does he know what he's talking about?*

A. He certainly knows how to talk you out of making him clean up his room. It's possible that some of that stuff will be worth something, but he'll have to be selective. Use the guidelines in this chapter to help him cull the best of the bunch. Then he won't have any excuse not to clean up the rest of his room.

They may not know how to read a stock table, but they spend hours poring over price guides. For lots of kids, sports cards and other collectibles have become a kind of mini stock market.

And no wonder. Lives there a kid in America who hasn't heard Mom and Dad lament—at length—that they'd be rich today if only *their* moms and dads hadn't pitched their childhood collections of baseball cards (or comic books or Barbie dolls)? It's no surprise, then, that there are legions of kids who don't flip cards, thumb through comics or braid Barbie's hair. Instead, the cards and books are tucked away in plastic sleeves and Barbie lies pristine in her box.

The kids are waiting for their ship to come in, and sometimes it does. Michael Faber of Gaithersburg, Md., got hooked on comic books when he was 4 years old and his grandmother bought him copies of *Archie* and *Richie Rich*. By the time he finished high school, Faber had 10,000 books stored in bins in his bedroom. He sold his collection for $6,000—enough to pay for his first three semesters of college.

But the collectibles market carries more than its share of risks, especially for kids. For one thing, it's anyone's guess which comics or cards or toys will be popular—and how many of them will be around—20 years from now when today's kids try to recapture their childhood. To take a current example, a 1952 Topps No. 311 Mickey Mantle in near-mint condition fetches more than $30,000 mainly because so few of the cards are still around. With millions of today's cards being carefully preserved, their future value is far from certain.

Then there's the tricky matter of selling a collectible that has gone up in value. A price guide might list a baseball card at $300, for example, but that's the retail price a dealer would charge. A seller won't get that much from a dealer, assuming the dealer is willing to purchase at all.

The real key to collecting is to just have fun.

Born to Save

Kids like teenager Faith Vettrus of Ridgefield, Minn., are natural pack rats. Vettrus collects key chains, pencils, stuffed animals, Pound Puppies, buttons and pins, rocks, shells, stamps and coins. "You get them one by one and after a while they just add up," says Faith, whose collections are kept in refrigerator-size boxes.

Faber, who is now in his twenties, recently sold his third comic-book collection. He got $5,500 for the

There's a market (and a price guide) for just about everything that catches a kid's eye.

3,500 books, which took him three years and $3,000 to collect. He used the money to pay off his student loans and credit card debts—and then started collection number four. It's become such a passion that Faber budgets anywhere from $20 to $50 a week to buy comics. Would he ever have considered bagging the books and putting the money he would have spent toward paying off his debts? "Never," says Faber. He emphasizes that he collects his comics for *fun* and never thinks about them in terms of money or as investments.

There's a market (and a price guide) for just about everything that catches a kid's eye, from traditional favorites such as baseball cards and autographs to offbeat items such as jelly glasses and Golden Books. But the market is fickle, so it's critical that kids collect for love, not money. "If you do it as an investment, it could go bad at any time," says teenager Tom Gordon III of Westminster, Md., owner of 5,000 to 8,000 comic books. "Then you're just left with paper held together by staples."

How to Spot a Winner

Yet it's possible that saving all that stuff may someday pay off. If that's what your kids are aiming for, encourage them to:

- **Focus on items popular with kids between the ages of 10 and 17.** That's the time in their lives they'll try to recapture when they're 30; they won't remember much before the age of 8.

- **Treat collections gently.** Better still, if you have the space and the cash, buy duplicates of some items— one to play with and one to keep in its box. The container can easily double an item's value.

- **Look for collectibles with tie-ins to movie or television characters or well-known personalities,** whether it's Ronald McDonald or G.I. Joe. That's what makes an item memorable.

Baseball Cards and Other Sports Addictions

When he was a kid, recalls Scott Kelnhofer, he and his friends collected cards of favorite baseball players, who might have worn the same number the kids wore in Little League. Now a kid's favorite player is more likely to be the rookie card that might be worth $5 in a few years, says Kelnhofer, who grew up to be editor of *Sports Cards* magazine.

The speculative frenzy in Mickey Mantles and Hank Aarons over the past few years has heightened interest in collecting and brought millions of new cards onto the market. That's good news for collectors who hold older, less common cards. But "if kids think prices will go up as they have in the past, they're sadly mistaken," says Kelnhofer.

Still, so many cards are being made that every kid can own a Cal Ripken Jr. or buy a 700-card set including every player in the league for as little as $15. To make collecting more fun, kids should start out with inexpensive cards of current players they like rather than trying to score big with older, more valuable cards from a generation of players they don't know and may not care about.

Besides, with older cards, rookie kids are at the mercy of seasoned dealers. "If they find a little kid to take advantage of, they probably will," says Jonathan Frent, a teenage collector from Ocean Township, N.J., who started his 200,000-card collection when he was 4.

Among today's cards, those likely to appreciate most are oddballs such as cards given as premiums with breakfast cereals or rookie cards of future hall-of-famers. Gary Sheffield flopped as a rookie with Milwaukee in 1989. But when he caught fire after being traded to San Diego, so did interest in his rookie card, which at one point had jumped in price from $1 to $12. Other players with superstar potential are Roberto Alomar of the Toronto Blue Jays, Mike Mussina of the Baltimore Orioles and Juan Gonzalez of the Texas Rangers.

Money Fun

What is the most famous baseball card? The 1910 Honus Wagner card from Sweet Caporal cigarettes. He was a nonsmoker and demanded that his picture be removed. The card is now worth as much as $300,000 if it's in near mint condition.

How to Satisfy Comic-Book Cravings

If your kids were turned loose with $50 to spend at their neighborhood comics shop, what would be the best buys? Alex Malloy, publisher of *Comics Values Monthly,* recommends that they should spend one-third on books that appeal to them and another third on comics the store owner recommends as up-and-comers. After reading their books, they can spend the final third on back issues of the series they enjoyed most.

More Kid Collectibles

Here's a list of popular collectibles, some of which you may recognize from your own youth. In each case, we've listed a reference guide available from public libraries and hobby stores.

- **Action figures:** *Tomart's Price Guide to Action Figure Collectibles,* by Carol Markowski, Bill Sikora and T.N. Tumbusch (Tomart Publications).

- **Hot Wheels:** *Tomart's Price Guide to Hot Wheel Collectibles,* by Michael Strauss (Tomart Publications).

- **Jelly, soft drink and other glasses:** *Tomart's Price Guide to Character and Promotional Glasses,* by Carol and Gene Markowski (Tomart Publications).

- **Baseball cards:** *Collector's Guide to Baseball Cards,* by Troy Kirk (Wallace-Homestead Book Co.).

- **Autographs:** *Collector's Guide to Autographs,* by George Sanders, Helen Sanders and Ralph Roberts (Wallace-Homestead Book Co.).

- **Comic books:** *Comics Values Monthly* (Attic Books, Ltd.).

- **Barbie dolls:** *The World of Barbie Dolls: An Illustrated Value Guide,* by Paris and Susan Manos (Collector Books).

- **Troll dolls:** *I Be Troll'n,* a monthly newsletter by Ellen Schmidt ($20 per year; P.O. Box 601292, Sacramento, CA 95860-1292); and *Trolls Identification and Price Guide,* which offers plenty of photos of '60s trolls and some new ones, by Debra Clark (Hobby House Press).

- **Little Golden Books:** *Tomart's Price Guide to Golden Book Collectibles,* by Rebecca Greason (Tomart Publications), or the *Bibliography of the Little Golden Books,* by Dolores B. Jones (Greenwood Press).

It's best to start small because, as with sports cards, the market can be treacherous, especially for youngsters who don't know the ropes. For example, publishers often hype sales by issuing the same book with several different covers. "It's sad to see kids buying books for the covers instead of the stories," says one veteran collector.

The value of a sports card waxes and wanes with the fortunes of the pictured player. Superheroes aren't plagued by mortal woes, but that's no guarantee that their comics will always appreciate. The recent *Death of Superman* blockbuster had seven printings, but only the first has increased significantly in value—and even that has fallen now that the Man of Steel has risen yet again. You can still get a copy of later printings for the cover price.

What collectors often prize are limited-edition books by small publishers such as Valiant and Image. But be warned: The definition of *comics* has changed dramatically since your youth. While you can still find *Archie* and *Richie Rich* (although not at every comics shop), many of today's hot-selling superheroes may be too violent or sexually explicit for young children. Go to the shop with your kids, especially if they're still in elementary school.

The Aftermarket for Happy Meals

Several years ago, Dolores Miller of Wichita was strolling through a flea market when she saw a woman buying a set of McDonald's Happy Meal toys for her grandchildren. "I thought they were cute," says Miller, who picked up a few sets for her own grandkids.

Today she has nearly 1,000 toys on display in her home, and "my dog has gotten awfully attached to cheeseburgers." Miller collects with her grandchildren, who live in different parts of the country. They talk long-distance to draw up lists of items they don't have, prowl flea markets to find them and report on their progress the following week.

What collectors often prize are limited-edition books by small publishers.

Among McDonald's aficionados, even Happy Meal boxes are collectible. Meredith Williams, author of *Tomart's Price Guide to Happy Meal Collectibles,* always asks servers to put the food on the tray and give him the box flat.

But the most prized possessions are a store's promotional displays. Jamie Riggs, a young collector from Nashville, was given the case that one restaurant used to spotlight its Barbie figures. At the annual convention of McDonald's collectors (yes, there is an annual convention), Jamie found out her display case was worth $200.

That's unusual, though. What makes Happy Meal toys attractive to kids is their low price—the cost of a meal or, if you find a cooperative store manager, 50 cents to $1 for the toy alone. At flea markets, the toys fetch anywhere from under $1 unboxed to $3 in mint condition with original packaging, or as much as $5 for toys intended for kids under 3, which are more rare.

Of course, the toys themselves are also attractive. "They're neat because you get to look at them and play with them," says Jamie.

Moving in on Action Figures

Jeff Denesen was only 6 years old when his parents got him a collector's case with ten action characters from the movie *Star Wars.* By the time the empire struck back, Denesen was hooked.

Eventually he collected all 108 *Star Wars* figures,

Calvin and Hobbes © 1989 Watterson. Reprinted with permission of Universal Press Syndicate. All rights reserved.

many in duplicate, a feat that wasn't easy to achieve. "We'd go to all the stores and ask when their next shipment was coming in so we could get first pick," recalls Denesen. "Once, when I was about 10, I was in a store holding one of the figures when a woman grabbed it out of my hand. I grabbed it back."

Kids are the best judge of which figures to buy; those that are most popular today are the ones they'll remember in 20 years. "If parents have a budget to buy five figures, I'd get four that the kids are asking for and an extra of the most popular one to keep in the box," advises Jeff Kilian, co-author of *Tomart's Guide to G.I. Joe Collectibles.*

Because toys can be faddish and their shelf life brief, some action figures have appreciated in value well before the 20-year benchmark. Figures from *Star Trek: The Next Generation* began flying out of stores right after making their debut. The figures carry serial numbers in order of their appearance, and a No. 1 Ryker soared to $100 within months.

In addition to acquiring the most popular items in a line, smart collectors also try to figure out what accessories are likely to be desirable yet scarce—for example, the Teenage Mutant Ninja Turtle blimp. Figures made in the smallest quantities—usually the female in a set—often have the biggest run-up in price. April O'Neil has outmuscled all the turtles.

Investing in the Blond Bombshell

If there's a blue chip among toy collectibles, it's Barbie. Math may be tough for her, but not for her maker, Mattel, which caters to the collectibles market with pricey limited editions or dolls made especially for particular stores. When Teen Talk Barbie was retooled after the infamous "math–is–hard" gaffe, collectors were willing to pay double the retail price for the original version.

Kids can start small with Barbies in the $10-to-$20 range. Look for dolls that seem particularly appealing,

Kids are the best judge of which figures to buy; those that are most popular today are the ones they'll remember in 20 years.

unique or attractive—one of the Dolls of the World Barbies, or Totally Hair Barbie in her black and brunette incarnations, which are less common than the blond edition.

With Barbie, neatness counts. Anything other than mint-in-box is much less attractive to professional collectors—although not to young girls. "I take them out of the box immediately," says Natalie Musser, a young collector from Columbus, Ohio. "I like doing setups [posing the dolls] and making different outfits." She does resist the temptation to comb their hair, but not because it would reduce their monetary value. "Eventually the hair will get straight and they'll go bald, and you'll stop wanting to look at them," says Natalie. And feasting your eyes on your treasures is, after all, what collecting is all about.

Adventures in Babysitting

And Other Fun Ways to Make a Buck

Q. *Dear Dr. Tightwad: My children, who are 12 and 14 years old, want to earn money next summer but they're too young to get a job. Can you suggest anything besides babysitting and mowing lawns?*

A. Don't knock the old standards; just give them a new spin. Instead of waiting for someone to call and ask for a sitter, your kids could organize a 5 P.M. play group to give parents relief during the arsenic hour. Instead of mowing lawns, they could sign up clients for full-service yard work that might include weeding flower beds, hosing decks and washing trash cans.

Kids get their first taste of the world of work by making their beds and picking up their toys. As they get a little older, they learn that their parents are willing to pay them to do more grown-up jobs, such as raking leaves or shoveling snow. One day it dawns on children that other people will pay them to rake *their* leaves and shovel *their* snow, and mom and dad have a fledgling entrepreneur on their hands.

Now, you'd think that most parents would be happy to nurture their children's interest in the free enterprise system. The extra cash would free parents

> *"My first work experience was in the first grade. I noticed that kids couldn't find fireworks to shoot off on July 4th, so I bought some from a mail order firm and resold them for three times what I paid."*
>
> **John Templeton,**
> **mutual fund pioneer**

from the enterprise of keeping the kids in clothes, cosmetics and video games. And the kids might even lay the foundation for their life's work. After all, business tycoon Warren Buffett bought stock at age 12, made enough money to pay taxes at 13 and bought a farm in Nebraska before finishing high school in Washington, D.C. And computer king Michael Dell started his empire in his college dorm.

Surprisingly, however, parents don't always encourage their kids' entrepreneurial instincts. "My gut tells me most people consider it an adult pursuit," says Joseph Vincent, executive vice president of Busines$ Kids, a company that, appropriately, helps kids get started in business. "Adults foster the myth that it's very complicated with lots of red tape." Emmanuel Modu, president of the Center for Teen Entrepreneurs and author of *The Lemonade Stand* (Bob Adams Inc.), calls it "a conspiracy of silence." Says Modu, "Parents don't tell their children that when it comes to earning a living, there are alternatives to working in a factory or joining a profession." He recalls that he took his first class in entrepreneurship as a graduate student at age 25, when "I could have used those skills in my teens."

The ABCs of Capitalism

Why are parents sometimes reluctant to teach entrepreneurial skills? Often because, unless they're in business themselves, they don't feel comfortable in the role. If truth be told, many Americans would probably be hard-pressed to explain the economic system that makes their country tick (and some might even feel vaguely guilty about it). In a study of Russians and Americans to determine their attitudes toward free markets, Yale economist Robert Shiller and two Russian colleagues found that Americans actually showed less understanding about how markets work and more hostility toward price increases and other kinds of capitalistic behavior.

But peel away the layers of econo-speak and the system really is quite simple. In fact, scratch the surface of the average American and you'll find an itchy capitalist. With the possible exceptions of eating and breathing, nothing is more instinctual than making money.

Brownies Equal Economics

Consider, for example, that American institution the fund-raiser—specifically, a fund-raiser undertaken a number of years ago by my son's nursery school. The school was a nonprofit cooperative run by the 30 families whose children attended. For several years demand for nursery school slots exceeded supply, so the school enjoyed a long waiting list and a modest budget surplus. One year, however, a new day-care center down the road siphoned off customers; as a result of the lower than expected revenue from tuition, the school faced a deficit of about $300.

How to close the budget gap? We couldn't cut expenses because most of our costs were fixed. Besides, our problem wasn't a bloated budget but a revenue shortfall. The quick and dirty expedient of a special mid-year assessment was dismissed; consumer resistance would be too great, and it would breach the informal contract agreed to in the fall when tuition rates were set. The idea of raising money through an auction or a book sale was more appealing but was rejected as not feasible. Our potential market—the 30 co-op families and members of the church at which the school was located—was too small. What we had to do, everyone agreed, was tap a larger market at the lowest possible cost.

Someone proposed a bake sale at a local shopping center, and that drew a flurry of interest. It had a number of advantages: a commodity product that everyone was familiar with and that wouldn't suffer for not having a brand name; ease of entry into the market (we could set up shop in front of Sears); no need for outside financing because parents would be investing the cost of materials (we'd bake the cookies). Another parent suggested a 50-50 raffle. Once the idea was explained—the winner gets 50% of the take—we were quick to see the potential. A ticket allotment of, say, $20 per family would go over better than an assessment because people would have a chance to make a return on their investment. Besides, we could sell tickets at the bake sale.

Eventually the raffle idea had to be scrapped because of regulatory difficulties: The church whose name the nursery school bears frowned on gambling. But the bake sale was a go. The goal, of course, was to maximize profits—or, as our bake sale organizer put it, "The more we bake the more we make." But we also had to determine the market-clearing price of homemade brownies and pineapple upside-down cake. In pricing my own nut rolls, I rejected a cost-plus approach; how could I put a price on my grandmother's research and development? Instead, I opted for market-based pricing: I called my mother in Pennsylvania and asked how much nut rolls fetch in bake sales there. Sell them for $5.50, she told me, and not a penny less than $5. Allowing for the higher cost of living in Washington, I figured we could get $6 easy.

We did. We also got $4-plus for cakes and did a brisk business in a scrumptious chocolate-and-cream-cheese concoction called black-bottom cupcakes (25 cents each, five for $1). We rotated our stock from the back of the table to the front, ran specials on slow-moving items and after four hours liquidated what little remained of our inventory with a special close-out sale. ("You couldn't even buy a mix at these prices.") The black-bottom line: a profit of $263.50.

And that's the economy in a nut roll.

Are Entrepreneurs Born or Made?

Everyone can spot the business "type"—glad-handing extroverts who are convinced they've built the better mousetrap and have no qualms about ringing doorbells and telling total strangers all about it at great length. No room here for shy, quiet kids who'd rather fiddle with computers or doodle in a sketchbook.

It's true that some personality traits can increase one's chances for success as an entrepreneur. It helps to be well organized and dependable, and to enjoy your work, for example. But building high-tech mouse-traps and talking a blue streak aren't necessarily on the list. While Linda Menzies was researching her book *A Teen's Guide to Business,* which she co-authored with Oren Jenkins and Rickell Fisher (Master Media), she talked to teens 13 and 14 "who had done so much that they made me feel old at 21," says Menzies. "I thought they'd be geniuses who had invented something, but they were just teens who had a good idea. It's a matter of finding a need and filling it with a skill you have."

Computer whizzes can offer their services tutor-ing other kids. Doodlers can create hand-designed T-shirts. If they cringe at the prospect of ringing door-bells, they can post notices on bulletin boards at school, shopping centers or places of worship; distrib-ute fliers in their neighborhood or enlist the aid of parents to pass the word, and the fliers, at PTA meet-ings. "There's no such thing as an entrepreneurial personality," Modu insists. "Anyone can be taught at an early enough age."

Walk into an average classroom of 13-year-olds and ask them for ideas on how to earn money, and it's likely that half will say babysitting and the other half lawn-mow-ing. Bonnie Drew, author with her husband, Noel, of *Fast Cash for Kids* (Career Press), breaks it down even further. "I go to a school to speak to the students, and maybe two of 30 kids in a class are real entrepreneurs, by which I mean interested since the age of 4 or 5. Five aren't motivated by money at all. But the others might be moti-vated to become entrepreneurs if they had a specific goal and you got them at the right time." The catalyst could be a long summer vacation when they're looking for something to fill the time, or their burning desire for a video game system that you aren't willing to buy.

It's a matter of finding a need and filling it with a skill you have.

Super Ideas at School

Or it could be a school assignment like the one that inspired Ronni Cohen's fourth-graders at Burnett Elementary school in Wilmington, Del. Cohen instructed her class of entrepreneurs (defined by the kids as "people who take risks and make choices so their company can make a profit") to invent devices that make it easier to eat pasta and come up with a marketing plan to sell them. On this day, Ian is showing off his Super Duper Spaghetti Scooper, a gizmo made of a tea strainer with a spoon attached at the other end (for eating spaghetti without losing the sauce). Using a hardhat, a clothespin and Legos, Courtney has created an elaborate pulley that hoists the spaghetti off the plate. All the kids rattle off the "factors of production" that they have used in building their inventions: "materials," such as tape, glue, rubber bands, string and empty soda bottles; "capital," or equipment that can be used again on other jobs, such as screwdrivers, scissors and staple guns; and, of course, "labor"—their own and that of various family members.

Each child has also done a marketing survey for his or her invention, measuring supply and demand at various prices and graphing the results to come up with a market-clearing price, the point at which supply meets demand. Eventually the kids vote Josh's creation—a fork attached to an electric screwdriver—as most marketable and launch into a dis-

Reprinted with special permission of King Features Syndicate

cussion of how to drum up demand for it. "Have a catchy ad." "Decorate it." "Make a small one for little kids." "Think of other things it can do, like whip potatoes, roast marshmallows and dig holes to plant seeds."

Closer to Home

School programs can provide the spark, but it's up to parents and other adults to fan the flames. Parents, family members and other entrepreneurs have the most influence on a kid's decision to start a business, according to Modu's survey of high school students attending a conference for teen entrepreneurs at the University of Pennsylvania's Wharton School. You don't need to be in business yourself; giving your child an opportunity to earn money around the house may be encouragement enough.

A family yard sale presents all sorts of entrepreneurial possibilities. Melodie and Ron Moore of Tampa, Fla., who publish the newsletter *Skinflint News,* practice their own penny-pinching advice by holding regular yard sales, at which their teenage son runs the food concession, selling coffee, soft drinks and popcorn. "Everybody buys something," says Ron. "He can make $25 or $30 in a couple of hours." He keeps half of what he earns as spending money and puts the rest in savings.

When Bonnie Drew's two sons were young, they helped organize family garage sales. On trash pick-up days, older son Jon would get up early and scavenge neighborhood cast-offs for old bikes and bike parts, then he'd rebuild the bikes and sell them at garage sales of his own. Kids began bringing their bikes to him

Encouraging Young Entrepreneurs

Lots of programs are available at all grade levels for teachers who want to introduce kids to entrepreneurship. Ronni Cohen's project, described on the preceding page, was part of "Choices and Changes," sponsored by the Delaware Center for Economic Education. Every state has its own such agency; to locate yours, write to the **National Council on Economic Education** (1140 Avenue of the Americas, New York, NY 10036; 212-730-7007).

"When our daughter was 12, she and her friends started running birthday parties for kids. She played the guitar and led the children in songs, and her friends led in games. They helped decorate and clean up and did everything but the food. The parents didn't have to hire an act, and she got paid very well."

Shari Lewis

for spare parts and repairs, and by the time he was 14 he was running a business fixing small engines. Younger son Robby, a "totally different personality," would buy boxes of candy at a warehouse store and then resell it to neighborhood kids. A musician, he eventually organized his own band. Whatever children end up doing, the impetus comes from home. "That's where they get the confidence," says Drew.

Three Success Stories

Now that you and your children are interested, you need to be inspired. There's nothing wrong with babysitting and lawn-mowing, but kids need to set their enterprise apart from the crowd. Add leaf-raking and snow-blowing and a summer lawn service becomes a year-long venture. Instead of accepting babysitting assignments haphazardly, your kids can drum up steady business by distributing fliers announcing they're available and listing their rates. Or sign up all their friends who babysit and match them with people in need of sitters, so frazzled parents only have to make one phone call.

Service Above and Beyond the Call

The latter falls into the category of carving out new niches, and one whittler extraordinaire is Daryl Bernstein, who by his own count had run at least 50 businesses by the time he turned 16 and wrote a book about his experiences (*Better than a Lemonade Stand,* Beyond Words Publishing). Included among the 50 is everything from cleaning the cages of neighborhood pets to planning and running birthday parties. Recently he was running only two ventures: a graphic design company that designs logos for small businesses, and a house-checking service that feeds pets, waters plants, brings in the mail and generally keeps an eye on houses when their owners are away.

Like most kids, Bernstein started out with a lemonade stand when he was 8 but gave it up because, he says, it didn't provide enough of a service. And service businesses are kids' strong suit because they don't require any special talent and they're easy for children to manage. Parents sometimes worry that starting a business can be risky, expensive and time-consuming, but it doesn't have to be. Bernstein's all-time favorite job was being an aide to the elderly. He ran errands for his elderly neighbors, read to them, watered their plants, cooked their meals, accompanied them on walks and did whatever else they requested. He recommends asking $3 an hour for such a job, noting that "Some of your older customers may not be able to afford a higher amount." He didn't charge for extra services, such as bringing his clients fresh flowers or baking them brownies. "You'll feel so good about doing this business, you'll forget about earning money," says Bernstein.

If helping the elderly was Bernstein's most socially conscious business, newspaper-moving was one of the cleverest. Observing that his neighbors, clutching their coffee cups in one hand and their bathrobes in the other, often had to dash to the end of the driveway to pick up the morning paper, Bernstein offered to do it for them. For $3 a month, he got up before his neighbors and moved their papers to the front door. It may not be a huge money-maker, but even ten customers means $30 a month, which for many kids is plenty.

Fresh Flowers for a Fee

What's attractive about any of these services is that they're feasible for kids of all ages, even younger ones without access to a car. But some jobs may require a helping hand and a set of wheels from mom and dad. When Brandon Bozek was 9, he and his mom brainstormed a number of business ideas. He considered starting a wake-up service but rejected that one because "I can't wake up myself." He loves to play miniature golf, but running a mini-golf course was "a weird idea."

Parents sometimes worry that starting a business can be risky, expensive and time-consuming, but it doesn't have to be.

At the time, his mother, who is in advertising, was working on a campaign for a flower shop, and that inspired the two of them to start a flower delivery service.

Brandon's "Bloomin' Express" sells monthly flower "subscriptions": For $16 to $20 a month, customers get weekly delivery of a bouquet chosen from Brandon's brochure. He purchases the bouquets from a distributor and his parents pick up the bouquets and ferry him to deliveries. But "I do everything but the driving," says Brandon, who makes about $100 a month.

Spelling Spells Profit

For three Texas schoolgirls, words like "LAM.buhr.kuhn" spell success. The Tarrant sisters, Valerie, Natalie and Huntley, publish study aids for students

Business Ideas for Kids

We've culled this list from the books recommended on page 133. Once your children have identified ideas of interest, they can use the questions on page 128 to choose endeavors that are appropriate for their age, ability and resources—including how involved you want to be.

❑ Window washing
❑ Curb address painting
❑ Outdoor painting (outdoor furniture, fences, doghouses, porches, decks or storage sheds)
❑ Garage cleaning
❑ Lawn-mowing
❑ Pool/driveway cleaning
❑ Housecleaning
❑ Carpet cleaning
❑ Plant watering
❑ Pet grooming
❑ House-sitting
❑ Picking up papers and mail for vacationing neighbors
❑ Pet and plant sitting

❑ Helping people move (packing, cleaning up)
❑ Golf caddie
❑ Bike repair
❑ Birthday clown
❑ Birthday party planning
❑ Tutoring
❑ Typing/word processing
❑ Buying and selling used books
❑ Sign making and painting
❑ Gift wrapping
❑ Errand service, including grocery and dry cleaning delivery
❑ Messenger service
❑ Flier distributor
❑ Odd-jobs agency set up with other neighborhood kids

preparing for the National Spelling Bee. In 1983, when Valerie was in the fifth grade and studying for her local bee, she spent hours looking up pronunciations and definitions for words in the official study guide. The results were impressive. "I was ready to give it away, but Dad said it was marketable," says Valerie. With the help of her parents, who run a data-processing business and contributed both their expertise and $7,000 during the business's early years, Valerie began publishing *Valerie's Spelling Bee Supplement.* That was followed by *Natalie's Spelling Bee Organizer,* a guide for teachers on how to conduct a spelling bee, and *Huntley's Spelling Mentor,* a computerized study system.

The girls worked weekends and holidays updating and editing their lists, taking things to the printer, filling mail orders, meeting customers and mastering the bookkeeping end of the business, which makes a profit of around $25,000 to $28,000 a year (their parents' loan has long since been paid off), and has helped pay for part of Valerie's and Natalie's college education. Valerie's studying psychology but considers the business "the most important thing I've done as far as education is concerned. I've learned a tremendous amount that most other people my age don't know and won't know for a long time." Postscript: All three Tarrant sisters made it to the spelling bee finals in Washington, and several national champions have used their material. (And the word is *lambrequin,* which is a scarf with slashed edges used to cover the helmet of a knight.)

Not every kid can start a mail-order business that generates thousands of dollars in orders, but the lesson here is to match your children's skills, hobbies or talents with money-making opportunities. The desire to earn money may be the catalyst that gets them to start a business, but it's their own interest that sustains it. In his survey of teen entrepreneurs, Modu asked the kids what they considered the most important thing about becoming an entrepreneur. Only 15% listed making money as tops, while 40% responded that "entrepreneurs can be as creative as they want."

The lesson here is to match your children's skills, hobbies or talents with money-making opportunities.

Getting Started

Lots of kids who babysit or mow lawns are already in business for themselves; they just don't realize it. Officially, their work becomes a business when they earn at least $400 a year, because that's when the self-employment tax kicks in. Unofficially it becomes a business when they begin to take it seriously, by giving it a name, making fliers, handing out business cards or generally being more professional and more formal about the way they run it.

Putting It On Paper

"Before I tell you my rates, I should explain that I'm not a babysitter, I'm an infant-care technologist."

In adult businesses, the first crucial step is to draw up a business plan, a blueprint of the business that describes in detail the product or service you're going to offer, your target market, advertising strategy, potential competitors and financial projections. For kids, of course, that has to be scaled down. "I never did a business plan," Daryl Bernstein confesses. "You're not going to get kids interested that way."

But kids will stand a better chance of success if they at least ask themselves some basic questions about what their business will do, whom it will serve, how much they'll charge, how much they'll have to pay in expenses and how they'll promote it. Their "business plan" can be as simple as a one-page work sheet with those headings (see the following list of key questions).

Older teens can be more detailed and more ambitious. Author Sarah Riehm (*The Teenage Entrepreneur's Guide,* Survey Books) recommends that they decide on a time period (will it be a summer job or a year-round occupation?), set up a work schedule, separate their costs into those that are fixed and those that are variable, establish prices and estimate how much business is expected each month.

The Busines$ Kit includes a work sheet that encourages kids to think about who their competitors might be and set goals for the business that are "specific, reasonable and measurable." For example, "I want to be the best lawn service in Center City" is good, but "I want to achieve 100% customer satisfaction with no refunds" is even better.

Raising Cash

A service business won't require much in the way of start-up capital, which kids will probably be short on. If they do need to raise cash, encourage them to rustle it up themselves by doing extra jobs around the house or holding their own yard sale. You can help finance the venture; Brandon Bozek borrowed about $70 from his parents to get Bloomin' Express rolling and paid them back in three months.

But it's more important for you to provide moral rather than financial support. Kids shouldn't expect their parents to be their main customers, provide unlimited free phone time or furnish raw materials gratis. If you're going to set up the table and provide the pitcher, the lemons, the sugar, the water and the cups, you're entitled to more than a free glass of lemonade.

Selling Themselves

One of the toughest steps for kids to take is the one that leads to that first door. Not to worry, says Daryl Bernstein, for whom knocking on doors has generally been a positive experience. "Adults are happy that kids are doing something other than sitting around flipping through channels," he says.

Nevertheless, kids have to be prepared to

Kids shouldn't expect their parents to be their main customers, provide unlimited free phone time or furnish raw materials gratis.

encounter cynical adults who don't believe that kids are disciplined or dedicated enough to follow through on their promises. When Bernstein solicits customers for his house-checking service, prospective clients sometimes ask how they can be sure he won't throw a party in their house while they're gone. To convince them he's trustworthy, he hands out a written biography, which tells that he's an honor student, details his

Questions Kids Should Ask Themselves

What will I do? _____

When will I conduct my business?
summers only?   year-round? _____

What will the name of my business be? _____

Is there a need for my product or service? _____

Who will my customers be? _____

How far from home can I conduct my business? _____

Who else is doing the same business in my
neighborhood? _____

How much are they charging? _____

Can I do the job better than the other guys? _____

How much will I charge? _____

How much time will each job take? _____

How much money do I want to make? _____

What's my goal for my business? _____

What do I need to know to do the job? _____

What kind of equipment do I need to do the job
and where can I get it? _____

How much money do I need to start my business? _____

What kind of help will I need from my parents? _____

How much of their time will I need each week? _____

Do I need to hire other people to help me? _____

How will I let my customers know that I'm available? _____

previous business experience and offers references. Being polite will win adults over, and so will dressing neatly. Even if you're selling a lawn service, don't show up in an old T-shirt and cut-offs. Instead wear a neat polo shirt or, better yet, a T-shirt imprinted with the name and logo of your business.

That kind of sight advertising also helps kids who would rather die than ring a doorbell. As noted earlier, shyness needn't keep kids from starting a business. At some point, however, they'll have to make direct contact with prospective customers. And when they do, Bonnie Drew has some advice on how to be a super salesperson: Use the same powers of persuasion you use on mom and dad when you're trying to get them to take you to the ice cream store or buy a new bike:

- **Tell them all the reasons they should buy your product or service and how it will help them.**

- **Tell them why they need your service right away.** Instead of asking them if they want you to lug their trash cans to the curb, tell them when you can start.

- **Don't give up if customers say no.** If they say they don't have time right now, ask if you can come back. If they say they don't need the service, ask if they know someone who does.

- **If they say yes, do the job promptly, courteously and thoroughly.** And always say thank you.

Mistakes Kids Make

Kids will be kids, even if they're entrepreneurs. At a time in their lives when they're particularly self-absorbed, it's often tough for them to live by the principle that the customer is always right. "When a customer tells a kid to show up at 3 P.M., the kid's tempted to say, oh, no, that's when I watch Bugs Bunny," says Bernstein.

It's often tough for children to live by the principle that the customer is always right.

Working weekends and once or twice on weeknights is plenty. After all, they're still kids and they need time just to have fun.

Not being professional enough in their attitude—by showing up late, acting rudely or speaking crudely—is perhaps the biggest mistake kids make, and it's the surest way of alienating skeptical adults. Here are some of kids' other foibles, with advice on how to correct them:

Getting bored

It's typical of kids to get excited about something, jump in with gusto and quickly burn out. If you recognize your children in this picture, encourage them to start their business as a short-term venture during summer vacation or over a holiday. With the end in sight, they can get out gracefully if they lose interest.

Getting in over their heads

Here are the three biggies:

- **Underestimating the cost.** A big problem even for adult entrepreneurs, being short of cash is best avoided by choosing a business in which your kids' biggest investment is their own effort. If they do need equipment—say, a computer to print fliers, or a lawn mower—they should use what they have or borrow what they can, instead of buying something new, shiny and expensive.

- **Underestimating time.** For young kids just starting out, ten hours a week is enough to devote to a business. Before they start, they should draw up a schedule to see when they can best fit in the time; working weekends and once or twice on weeknights is plenty. After all, they're still kids and they need time just to have fun.

- **Overestimating their strength.** Children can be tempted to take on a job that's too physical—moving furniture, for example—or just plain unrealistic—mowing ten lawns in two days. Making the effort to think through a business plan, even a rudimentary one, can help here. So can the timely intervention of mom and dad.

Milking the business

Many kids, after all, start businesses to make money, and they're tempted to spend everything, when it may be prudent to plow some money back into the business. Starting a lawn service by borrowing mom and dad's mower is fine, but if the business takes off, it's time for kids to consider investing in a machine of their own.

Over- or underpricing their products or services

Kids often don't have a good sense of what their costs will be or what their services are worth. As in the bake sale example that introduced this chapter, kids have a couple of options in setting prices. In the so-called *cost-plus approach,* they tot up the cost of any raw materials they might need, such as cleaning supplies for washing cars, add in how much they want to make and come up with a figure. In the *market approach,* they find out what competing businesses are charging and set their prices accordingly. Their competitors can be anyone from the kid down the street who's also mowing lawns to a professional lawn-care service. Sarah Riehm recommends that a kid-run business should charge 25% to 30% less than its professional competition.

When *Zillions,* the consumer magazine for kids, asked hundreds of children what they had earned on summer jobs, the survey turned up a two-tier price system: one (lower) price for parents and another price for everyone else. For example, the median price for babysitting was $2 an hour at home, $3 an hour away from home; for mowing, $5 per lawn for parents, $10

What's Good for the Goose...

• •

Q. *Dear Dr. Tightwad: My daughter has started babysitting for neighbors to earn money. Now when I want her to watch her younger brother and sister, she wants me to pay her. Isn't she being mercenary?*

A. Possibly, but she has a point. She shouldn't expect to be paid for watching the kids for a few minutes while you run to the store. But if you're taking her away from a paying gig on a weekend, add her fee to the cost of your night out. In return, however, it's reasonable for you to expect a family discount.

Encourage them to set their sights high while engaging in some down-to-earth planning, and they stand a good chance of pulling it off.

per lawn for others; for walking dogs, $1 a day at home, $2 a day away from home. To set their prices, kids asked other kids what they were charging or sought advice from their parents. Some enterprising youngsters visited customers in advance and set their prices based on the difficulty of the job. One babysitter ups her fee if the kids look wild. If they look "really bad," she might not take the job.

Kids can also ask potential customers how much they're willing to pay, or do some informal market research by surveying their parents and other adults. That can work to a child's advantage because adults often put a higher value on the service than the child does. If the price is too low, the kids can bargain, or turn down the job. (For a fun lesson in how not to set prices, rent the video *The Gravelberry Pie King*, in which Fred Flintstone becomes a pie tycoon by selling Wilma's famous gravelberry pies for a price that doesn't cover the cost of the ingredients.)

Lacking confidence

Some kids are doomed to failure because they don't really believe they can succeed. Encourage them to set their sights high while engaging in some down-to-earth planning, and they stand a good chance of pulling it off.

Nuts, Bolts and Red Tape

Starting a business is, after all, an introduction to the real world, so it shouldn't be surprising that as entrepreneurs your kids will be introduced to regulation, taxes and the fine points of the law.

Red Tape

They will probably set up shop as a sole proprietor, which is the easiest way to start a business: You just do it. Federal and state child labor laws restrict the age at which kids can get a job, the kinds of work they can do and the hours they can work. Under federal law, for example, 14 is the minimum age for most nonfarm work. But the federal law applies to employer-employee relationships. So if the kids run their own business or are independent contractors who babysit or mow lawns on a part-time, irregular basis for lots of different customers, they're not covered by the law. There are specific legal exemptions for kids who deliver newspapers, perform in show business or work for parents in their solely owned nonfarm business. For more information, call the Department of Labor at 202-219-4907

More Ideas and Advice for Kid Business

If you or your kids need more inspiration, a number of sources can help:

- Daryl Bernstein's *Better Than a Lemonade Stand* (Beyond Words Publishing) describes 51 businesses, with hints on which supplies and how much time you'll need, what to charge, how to advertise.

- Bonnie and Noel Drew's *Fast Cash for Kids* (Career Press) lists 101 money-making projects for children under 16, arranged by season of the year. Also includes age-appropriate tips on how to handle the financial end of the business.

- *The Teenage Entrepreneur's Guide,* by Sarah L. Riehm (Surrey Books), picks up where the Drews' book leaves off, with 50 money-making business ideas for older teens, and more detailed information on preparing a business plan, setting up a bookkeeping system and paying taxes.

- *A Teen's Guide to Business,* by Linda Menzies, Oren S. Jenkins and Rickell R. Fisher, offers anecdotes from successful teen entrepreneurs and includes a section on how to land a job working for someone else.

- *The Lemonade Stand: A Guide to Encouraging the Entrepreneur in Your Child* (Bob Adams Inc.) is Emmanuel Modu's comprehensive guide for parents that includes chapters on legal and tax issues, business ethics, and business concepts your kids should know.

- **The Busines$ Kit** is a package of manuals, tapes, stationery and other tools designed to teach kids ages 10 to 18 how to start and run a business; includes access to a toll-free hotline that kids can call for advice on business problems. The cost is $49.94, plus $11.75 for postage and handling. For information, call 800-282-5437.

- *Start your Own Lemonade Stand,* by Steven Caney (Workman Publishing), a do-it-yourself kit with apron, lemon juicer and recipes, plus a booklet with strategies for success.

At the very least, your kids will have to contend with homeowners associations and local zoning ordinances.

and order its free publication, *A Handy Reference Guide to the Fair Labor Standards Act.*

Once kids have decided on a name for their business, they should register it with the county government through the county clerk's office. Registration is required if they're going to be doing business under a name other than their own; it's recommended if they'll be using their own name. In some cities, kids may also need to get a license to operate certain businesses; check with your local authorities.

At the very least, your kids will have to contend with homeowners associations and local zoning ordinances, which may not allow them to run a business in a residential neighborhood, post signs on their lawn or store equipment in the yard. In reality, however, neighbors, who tend to be the most vigilant enforcers of zoning laws, aren't likely to object to the kinds of service-oriented businesses kids are likely to start.

If your children will be selling directly to the public goods or services that are subject to state or local sales tax, they'll have to collect the tax. That means applying for a sales tax permit. If they'll be selling to a store for resale to the public, they probably won't have to collect the tax but may have to apply for a wholesale exemption certificate.

Taxes

If your child has net business earnings of at least $400 a year, the federal tax law kicks into gear. Technically your son or daughter is expected to file three tax forms:

- *Form 1040,* the basic two-page tax return;
- *Schedule C,* to report the business income and any expenses;
- *Schedule SE,* to figure the social security tax on self-employment income. (There's one important exception to the self-employment tax rules: They don't apply to newspaper carriers under age 18.)

Although a child claimed as a dependent on the parents' tax returns can't claim a personal exemption, he or she does get a standard deduction. That deduction is either $600 or, if greater, equal to the child's earned income up to $3,700. (Those are the 1993 figures; they may rise in the future with inflation.) That means there may be no income tax due on up to $3,700 of earnings from the business. But there's no standard deduction to offset the self-employment tax. That 2.9% levy starts with the first dollar of net self-employment earnings. On $500 of income, this tax would cost $14.50. (If you have a sneaking suspicion that few children with such low incomes go through the hassles to file these tax forms, you have a lot of company.) Check with your local Small Business Administration office or chamber of commerce to see if any state or local taxes are due.

Points of Law

If your children's business employs other children, their working hours will have to be limited as required by child-labor laws. Under federal law, for example, children who are 14 and 15 can't work more than three hours on a schoolday or more than 18 hours during a schoolweek. Kids under 14 can't work at all, unless it's in an occupation that the law specifically exempts: acting or performing, delivering newspapers or making wreaths at home (the state of Maine requested that exemption back in the 1930s, when making pine wreaths was a major state industry).

Minors can enter into contracts, but they're not legally bound to fulfill them. This may put off some adults, who may be reluctant to do business with a minor. To reassure skeptical adults, parents could become a party to the contract (although this would also make you liable if the customer was dissatisfied with your child's product or service). The best solution is for your children not to back out of a contract.

Check to see whether your homeowners policy covers any business-related injuries, say, to customers

If they lose a customer because they show up late to do the lawn, they learn a lesson parents can't teach.

or employees. Some policies have so-called business pursuits clauses that specifically exclude such injuries. Even if yours doesn't, make sure you're covered.

All in all, the red tape shouldn't be sticky enough to discourage kids from starting a business. Most children don't make big bucks, so the procedure is fairly simple and straightforward. "I do a little of my tax return and my mom does the rest," says Brandon Bozek. "I don't look forward to it, but it's not horrible."

Why You Should Care

Why go to the trouble of encouraging your kids to start their own businesses? "It's lots of fun," says Bozek. "It takes up some of your friend time, but it's a great way to earn some spending money and it's not all that hard to do."

The whole issue of how much, or even whether, young people should work is a hot potato (for more on that debate, see the next chapter). But if your kids are inclined in that direction, there's a lot to be said for having them be their own boss and set their own hours in a job they enjoy doing. And it will yield dividends to you. Kids may not pay attention when you talk about being dependable, but if they lose a customer because they show up late to do the lawn, they learn a lesson parents can't teach. In addition, they learn to converse with grown-ups, use the telephone and budget both their time and (you hope) their money.

Entrepreneurship is also an avenue for channeling the creativity and hustle of inner-city kids into productive ends. A number of organizations—Modu's Center for Teen Entrepreneurs, the National Foundation for Teaching Entrepreneurship, the University of Pennsylvania's Young Entrepreneurs at Wharton—teach business skills to at-risk youth to build their self-esteem. "A lot of these kids don't even believe they can start a business. But once they see it's a way of making money and getting praise from family and friends, they become excited and involved," says Alia Walker A. Rashied, director of Young Entrepreneurs at Wharton.

Zakia Andrews, a 1989 alumna of that program, started her own business selling lingerie at house parties and took it with her when she went to college. When Michael Freeman started the program at the National Foundation for Teaching Entrepreneurship, he didn't even know what the word meant. With a $25 stake from the course, he went to New York's wholesale district and bought novelty items like nail clippers and pens, then resold them to people in his Bedford-Stuyvesant neighborhood. Later he graduated to selling calculators and watches that store phone numbers, and now he teaches future entrepreneurs.

> ## Organizations That Help
> ●
>
> - **The Center for Entrepreneurship** offers a variety of resources and educational opportunities for prospective entrepreneurs, including students. For more information, write or call the Center for Entrepreneurship (Wichita State University, 1845 N. Fairmount, Wichita, KS 67260; 316-689-3000).
>
> - **Junior Achievement** works with schools and businesses to introduce students to practical economic concepts, business organization, management, production and marketing. For more information, write or call Junior Achievement (1 Education Way, Colorado Springs, CO 80906; 719-540-8000).

For kids (and adults) of any age, running a business gives a glimpse of the real world and a look at a career option they might not otherwise have thought of—and one that may look increasingly attractive in the years ahead. As traditional employers attempt to stay lean and mean, jobs will become more competitive and more vulnerable. "We need to make young people aware that you can have the opportunity to make your own living and not have to rely on someone else for a job," says Joseph Vincent of Busines$ Kids. "If I work for Wal-Mart, I have a job. If I am Sam Walton, I am the job."

Working Teens: Take This Job and Love It

Q. *Dear Dr. Tightwad: I encouraged my 16-year-old to get a job because I thought it would give him a taste of the real world. But I've created a monster. He buys expensive clothes that even I can't afford, and now he wants to work longer hours so he can buy more.*

A. Your son isn't getting much of a reality check if he is working to put clothes in his closet without having to put food on the table. You're entitled to limit his hours if you think he's overdoing it and even to put restrictions on how he spends his money.

By the time your kids are 16, and maybe even sooner, they're likely to broach the subject of getting a job to earn extra money. And if they don't, you probably will. You'll figure it's about time for them to start pulling their weight when it comes to buying clothes, cosmetics and cassettes—not to mention gasoline (and insurance) for the car they'll soon be driving. And besides, wouldn't a job be just the ticket for teaching them responsibility and the value of a dollar?

Lots of parents and teens have the same idea. Teenage Research Unlimited's 1992 annual survey showed that 33% of 12- to 19-year-olds worked at a regular paid job (as opposed to seasonal or occasional work). Teens in that age group earned $88 billion in 1992, up from $65 billion in 1986, and they took home an average of $57 per week (12- to 15-year-olds averaged $25 per week; 16- to 17-year-olds averaged $57 per week; and 18- to 19-year-olds averaged $123 per week). According to Simmons Market Research Bureau, 12- to 19-year-olds work an average of nearly 11 hours per week (12- to 17-year-olds average 8.6 hours per week).

Dr. Tightwad has to wonder whether this is too much of a good thing. Although teens earned $88 billion in '92, they spent $93 billion of their own and their parents' money, reports Teenage Research. By encouraging kids to work, have we created a generation of teenage werewolves, obsessed with feeding their ravenous appetites for even more clothes, cosmetics and cassettes?

Sometimes it seems so. Barbara Johnson and Barbara Bellinger, both vice-presidents of People's Bank in Bridgeport, Conn., conduct a program on money management for high school students. In one exercise, they ask kids to assume they work 15 hours a week earning $5.50 an hour. Out of their pay, they have to cover transportation to and from work, entertainment, and food other than school lunches. The challenge: Work out a plan for buying a $700 stereo without charging it or laying it away. "Most of the kids will opt for working more hours," says Johnson. "When we raise the question of how that would affect their homework, they say they hadn't thought about it." A few are willing to cut back their spending and save more money out of current income, in which case it would take them about six months to accumulate enough cash to buy the stereo. "But that's rare," says Johnson. "They want to get it as fast as possible."

Ever more conspicuous consumption is just one not-so-desirable side-effect of teen jobs. Others are chronicled in studies of working teens in Orange County, Cal., by researchers Ellen Greenberger and Laurence Steinberg and in Wisconsin by Steinberg and S. M. Dornbusch. Among teenagers who put in more

By encouraging kids to work, have we created a generation of teenage werewolves, obsessed with feeding their ravenous appetites for even more clothes, cosmetics and cassettes?

Kids & Money

When Macaulay Culkin was 12, he earned a reported $5 million for Home Alone 2, *but it all went into a trust. He said he didn't even get an allowance. "When I, like, need money or something, I just ask my mom if I can borrow $10," he told* USA Weekend.

than 20 hours per week—the national average among high school seniors who work—these studies found that the negatives significantly outweigh the benefits:

Grades suffer.

"When kids work a lot, they disengage from school," says Steinberg, professor of psychology at Temple University and author, with Ann Levine, of *You & Your Adolescent* (Harper Perennial). They're absent more, spend less time on homework, participate in fewer extracurricular activities and have more trouble staying alert in class. Even teachers are aware of it. Responding to increased working hours by their students, teachers at four Wisconsin high schools said they assigned less homework and cut down on the number of long-term assignments and the amount of required outside reading, according to a study by Linda McNeil, a professor at Rice University.

Drug and alcohol use go up.

Kids who work have more money to spend, but that's not the whole story. After comparing kids who get allowances with kids who earn the same amount of money by working, Steinberg and others have concluded that "there's something about working that contributes to drug and alcohol use." A couple of possible culprits: exposure to older adolescents and stress on the job.

Parental authority declines.

Working kids have less contact with their parents, and parents grant them more freedom. In the Orange County study, more than half of the students interviewed reported that they ate dinner with their family less often, helped out less around the house and spent less leisure time with their family.

Further, there's some evidence that all the real-world lessons picked up on the job weren't necessarily positive. "Our research finds kids more likely to become cynical," says Steinberg. "Over time, they're more likely to agree with such sentiments as, 'People who work harder than they have to have to be crazy.' "

Limit Your Kids' Work Hours

Does that mean you have to resign yourself to supporting your kids with precious little contribution from them? Do you have to put up with them sitting around the house wondering what to do with themselves? Not necessarily. Before you march up to your children and demand that they quit their jobs tomorrow, remember that studies showing the negative effects of working, while thought-provoking, aren't the last word. It's not clear, for example, whether working long hours caused the lower grades and other ill effects experienced by some students, or whether a lack of interest in school prompted the kids to work long hours in the first place. "It's hard to know what causes what," says Jerald Bachman of the University of Michigan's Survey Research Center. "If a kid doesn't do well in school, that makes it easier for him to work longer hours."

In fact, some research shows that working doesn't have an adverse effect on teens. A study of 1,000 ninth-graders in St. Paul, Minn., found "no differences between kids who work and kids who don't" in such areas as school achievement and mental health, says Jeylan Mortimer of the University of Minnesota, who conducted the study with Katherine Dennehy and Chaimun Lee. "Any attempt to portray working as the greatest thing or the worst thing that ever happened to youth is oversimplification."

Even Steinberg's studies show that teens who worked less than ten hours a week got better grades, on average, than kids who didn't work at all. And the kids said they learned other things as well: how the business world works, how to find and keep a job, how to manage both money and time, and how to get along with other people. Girls who worked had a greater sense of self-reliance.

Kids & Money

In a survey commissioned by Childreach, a nonprofit organization in Warwick, R.I., that helps children in other countries, 56% of 10- to 14-year-olds said they expected to earn more than their parents.

The Moderate Approach

So what's a parent to do? Trust your instincts. Yes, it's great for kids to get a taste of the real world, and the extra money doesn't hurt either, but don't give them carte blanche. Get them thinking about what activities they might have to give up to fit a job into their schedule. Have them start with a summer job. Since there's no conflict with school—which is, after all, their primary responsibility—holding a job has fewer negatives. If the kids want to continue working during the school year, limit their hours, at least at first, until both you and they are satisfied that they can balance the job with schoolwork, family time and extracurricular activities.

Steinberg himself isn't against working, as long as it's in moderate doses. He recommends that sophomores be limited to ten hours a week, juniors and seniors to 15. That should be plenty of time for your kids to learn the virtues of showing up on time, getting along with co-workers and customers, and not loafing on the job. As your children get older and more experienced, and more adept at managing their time, you can consider letting them increase their work hours—but not to the detriment of their schoolwork.

When family psychologist John Rosemond's son, Eric, turned 16, getting a job wasn't an issue. He started looking for one as soon as his parents told him that if

---

What the Law Says

● ●

Federal child-labor laws limit the number of hours a 14- or 15-year-old may work: No more than three hours on a schoolday or 18 hours in a schoolweek; and no more than eight hours on a nonschoolday, or 40 hours in a nonschoolweek. (Also, work may not begin before 7 A.M. nor end after 7 P.M., except from June 1 through Labor Day, when evening hours are extended to 9 P.M.) The law doesn't restrict working hours for children 16 and older.

In fact, to encourage teenagers to stay in school, a group called the Child Labor Coalition is pushing for state legislation limiting 16- and 17-year-olds to 20 hours of work a week (excluding agriculture) when school is in session. A few states have already done that. But the National Child Labor Committee feels that's too dramatic a reduction in work time for older teens, according to executive director Jeffrey Newman. At a certain age, says Newman, there has to be a "reasonable opportunity" for kids to work, especially kids who are unhappy or unsuccessful in school.

he wanted to drive the family car he'd have to foot the bill for his own gas and for the increase in the family car insurance policy. The Rosemonds promised to cover Eric's insurance for two months, and about a month later he was stocking shelves in a drugstore. But they also limited his work time to 15 hours a week and told him that he could stay on the job only if his grades didn't slip. If they did, he'd have one report card period to bring them back up. After that, he'd be out of a job and getting around on foot as well. Eric was equal to the challenge and never had to hoof it.

Volunteering: An Alternative

Kids are often given more responsibility in volunteer positions than in paying jobs.

If you don't need the money and you're more interested in having your teens learn job skills such as leadership and responsibility, as well as how to take orders and work with people, you might look into volunteer positions—working at a hospital, a child-care facility or a museum. Kids are often given more responsibility in these positions than in paying jobs, and they get exposure to a variety of careers and to slices of life that they might not normally come in contact with. If you would otherwise ask your children to divide their earnings among college savings, discretionary spending and charitable giving, you might consider waiving the giving requirement if the kids are doing volunteer work. Or agree to provide a bigger allowance in exchange for their willingness to forgo income.

Don't underestimate the value of extracurricular activities. Stephen Hamilton, director of the Youth and Work Program at Cornell University, points out that even more than school itself, extracurriculars give students a taste of life in the outside world because they often involve working with a group of people to accomplish a goal or task. In extracurriculars, as in the workplace, teamwork can be so important that if you're late you let everyone down. In school, on the other hand, the emphasis is on the individual, says Hamilton, and "cooperation is called cheating."

Which Job is Best?

If your kids are dead set on earning money—and, face it, that's likely to be the case—you can at least exert some influence on where they work. Academic researchers generally agree that the nature of the job has as much influence on kids as the number of hours they spend doing it. Who are they working with? Is the job interesting? Is it stressful? How much responsibility do they have? Do they get to make independent decisions?

In Steinberg's studies, two jobs stood out as having fewer negative effects:

- **Retail sales in a small business.** One teen who worked for a small, family-run florist spent most of her time working side by side with the owner and got a unique perspective on the whole operation. Instead of just ringing up sales, she became experienced in ordering flowers, taking inventory and setting prices.

- **Babysitting.** Believe it or not, this job ranked high on Steinberg's scale because sitters worked in relatively pleasant surroundings and were given a fair amount of responsibility for making decisions. In addition, babysitters tend to be independent contractors who can set their own work schedules and enjoy the benefits of self-employment. (Babysitting also paid less than other jobs, according to Steinberg's studies. For

PEANUTS reprinted by permission of UFS, Inc.

suggestions on how to build a steady business and earn more money, see the preceding chapter.)

It's probably unrealistic to expect most 16-year-olds to know what they want to do with their lives, but some of the most rewarding jobs are those that give kids experience in a field that might turn into a future career—being a copykid at the local newspaper, working in the mail room of a bank or other major corporation, helping out in an animal hospital, even working in a local T-shirt shop. Linda Menzies, who at age 19 started her own graphic-design business, began her working life at 16 as a graphic designer creating packaging for a man who invented kids' toys and other novelty items. Even if jobs like these are not paid positions, they can be invaluable as an investment in the future.

Best of all, especially for kids who don't plan to go on to college, are jobs that exist in a school setting, such as vocational/cooperative education programs. Bachman thinks work could be more meaningful to all teens if employers' reports of their job performance could become part of their school records and be used as a credential when they apply to college or enter the job market full time. Cornell's Hamilton is also director of a Youth Apprenticeship Demonstration Project that goes a step further and actually provides the full-time job after high school. In pilot programs involving hundreds of teens around the country, students enter apprenticeship programs in fields as diverse as health care and metalworking that begin with their junior year

in high school and last four years, including two years of college. By the time the kids are 20, they have had the benefit of on-the-job training and are ready to take on adult work responsibilities.

Hamburger Heaven

So far, however, such programs aren't widespread. When push comes to shove, many kids are going to end up, you guessed it, flipping burgers. That kind of work doesn't rank high on the list of stimulating, meaningful employment preferred by most academics. One summed up the prevailing opinion like this: "I try to acknowledge the important learning one can acquire from that kind of job: punctuality, teamwork, smiling at customers, working under pressure. The problem is that after three or four months you've probably learned those lessons, and what else is there?"

The "what else," of course, is the opportunity to earn money in a job that's readily available and not too far from home. Most parents would probably be proud if their kids could survive, and even thrive, in what's perceived as a pressure-cooker atmosphere. It's a teen milieu, and many kids apparently aren't being harmed by the experience. In a study of fast-food workers by Ivan Charner and Bryna Shore Fraser of the National Institute for Work and Learning, 63% of the respondents expected to graduate from a four-year college, and 19% more planned to attend some college or graduate from a two-year program. Overall, 67% of all fast-food workers and 64% of younger employees said they enjoyed their jobs.

It's also true, however, that not all burger joints are alike. In the Charner/Shore Fraser study, workers were more satisfied with management personnel in franchised stores owned by an individual or small corporation than in company-owned stores. Company policies do make a difference. For example, the owners of some McDonald's stores have offered bonuses to kids with good grades; a 3.0 average earns an extra

15 cents per hour. Burger King runs 18 Burger King Academies, private high schools where at-risk kids can study while working at the chain, and most Burger King managers come up through the ranks, says Ray Krause of Grand Metropolitan, the British conglomerate that owns Burger King. Krause notes that "this is not necessarily the place you go and stay for the rest of your life, but for many kids it's a first step."

How You Can Help

For parents, the lesson once again is to stay in touch with your kids' work life. Yes, it's great that they're out on their own, but they're not independent yet. They're still kids, and you're still their parents. Get the scoop on where they're working from other kids who work there, or "interview" the manager yourself and ask about policies on teen work schedules. Would your kids have to work a minimum number of hours a week? How many nights? Is the manager flexible enough to accommodate studying for a big exam, playing in a big game or appearing in the school play? If the answers aren't satisfactory, steer your teens to another employer.

Barbara Johnson tells a personal anecdote about her son, who was in his twenties when he decided to settle down and attend a rigorous college, then announced that he had saved enough money to get an apartment off-campus for the spring semester. "But how will you keep the apartment over the summer?" his mother asked him. "I'll keep living there and get a job to pay the rent," he replied. "Then how will you save the money to pay for the apartment when school starts?" she countered. "I'll work during school," he replied. "But," she reminded him, "your primary responsibility is to get good grades so that you can achieve your goal of getting into grad school." As a result of that conversation, her son abandoned the idea of the apartment and started talking about being a resident adviser in a dorm. "At first I thought it would be

Get the scoop on where your kids are working from other kids who work there, or "interview" the manager yourself and ask about policies on teen work schedules.

It would seem, ironically, that they've learned the lesson: A buck will buy stuff, and lots of bucks will buy even more.

good for him to have an apartment and be independent, but what he really needed was someone to say no," says Johnson. "Parents don't set up boundaries as often as they should or remind kids of all the other things they have to do."

The Pitfalls of "Premature Affluence"

In a *Newsweek* article on teens who work, dozens of young people bared their souls—and their closets. One revealed a young man's back-to-school wardrobe: Two leather jackets, six sweaters, 12 pairs of jeans, four pairs of shoes, two belts and loads of shirts, including a half-dozen silk ones. One senior girl had 20 pairs of dress shoes, with a purse to match each one, plus ten pairs of sneakers.

And it's all financed by those jobs that are supposed to teach teens the value of a dollar. It would seem, ironically, that they've learned the lesson: A buck will buy stuff, and lots of bucks will buy even more. In its annual High School Financial Awareness Survey for 1992, the College for Financial Planning found that of responding teens who worked, the typical weekly paycheck, less deductions, was $80. The typical weekly savings was $5.

Bachman has even coined a term for the phenomenon—premature affluence. Teenagers have so much income for discretionary spending that they can often afford the designer clothes and electronic gizmos their parents can't. But when they go off to college or out into the world and have to pay a bigger share of their own living expenses, they can no longer spend $200 a month on compact discs and their standard of living actually declines.

Bachman knows whereof he speaks. His deal with his own daughter, Terri, was that mom and dad would pay part of the bill for college and she would have to pay the rest. While she was in high school, however, she didn't think she wanted to go to college so she spent her money freely. When she decided to attend school after all, it meant cutting way back on her spending. "She came through it fine and she's now a careful money manager, but she did it the hard way," says Bachman.

How can parents make it any easier? By not being so quick to accept your kids' argument that it's their money so they can do what they want with it. Although you may not be aware of this, it actually *isn't* their money. As long as you're supporting your children, you're entitled to at least a portion of their income unless you give them, either by formal agreement or practice, the right to spend and manage their own earnings. (In a number of states, the amount you can take is regulated. For example, the "Coogan law" requires that a percentage of the wages earned by child performers be put in trust for them until they reach the age of majority.)

Most parents wouldn't go so far as to confiscate their kids' income, but there's nothing wrong with sitting your teens down before they start working to hash out an agreement on how the money will be spent. When they were young and you were giving them an allowance, it was appropriate for you to require that they save some or give some to charity. Now that they have the opportunity to earn serious money, it's appropriate for you to require, for example, that they contribute to the family's welfare, if that's an issue; save a percentage of their income for college; or get your approval for purchases above a certain dollar amount.

©1993, Washington Post Writers Group. Reprinted with permission.

*Kids should start
looking early,
presuming that it
will take a couple of
months to land a job,
and be creative in
their search.*

That, of course, can mean swimming against a tide of teen materialism. In this latest "just say no" campaign, researcher Bachman proposes that parents get help from other parents. Just as they conferred on guidelines for things like curfews and substance abuse, they could come up with guidelines on the number of hours it's appropriate for students to work and how much of their income should be theirs to spend as they please. That's especially important if parents believe that letting their kids spend most or all of their earnings isn't a realistic way to teach them the value of money. (For more on budgeting and other teenage money-management issues, see Chapter 12.)

Tips on Finding a Job

Unless you're willing to give your kids all the money they want, or unless they're satisfied with what you're willing to give, they'll probably have a job at some point during their high school years. Studies show that children who receive allowances when they're younger are even more likely to work when they're older.

For most kids, job hunting means keeping an eye out for stores with Help Wanted signs in the window, putting in an application and waiting to be called. But they can improve their chances of getting a job—and, in particular, getting a job they want—if they approach their search more professionally. They should start looking early, presuming that it will take a couple of months to land a job, and be creative in their search. Don't assume, for example, that want ads are just for adults. Watching the classifieds could turn up a position as part-time receptionist in a doctor's office during after-school hours.

Other job-hunting tips for kids:

Prepare a resume.

"Kids don't always give themselves enough credit for leadership skills and organizational ability that can translate into the workplace," says Karen Webster, Director of Marketing with Price-Waterhouse, who presents a seminar on job skills to teenage participants in the Loyola Money Management Camp each summer in Baltimore. Making the honor roll, being editor of the school paper, directing the school play, babysitting or volunteering at a local hospital can all look impressive to employers (especially if most of the other kids they've interviewed haven't bothered to spell out their accomplishments).

If they're applying at a more laid-back operation they can afford to be more casual but never sloppy.

Dress appropriately.

At a large corporation or small business, dress is conservative but not necessarily formal—jacket and slacks for a boy (a suit isn't necessary unless the company is super straitlaced), dress or skirt and blouse for a girl. If they're applying at a more laid-back operation such as a summer camp or amusement park, they can afford to be more casual but never sloppy—shirt (with collar) and trousers for boys, skirt or slacks and blouse for girls (never jeans for anyone).

Observe the niceties of interview etiquette.

In Webster's class, kids run through an exercise in which they are interviewed for hypothetical jobs ranging from astronaut to chef. The kids "tend to be quite cavalier about it," Webster says. "They'll saunter up and slouch down in a chair." What they really need to do is look the interviewer in the eye, shake hands, address him or her as Mr. or Ms., sit up straight, and not be afraid to make small talk or ask questions.

Chalk it up to inexperience. But kids can be a quick study. To encourage her students to speak up, Webster suggests a list of questions they can ask an interviewer. As instructed, one girl, who was being interviewed for a position as assistant zoo keeper, asked the chief zoo keeper why the previous assistant had left. "Oh, there was a terrible accident," deadpanned the zookeeper. "He was killed by a bear." "Then I think you need better training and safety procedures," the girl shot back at the surprised counselor. "I'm not interested in working at your zoo."

An Unexpected Tax Bill
. . . .

Q. *Dear Dr. Tightwad: This year my son earned $1,351 working at a summer job and $465 in interest from a savings account. I know the standard deduction for single people is $3,700, so I thought he wouldn't owe any tax. But our accountant says taxes are owed. How can this be?*

A. Your son's thrift threw a wrench into the works. Children who are claimed as dependents on their parents' return don't automatically get the full standard deduction. For 1993, their deduction is either $3,700 or the total of their income from a job, whichever is less. So your son's standard deduction is $1,351, precisely enough to wipe out the tax bill on his summer earnings. But the $465 in interest isn't protected. He'll owe $69 in tax.

A Word About Taxes

One bit of real-world experience that goes along with holding a job is filing a tax return. Your children may not actually have to file but it's a good idea to do it anyway—and not just because they're good citizens.

Assume, for example, that your 16-year-old son earned $2,000 at a summer job. If that's his only income for the year, he doesn't have to file. But filing is the only way he can get back what was withheld from his paychecks. Assuming your son earned $200 a week, at least $10 probably was withheld from each check for federal income taxes. He'll get it all back in the form of a tax refund.

If your son also had investment income—interest on a savings account, perhaps—he must file a return. When the only income is from a job, a dependent child could have earned up to $3,700 in 1993 before having to file a return. If there is any investment income, though, the trigger point is $600 for job earnings and investment income.

Since you'll claim your son as a dependent on your tax return, he can't claim a personal exemption on his own. But he does get a standard deduction, equal to $3,700 or the total of his earned income, whichever is less. His $2,000 deduction will wipe out the tax bill on his wages, but his investment income will be taxed in the 15% bracket.

How to Succeed in Business

Much has been made of the fact that U.S. schools don't adequately prepare teens to succeed in the job market. Sometimes the skills that are lacking are academic ones in reading, writing and math. Sometimes kids are handicapped by their unfamiliarity with the workplace and an inability to connect what they're learning in school with the jobs they'll hold when they graduate. When Grand Metropolitan commissioned a poll of elementary school students, only 48% said they knew a lot about what their father did at work, and 57% said they knew a lot about what their mother did. Among disadvantaged youth, many didn't have exposure to an adult who was working.

As a result, Grand Met launched Kapow (Kids and the Power of Work), a program in which employees of Grand Met companies come to elementary schools to act as role models and talk to the students about their jobs and the skills they need to do them. Comments from the kids indicate that often they don't appreciate the variety of jobs out there and

Beating Withholding

Q. *Dear Dr. Tightwad: Last year my teenage daughter earned about $1,500 at a summer job, and money was withheld from her salary for income taxes even though she didn't end up owing any tax. Is there any way we can avoid withholding this year so she won't have to file a tax return to get her refund?*

A. Theoretically, yes. Practically, probably not. When she files her Form W-4 with her employer, your daughter can claim exemption from withholding if she meets all three of the following conditions:

- She had no tax liability in the preceding year.

- She expects to have no tax liability during the current year.

- If her income will exceed $600 and you claim her as a dependent, she can't have any nonwage income, such as interest from savings.

Since it's likely that your daughter's income will exceed $600 and include at least some unearned income, she probably won't qualify for the exemption from withholding. Note: There is never an exemption from withholding for social security taxes, which are not refundable.

don't realize all the things they need to know to, say, create a new flavor for Häagen-Dazs. (As part of Kapow, kids used Skittles and other goodies to create their own flavors for Häagen-Dazs, a Grand Met company.)

Sometimes the skills that are lacking have to do with basic attitudes toward responsibility and team-work. In that case, a part-time job can help, especially if the hours are manageable and the setting is conducive to learning.

That's the way it was for Danielle Schneider. The Florida teen started working as a camp counselor when she was 15 and held several jobs in retail sales before finding her "niche," working 12 hours a week at a family-owned clothing and accessories store. The owners, she says, were "really good" about scheduling her work hours around her school activities—she was a cheerleader, vice-president of the student council, a member of the debating team, and acted in school plays.

Schneider thrived on the busy schedule, and on the work itself: "I think I have a good sense of fashion, and I like helping people pick out clothes." Her co-workers were "like a family," and the atmosphere was friendlier than in the big mall stores "where you're always selling, selling, selling." Sure, there were days when she'd rather have stayed home, but having to get up and go taught her "how to be responsible and budget my time, which you have to do when you go to college." If they could be as contented as she, says Schneider, "all kids should work."

Family Matters: Gift-Giving & Other Problems Solved

Q. *Dear Dr. Tightwad: My kids get so much stuff over the holidays that it's downright embarrassing. How can I bring things under control without disappointing them?*

A. Don't worry so much about the kids. They take their cue from you, and if you lay down ground rules about how many presents they will get and what's appropriate for them to ask for, they'll accept them. Telling them, for example, that Santa will bring one big present and mom and dad several smaller ones will help them focus on what they really want instead of asking for everything they can think of.

Even if you get a grip on your own gift-giving impulses, what do you do about everyone else's? The dilemma begins at birth, as doting grandparents bring material offerings. It's aggravated throughout childhood by extravagant birthday celebrations. And it's altogether complicated in situations of divorce. But take heart, you can depend on Dr. Tightwad for some commonsensical—and diplomatic—solutions.

Take the money you would have spent on presents and spend it instead on a quiet family getaway or some other nontraditional gift.

Making Sense of the Holidays

It's possible to cut back on holiday gift-giving without your kids' even being aware of it if you give them as gifts what you would have bought anyway: a new backpack for school, ice-skating lessons, a family outing to the circus. In one family, parents who were planning a winter trip to Walt Disney World stuffed the tickets into their kids' Christmas stockings, along with guidebooks and other Disney paraphernalia. Planning the trip kept the kids happily occupied long after the post-holiday blahs might ordinarily have set in.

If you want to make a clean break with commercial holidays past, take the money you would have spent on presents and spend it instead on a quiet family getaway or some other nontraditional gift. Author and family counselor Eda LeShan recalls that when her daughter was around 8 years old, the child was part of a family conspiracy to surprise her grandparents by flying Aunt Lilly, one of their oldest friends, from California to New York for a visit. When Aunt Lilly, wrapped in tissue paper and a bow, appeared on the stairs, "it was a Christmas that all of us will remember more than any other," says LeShan, author of *When Your Child Drives You Crazy* (St. Martin's Press).

Q. *Dear Dr. Tightwad: I love the holidays but I resent all the toy advertising that's directed at children. My kids make lists a mile long and ask for one outrageous thing after another. How can I cope with all the commercialism?*

A. You can trash the tube, you can make good on your threat to put coal in their stockings to teach the little darlings not to be so greedy—or you can turn the commercialism to your advantage. If the kids want to make lists a mile long, let them. With their minds so focused on acquiring things, it's a perfect time to slip in a few lessons about consumerism.

First of all, sit down with them and go over their lists, helping them separate things they need from things they want. (It may sound obvious, but children, and even some adults, have trouble making the distinction.) Have them set priorities: Which things do they want most? And which things are you unwilling to give them, regardless of their priorities? If the motorized Barbie convertible isn't in the cards, tell them why. If they're older, you can have them work within a budget, choosing which toys they'd buy if they had, say, $300 to spend. It's a win-win game: They get experience in making choices, and you make your holiday shopping a whole lot easier by whittling down the lists.

Don't be too hard on your children. You're more frazzled than usual at this time of year, so it's easy to lose patience with them. But by coming to you with their wants, they're only doing what comes naturally, says James McNeal, marketing professor at Texas A&M University, who has studied the consumer behavior of children. Preschoolers will pretty much ask for everything they see and promptly forget about most of it. Older kids will be more discriminating, but they'll still push the envelope in hopes of stuffing it with as much as they can. They'll expect you to say no, so don't disappoint them. If they don't get what they want, they're not going to pack up and leave home.

As for those "outrageous" toys, look at them from a kid's point of view. Adults tend to prefer toys that are scaled-down versions of grown-up things, such as kitchen sets and cars. But toys that rank high in what McNeal calls "kidness value" really are outrageous things that have no counterpart in the adult world—such as Ninja Turtles or Gak (or remember hula hoops and Silly Putty?).

Have them set priorities: Which things do they want most? And which things are you unwilling to give them, regardless of their priorities?

Emphasize the Meaning

Q. *Dear Dr. Tightwad: My daughter will make her First Communion this year, and she's sure to get a lot of financial gifts from family members. I'm worried that she'll get so carried away by the money that she'll forget the religious significance of the occasion.*

A. Dr. T put this question to parents of different faiths whose children celebrated religious milestones and came up with a number of suggestions.

The most extreme was simply to ask family members not to give any financial gifts. Or you and your child could agree to contribute any money to charity, perhaps using it to buy food baskets for poor families in your community. If you're inclined to let her keep the money, have her treat it as serious savings by putting most of it in the bank.

If everyone else in your family will be giving financial gifts, you should give one

Dialing for Dollars

• •

If you've been trying to figure out what to give your child as an unusual birthday gift, consider this money-smart idea: Buy your kid big bucks. You can buy sheets of uncut currency in $1 and $2 denominations from the **U.S. Bureau of Engraving and Printing;** 202-874-3316. For an order form and catalogue, write: the Bureau of Engraving and Printing, Office of Public Affairs, Room 533-M, 14th & C St., S.W., Washington, DC 20228. Allow four to six weeks for delivery. If you're visiting in Washington, you can buy your bucks at the Bureau's Visitors Information Center at 15th St. and Independence Ave., S.W., from 8:30 A.M. to 3:30 P.M., Monday through Friday.

that has religious significance, such as a prayer book or Bible. Your daughter will take her cue from you. As long as you don't lose sight of the real meaning of the occasion, neither will she.

Put Birthdays in Perspective

Q. *Dear Dr. Tightwad: My daughter recently celebrated her third birthday. I'm embarrassed to admit this, but she got 17 presents just from family members and another ten at the party she had for children from nursery school. She got bored opening them and toddled off to watch a tape. What is the "right" number of presents for children to receive?*

A. That's easy. The "right" number of gifts is the number that won't embarrass you.

That's not as flip as it might sound. All parents have a sixth sense telling them when enough is enough. Knowing when to quit isn't the problem. Quitting is the problem, because parents naturally want to indulge their children. For suggestions on how to kick the habit, see the following answer.

In your situation, you might have quietly put away the rest of the gifts to be opened on rainy days throughout the year. To cope with doting grandparents and aunts, set up a college savings fund for your child with a bank or mutual fund and ask family members to contribute in lieu of buying presents.

As for the generous preschoolers, you can solve that problem by inviting fewer children. Kids that age don't need a big blowout; asking the neighbor kids to drop by for cake and ice cream is excitement aplenty for both you and your child. One old rule of thumb is to invite a number of children equal to your child's age, with perhaps one more to grow on.

Q. *Dear Dr. Tightwad: I've had it with kids' birthday parties. Parents have upped the ante too high: First clowns, then ponies, now my son has been invited to a party with a merry-go-round on the lawn. You feel obliged to buy expensive gifts, which the birthday child gets too many of. My kids are even starting to compare the size of the party bags they bring home. Am I just a voice in the wilderness?*

A. Dr. T will join you to make a chorus of at least two. Perhaps what we need is a group called Birthdays Anonymous to support parents who want to withdraw from the party circuit. Some parents have made the break, and here's their advice on how to kick the habit:

Don't get hooked in the first place.

One mom from Philadelphia simply held off on having nonfamily parties until her kids were in kindergarten. Then she held traditional at-home affairs with games of charades, penny pitch and pin-the-tail-on-the-donkey. By the time her children were in fourth grade, they were ready to invite a handful of kids for a sleepover or a matinee, and she was home free.

A variation on this is to have a big blowout every other year instead of annually, or perhaps for certain "milestone" birthdays—6, 10 and 13, for example. In

Perhaps what we need is a group called Birthdays Anonymous to support parents who want to withdraw from the party circuit.

If you must have a crowd and don't want your children inundated with gifts, set a price limit of, say, $5 per gift.

the off-years, you can invite Grandma, Aunt Sis and all the cousins for cake and ice cream.

Be creative.

If you must do something out of the ordinary, do it on the cheap. Take a group of kids fishing at a local pond; to a field for a pickup game of soccer or baseball; to a playground or a children's museum. Pack a picnic lunch.

Be radical.

If you must have a crowd and don't want your children inundated with gifts, set a price limit of, say, $5 per gift. Or ask guests not to bring any presents. "We did that once and our friends told us it was seditious," laughs one father from Washington, D.C. "But we told them their children's company was the best present they could give."

Grappling With Grandparents and Other Gift-Givers

Q. *Dear Dr. Tightwad: We try to hold back on giving our children too many toys and teach them to live within their allowance, but then their grandparents shower them with gifts or checks on birthdays and holidays. How should we handle this?*

A. Have your children write a polite thank-you note. Grandparents need to do things for their grandchildren, so you might as well let them have their fun. It wouldn't hurt to let the kids have some fun, too. Instead of dutifully encouraging your children to trot down to the bank and deposit grandma's check (or dutifully depositing it on their behalf), let them cash it and spend at least some of the money. (It's okay to have them save a portion if the check is large or if they don't get an allowance and need to learn the virtues of thrift.) Here's the note one wise grandmother enclosed with a birthday check for her 4-year-old grandson:

Dear Peter, This check is for your birthday. Have mommy buy something for you, or you can save it to put in your billfold. Daddy can change it all into "ones"!

You might even hide the bills and have your children find them in a game of treasure hunt.

If you think things have gotten out of hand, try this technique to steer grandparents to gifts kids will like (and you'll approve of): Send them toy catalogs with a selection of things circled and let them choose what they'd like to give. One mother who went this route says she's been "getting great presents ever since." Or have your children keep a running wish list of things they'd like but won't necessarily get. On birthdays and holidays, gift-givers can take their pick.

A wish list serves a couple of other purposes. Over time, children may decide they no longer want a must-have toy and cross it off. Or the list may spark some lively discussions between you and your children. Your interest alone may be enough to satisfy them.

Katharine Lustman-Findling is an education consultant and lecturer at the Yale Child Study Center. She's also a grandmother. Instead of trying to guess what her grandchildren want, she got into the habit of taking them shopping individually and letting them choose, setting a price limit of $100 for the teenage girls and $50 for the younger boy. "The girls shopped

If you're concerned that your parents are undermining your authority, you'll just have to bite the bullet and discuss it with them.

with an eye on price. I had to tell them that if it cost $5 or $10 more and they really love it, don't look at the price," says Lustman-Findling. "My grandson, on the other hand, tried to talk me into everything. By the end of the day I was completely exhausted." But her shopping sprees had an ulterior motive: While the kids spent money, she spent time with the kids.

Q. *Dear Dr. Tightwad: My children have one set of grandparents who shower them with gifts and another who can't afford to do that. I'm afraid the kids are going to start favoring the grandparents who buy them more. What should I do?*

A. Don't worry about a problem that may not exist. Children aren't mercenaries. Expensive gifts won't buy their affection, especially if the poorer grandparents are generous with their time and love. If you must say something, just tell the kids that both sets of grandparents love them equally but have different ways of showing it.

It may be that this situation is a bigger problem for you than for your children, especially if you think your parents or parents-in-law are buying things you'd rather your kids didn't have. In that case, see the preceding response. If you're also concerned that your parents are undermining your authority, you'll just have to bite the bullet and discuss it with them. Standing up to your own parents can be tough. It might carry some weight with them, and ease the burden on you, if you stress that you're trying to teach your children the value of a dollar—a virtue prized by grandparents, who often find it lacking in their own children.

Or let a third party intervene. Show your parents this book and let Dr. T take the heat.

Q. *Dear Dr. Tightwad: Now that my kids are 12 and 13 they're a little too old for the cute birthday presents their grandmother sends. It would be easier if she just gave money, but I don't want to hurt her feelings.*

A. Then suggest gifts the children might like. Or simply tell her that since they're into the terrible teens, it's difficult even for you to find something that pleases them, so it's best to send a check or a gift certificate. She may even be relieved. Just remember to have the kids thank Grandma and tell her how they used the gift.

Q. *Dear Dr. Tightwad: During the summer my children are often invited to spend a week with their grandparents or to go on vacation with a friend's family. Should I expect their hosts to pay for meals out and other activities or should I send them with money to pay for themselves?*

A. It all depends on which hosts you're talking about. The closer the relatives, the more likely they are to want to pay your kids' way. In any case, you ought to feel freer to broach the subject in advance with your parents or parents-in-law. Even if they insist on treating your kids, however, the children should still have their own pocket money for souvenirs or other small expenses.

In the case of a friend's parents the etiquette can be trickier, so Dr. T consulted with Judith Martin, a.k.a. Miss Manners. If you bring up the subject with your children's hosts and they brush

Minimizing Messiness

Q. *Dear Dr. Tightwad: My kids and I are always fighting about their messy rooms. I don't want to resort to bribery to get them to clean up, but what else can I do?*

A. You could simply shut their doors. If you get along well with your children otherwise, and if the chaos doesn't seem to interfere with their schoolwork, think twice before you fight this battle.

But if the mess really bugs you, try cooperation rather than confrontation. Take the kids with you to buy brightly colored storage bins, labels and markers, and anything else that will make the job more appealing. Then set a time when you and they can tackle the clutter together, deciding what to toss and what to keep.

Sometimes children just need help getting organized. Donna Goldberg, who runs a service called the Organized Student in New York City, helps kids get their act together by breaking down the task—telling them, for example, to line things up on a shelf in size order or put them in drawers by category. "If you want it neat, you have to show them how to do it," says Goldberg.

That includes introducing them to the vacuum cleaner and the washing machine. But you can make the job fun, too, by letting them rearrange furniture or asking a friend to help (you provide the refreshments). Maybe they can even make a few bucks by selling castoffs at a yard sale.

aside the inquiry by saying, "Oh, don't worry about it," don't take them literally, advises Miss Manners. "Hosts should not be reaching into their pockets for their houseguests."

On the other hand, you don't want your kids to be put on the spot by offering to buy their own tickets at an amusement park and being told by the hosts that it's their treat. If they insist on paying, tell your children to offer to buy everyone a treat in return. "Reciprocation is always better than flat-out paying the bill," says Miss Manners.

Remind your children to be helpful while they're guests and to watch for something appropriate to send as a thank-you gift later.

Q. *Dear Dr. Tightwad: After I had told my children they absolutely, positively couldn't have a new video game system, their doting great aunt arrived for a visit and presented them with one. I felt put on the spot and accepted the gift. But now I'm seething. I feel I should have stood my ground and turned it down. What do you think?*

7-15
©1993 Bil Keane, Inc.
Dist. by Cowles Synd., Inc.

"A penny for your thoughts, Billy."

"Make it a quarter and we've got a deal."

A. There are certain niceties that have to be observed in life, and accepting a gift graciously is one of them.

But enough is enough. Dr. T suggests that you take a deep breath and follow this three-step plan:

1. Set limits on the time your kids can spend playing video games.

2. Have a polite but firm talk with the doting aunt and ask her to please consult with you before giving gifts. Tell her that you'd like an opportunity to discuss what the kids need, want, and are allowed to have.

3. Sit down and play a game or two with your kids, compliments of Great Aunt Sadie.

Dealing With Divorce

Q. *Dear Dr. Tightwad: I'm a recently divorced mother with custody of my two children. We're just scraping by financially, but when the kids go to visit my ex on weekends, they come back wearing expensive sneakers, toting boom boxes and talking about their trip to the amusement park. I'm tempted to tell them that if their father is that well off, he can afford to pay more in child support.*

A. Bite your tongue. You're experiencing a common complaint we'll call the Santa Claus Syndrome. If you're still on speaking terms, talk things over with your ex. It may be that the gift-giving isn't an attempt to get back at you but simply a way of compensating for not being around much.

If talking is out, keep in mind that bad-mouthing their father to the children won't give you much relief. In more than 30 years as a divorce adviser to the rich and famous, New York City lawyer Norman Sheresky has seen couples so embittered that they have asked for court transcripts to prove to the kids what a villain their former spouse is. But it's too much to ask that children sit in judgment in a case that would have been difficult for Solomon to decide. And it can backfire as well because kids can be fiercely loyal to both parents.

If you think you can get more money, take your ex to court and tell it to the judge. Better yet, couples can short-circuit future problems by addressing as many child-related financial issues as possible in the divorce agreement. Do your children have special needs or gifts

Couples can short-circuit future problems by addressing as many child-related financial issues as possible in the divorce agreement.

that will require special expenditures? Who's going to pay for piano lessons? Is summer camp still in the picture? If the kids are approaching driving age, who's going to pay for insurance? Who's responsible for college tuition? When Sheresky negotiates a settlement, he includes everything from the cost of schoolbooks to the number of trips home each semester.

Margorie Engel, an author and speaker on families and divorce in Boston, recommends building into the agreement a procedure for reviewing the settlement periodically through your lawyers to allow for changes in your children's health, growth patterns or emotional needs. "The biggest difficulty with divorce agreements is the assumption that this snapshot is going to be good for years. It never is," says Engel, author with Diana Gould of *The Divorce Decisions Workbook* (McGraw-Hill).

In the real world, rewriting divorce agreements often isn't an option, especially when child-support payments are spotty or nonexistent. In those cases, you need to have a straightforward discussion of your new economic circumstances with your kids. Involve them in brainstorming to find ways in which they can help cut back on expenses or contribute money or sweat equity to the household. Says one divorced dad with custody of three children, "I don't hide the time and money pressures from my kids. We work together to do the household chores, and they no longer beg me for toys I can't possibly afford."

If you have an ex who *can* afford them, try not to

Neither a Borrower...
● ●

Q. *Dear Dr. Tightwad: Parents are always telling you how their kids bug them about money. Well, I'm a kid and let me tell you how my parents bug me. They're always borrowing money from me to pay the babysitter or the guy who delivers pizza, and then they forget to pay it back.*

A. On behalf of parents, Dr. T pleads guilty. We borrow spare change from our kids because you're the only ones who ever seem to have any. It goes with being part of a family; if we can learn to put up with you leaving wet towels on the bathroom floor, you can learn to put up with us raiding your cash stash. However, you do have a right to be paid back. Your parents probably just don't get around to doing it, and you have Dr. T's permission to remind them, nicely.

overreact in front of your kids. Explain that parents give their children many things, not all of which can be purchased with money. Watch how the children are reacting to their other parent's largess. You may worry that they're being bought off, but they may be quite well aware of what's going on.

Q. *Dear Dr. Tightwad: I'm a noncustodial father who pays child support regularly. But when the kids come to visit me they always seem to be dressed in rags and in need of money for some school or sports activity. I give it to them, but I feel like a chump.*

A. You sound like a victim of what we might call the Ransom of Red Chief Syndrome, a complaint of some noncustodial parents, mainly fathers, who feel that they are already giving enough and resent the fact that their ex-spouses aren't accountable for how they're spending the money.

Children themselves have been known to manipulate this situation to their advantage. One woman recalls that when her parents divorced, her younger brother managed to collect an allowance from both mom and dad. When her parents found out what was going on they put a stop to it, but only after a major shouting match with each other.

If you and your ex are on speaking terms regarding your children, you need to get together and discuss what's going on. Do the kids need things that weren't budgeted for? If so, who's going to pay for them? Who should be responsible for taking the kids shopping for

---

...Nor a Lender Be

• •

Q. *Dear Dr. Tightwad: My 10-year-old son is always borrowing money from his eight-year-old sister and forgetting to pay it back. How can I teach him that it's important to repay his debts?*

A. First, have a frank discussion about the meaning of the words "deadbeat" and "garnishee." Then tell your son that henceforth any borrowed money is expected to be repaid within, say, one week of the date borrowed. After that, interest will start to accrue at the rate of five cents a week (or whatever seems appropriate for the loan in question). If at the end of a certain period—perhaps one month—the debt is still outstanding, tell him you'll begin deducting the money from his allowance and will instruct his sister not to advance him any more cash.

Don't be infected by the Fairy Godparent Syndrome, in which an overeager stepparent showers the children with stuff in an effort to buy their affection. It isn't going to work.

new clothes? If money is tight, include the kids in the discussion and allow them to choose between, say, one pair of better jeans or two less expensive pairs. If you and your ex aren't on speaking terms, it's a bit trickier. Assuming the children are old enough, you can discuss with them what they need and want, how much each parent can afford and how the children themselves can contribute.

Q. *Dear Dr. Tightwad: I'm a widow with two children, and I'll soon be marrying a divorced man who has custody of his three children. How should we treat each other's children financially to avoid conflicts?*

A. You'll be wise not to fall into the Cinderella Syndrome, a phenomenon of blended marriages in which one spouse shows financial favoritism toward his or her own children. (Members of the spouse's family, such as grandparents, can be guilty of this as well.) Parents who buy a toy or a shirt for their own kids but not their stepchildren risk creating a tremendous amount of ill will that could easily be avoided with a relatively small outlay of cash. When Margorie Engel remarried, her husband's mother "opened her arms to my two daughters," she recalls. "My kids got birthday cards and valentines just like her own grandkids did. They got checks, too. The checks were smaller, but the kids were never forgotten. It's not the amount but the thought."

In most cases, says Engel, stepfathers tend to step in and provide financial support even when they're not legally obligated to do so. But if at any time you feel that your kids are getting short shrift, you need to raise the point with your new spouse, who presumably is easier to communicate with than your former one is. Rather than simply complaining about the unfairness, it might be better to put your case in writing, listing expenditures on each child and suggesting ways they might be equalized.

At the other extreme, don't be infected by the Fairy Godparent Syndrome, in which an overeager stepparent showers the children with stuff in an effort to buy their affection. "It isn't going to work," says Kenneth Doyle, a financial psychologist from the University of Minnesota. "The new parent is automatically seen as an interloper, and if that person comes on like gangbusters, it's going to look awfully crass." Give the children time, not money.

Q. *Dear Dr. Tightwad: I'm a recently divorced woman with custody of two young children. I'm getting child support, but suddenly I feel financially responsible for these kids and I need some guidance on what I should be doing.*

A. For starters, don't let your feelings of responsibility (and possibly even guilt) lead you to try to maintain a lifestyle that you can no longer afford. If you have been given the house but are struggling to pay the mortgage, consider trading down. Alan Ungar, author of *Financial Self-Confidence for the Suddenly Single: A Woman's Guide* (Lowell House), notes that "too often people believe they, or their kids, need the security of not being uprooted. That creates more instability because they can't make the payments and end up losing the house."

Single parents are often tempted to be more indulgent with their kids because they feel guilty. Resist. Instead, be candid in explaining to them that (through no fault of theirs) there isn't as much money for toys and treats as there used to be.

How Active is Too Active?

Q. *Dear Dr. Tightwad: My 8-year-old daughter wants to sign up for every activity in sight. She's running me ragged, and I'm going broke paying for it all. But I want her to have a chance to try as many things as she can. Help!*

A. Get a grip. Then get a life; sounds like your daughter has taken over yours. It's fine to get her involved in lots of activities, but you have to strike a balance. David Elkind, author of *The Hurried Child* (Addison-Wesley), recommends that parents limit elementary-school-age children to one sports activity a season, one social activity and one artistic endeavor (for example, soccer, scouts and music lessons). Dr. T has a personal variation on the rule of three: no more than three days a week of activities that require being chauffeured (so ice hockey practice twice a week counts as two, but piano lessons at school don't count). If your daughter needs more direction, you might require her to choose two activities per season, which she can change until she zeros in on what most interests her.

Don't let your feelings of responsibility (and possibly even guilt) lead you to try to maintain a lifestyle that you can no longer afford.

That will free up cash for expenses you shouldn't avoid, such as insurance. Your children should benefit from your former spouse's life insurance, but don't neglect to insure your own life. One guideline is to buy coverage equal to around eight times your annual salary. Your least-expensive option is a guaranteed-level term policy. For a 45-year-old woman, a 15-year level-term policy for $100,000 would cost about $250 a year. (In naming beneficiaries for life insurance policies, keep in mind that an insurance company will not pay proceeds to a minor. You should name a trust set up by your will as the beneficiary.)

Don't forget disability insurance. You may be eligible for benefits through your job or social security, but that coverage is often limited. You'll probably need to buy your own insurance to fill the gap. Benefits you receive from a policy that you have paid for are tax-exempt.

You also need to make a will. The court would probably name your ex-spouse as guardian of the children (unless you could make a strong case, in writing, against it). But you also need to name a property guardian, since in most states children under 18 aren't considered legally competent to deal with substantial assets. The property guardian can be the same person as your children's guardian, although a divorced parent is sometimes inclined to choose a separate property guardian if the ex-spouse gets custody. (For more on insurance and estate-planning issues for parents, see Chapters 15 and 16.)

Save as much as you can, even if it's only $25 a month. That's still enough to buy a series EE U.S. savings bond.

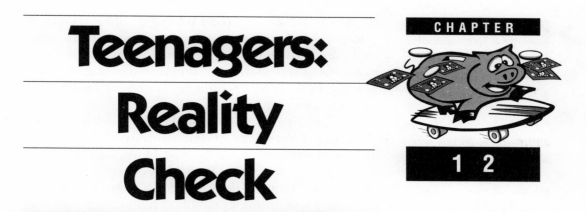

Teenagers: Reality Check

Q. *Dear Dr. Tightwad: My teenagers think I'm cheap because I won't spring for rock-concert tickets. How can I make them understand that it's expensive to run our household?*

A. The next time you pay a month's worth of bills, let *them* write the checks and see how much is left in the account.

Mom: *Your checking account is overdrawn again.*
College student: How could it be? I still have checks.

That about sums up the average teenager's Achilles heel when it comes to money. By the time children reach their teen years, they're hemorrhaging cash; in 1992, kids between the ages of 12 and 19 spent $93 billion of their own and their parents' money. Yet they can still be notoriously ill-informed about how much it costs to live in the real world.

Kids are under two misconceptions: "They think they're going to make a lot more money than they will, and they think things cost less than they do," says Darlene Todd, who heads her own financial planning firm in Chicago and has worked with older high school students in association with the Illinois Council on

Economic Education. Todd tells of a young co-worker who got the financial shock of her life when she married. She had been living at home, paying for her car, clothes and telephone and thinking that she was supporting herself. She hadn't reckoned on the cost of rent, insurance or food.

In extreme cases, you could end up with every parent's nightmare: the classic underachiever. Peter Spevak of the Center for Applied Motivation describes the type: As a child, an underachiever would rather play video games than study for the math exam; as a young adult he's still at home, dabbling halfheartedly in college courses and hanging around with younger kids. He figures he's entitled to the same kind of house and middle-class circumstances his parents enjoy, but he never stops to think that his parents had to work to get them. Delayed gratification frustrates him, and he can't deal with frustration. Well-adjusted adults would handle the disappointment of not being able to vacation in Florida by making alternate plans or saving to take the trip next year. Underachievers, explains Spevak, would "sit there and whine."

The best prevention is early intervention. Darlene Todd gave her daughter Susan a dose of reality therapy when she was 18. The two of them scoured Chicago newspapers looking for apartments that Susan could rent for $500 to $600 a month. They started out with three bedrooms in mind and ended up looking at studios—that Susan could share with a friend.

What Teens Know —and Don't Know

Today's teenagers are hardly babes in the woods when it comes to things financial. They are, after all, children of the revolution that popularized personal finance in the 1980s, and they couldn't help being caught up in it, at least peripherally. Trouble is, the little they know is enough to make them dangerous.

Checking Accounts

Teens know, for example, that checking accounts exist, but they don't always know how to balance one. That old joke about not being overdrawn if you still have checks is sometimes painfully on the mark. Kathleen Hennessey, a faculty member at Texas Tech in Lubbock who has counseled students on financial matters, recalls one student who came to her in tears with a sheaf of checks. She feared the checks had bounced, but they were actually canceled checks that had been returned to her routinely by the bank.

Credit Cards

Teens know how to use a credit card to buy things, but they're not always clear on how they're supposed to pay the bill. They think plastic is just another form of currency and don't understand that using a card is like taking out a loan. So they're vulnerable to the experience of the Maryland teen who went off to college, ran up $600 in credit card debt, faithfully made the minimum monthly payment, then suddenly realized she was hardly making a dent in paying off the bill. Her parents eventually bailed her out.

Saving

Teens know that saving money is a worthwhile goal—especially to pay for the expensive college education their parents have been fretting about for years—but for most of them CD means compact disc. In the 1992 High School Financial Awareness Survey sponsored by the College for Financial Planning, about 70% of the 1,836 teens responding said they plan to attend college. But more than half of those students had not saved for their postsecondary education costs. (Those who did save reported having, on average, about $2,614 in the bank.) Among the 60% who reported having a job, the median take-home pay was $80 a week; the median weekly savings was $5.

Teens think plastic is just another form of currency and don't understand that using a card is like taking out a loan.

Planning for college actually provides a convenient opening for parents to introduce their kids to the fine points of budgeting, saving and even investing. Yet when parents come to her to discuss how to pay for college, "very few of them even bring their kids," says Bonnie Hepburn, a financial planner in Acton, Mass.

That's partly because they're naturally reluctant to discuss the family's financial situation with the kids—and partly because they often share their kids' casual attitudes toward budgeting, credit and saving. But now may be the last chance for the whole family to shape up before the kids graduate and go off on their own, either to manage a household and pay bills they didn't even know existed or to attend college, where credit cards are as easy to get as pizzas at midnight—and just as habit-forming.

On-the-Job Training

You might have gotten a chuckle (or at least a knowing smile) out of the question and answer that began this chapter, but we weren't kidding. Teens are old enough to learn the nitty-gritty of household finances, so you might as well use your bill-paying chores as a learning opportunity and let your children write a month's worth of checks. To make your point more dramatically, adopt the tactic of one father. He brought his teens into line by getting his pay in dollar bills, sitting his family down with the stack of cash and a pile of household bills, and asking the kids to parcel out the money to pay them. By the time his kids saw how little was left, they were talking about getting part-time jobs.

Holding down a job is one way for kids to get an introduction to Life 101. Your kids will find it easier to appreciate the cost of adding them to your auto-insurance policy if you can put it in terms of how many hamburgers they'd have to flip to cover the cost themselves.

Whether you want your child to work and for how many hours merits separate consideration (see Chapter 10). If you prefer that your kids concentrate on school-work and extracurricular activities rather than a job, that doesn't mean they have to miss out on real-world experience. Simply holding family meetings to discuss such financial matters as which car to buy and how to pay for it, how to cope with an impending layoff or how much to spend on holiday gifts can give your kids an invaluable insight into the decisions they'll have to make someday. And there's an immediate payoff for you. By

Who Pays?

Q. *Dear Dr. Tightwad: My daughter was invited to homecoming by a boy, but she offered to buy her own ticket (and he accepted) because she was afraid he couldn't afford it. I think he should have paid. Am I old-fashioned?*

A. Probably, but so is Dr. T. He (or she) who does the asking should pick up the tab. Tell your daughter to save her money for group outings, when it's okay to go Dutch.

seeking their input, you short-circuit any grousing later on if you wind up with a station wagon instead of a sports car or if the customary Christmas pile is smaller than usual.

By the time your children graduate from high school, it's reasonable to expect them to be able to manage their own checking account (although you'll probably have to co-sign for them to open one if they're under 18). Only about 17% of teens have checking accounts, and that's heavily weighted toward 18- and 19-year-olds, 43% of whom have accounts. But at Young Americans Bank in Denver, the average checking account holder is 15, has a balance of $240 and no illusions about the money lasting as long as the checks. Cindy Culkin, a bank representative, says that the bank's account holders are very responsible and have very few problems with their accounts.

Victoria Felton-Collins, a financial planner in Irvine, Cal., opened checking accounts for her kids, with herself as co-signer, when they were in their early teens. Once, when her son was about 14, he injured his leg on a skiing trip. Before he could be treated, the hospital wanted some evidence that the bill would be paid. Felton-Collins's son wowed them by whipping out his checkbook and writing a check, which the hospital accepted.

The Budget Bugaboo

What gives teens fits is budgeting. In fact, adults and teens both have such a distaste for its eat-your-spinach overtones that the word *budget* has all but disappeared from the lexicon of financial planners. Instead the focus is on dessert, in the form of a "spending plan," that's more freewheeling and less constraining than a budget. Here's how:

Record expenses.

Encourage your teens to write down everything they spend for a month, not necessarily to cut back on their outgo but to get control of it. "It may change their behavior and it may not, but the next time they go out to buy fries and a Coke they'll remember that 60% of their money is going toward junk food," says Kathleen Lenover, a financial planner in Denver who teaches high school students a course in personal finance. (To help them develop a basic spending plan, suggest that your teenagers use the accompanying record-keeping work sheet.)

Reprinted with special permission of North America Syndicate

Set goals.

You stand a better chance of getting your teens to change their behavior if you encourage them to set goals. Saving money because it's the right thing to do is too abstract, even for teens. They need something to work toward, whether it's a new stereo, a college education or a vacation.

Make goals tangible.

Whatever goal your kids settle on, have them write it down, which seems to provide a psychological boost. "When we write down what we're passionate about, there seems to be some sort of power that helps us accomplish it," says Lenover. "Kids eat this up."

Make goals straightforward.

Lenover emphasizes what she calls the 70-20-10 rule of money management—70% to spend, 20% to save for future big-ticket purchases and 10% for long-term investing. When a spending plan is that cut-and-dried, it becomes more manageable and less off-putting. (To make it even less scary, for both you and your kids, read the introduction to investing in Chapter 7.)

Decide what's important.

Teens also need help with setting priorities—deciding which things they really need and which they merely want. Maybe this sounds obvious to you, but with teens you can't belabor a point.

- **Have them draw up a list of needs and corresponding wants.** For example, they need school clothes but they want a fringed leather jacket that will exhaust their entire clothing budget. They need shoes; they want a pair to match every outfit, plus a few extras. They need transportation to school; they want a new car—and they want you to buy it for them.

Teens also need help with setting priorities—deciding which things they really need and which they merely want.

continued on page 180

Where Your Money's Coming From, Where It's Going

As a teen, you probably have a steadier stream of income—and more of it—than when you were a kid. Your regular expenses have probably expanded, too. So it's never too soon to start tracking where your money comes from and where it goes.

This work sheet will help you achieve your goals. Make one copy of it for each month of the year. By recording your income and expenses this month, you can identify where you'd like to make changes next month. Maybe you want to increase your income by asking for more odd jobs at home or by taking a part-time job. You could stop buying CDs or comics for a while to save money for a stereo or your prom. Maybe you want to save more for college or give more to charity.

Remember, your parents will still expect to have some say about your choices. They may limit the hours you can work each week or not allow you to buy a car. They may expect you to save a percentage of your income for college or to pay for your share of the family's car-insurance bill. Fill in those regular "fixed expenses" first thing each month and set aside the necessary money.

Month _____

Income

Allowance $ _____

Odd jobs   _____

My job or business   _____

Gifts   _____

Money I borrowed   _____

Total Income $ _____

Expenses

Money I owe $ _____

Savings   _____

College savings   _____

Church or other charity   _____

Gifts for family and friends   _____

Car payments and/or insurance   _____

Gas, oil, repairs, fees and taxes   _____

Public transportation (bus, subway) _____

Lunch money _____

Eating out and snacks _____

Clothing and accessories _____

Personal care _____

School supplies and fees _____

Telephone bills that I pay for _____

Recreation and hobbies

    Sporting equipment and fees _____

    Entrance fees for the skating rink,
       rec center, and so on _____

    Club dues, uniforms and other expenses _____

    Art and craft supplies _____

    Things I collect _____

    Stuff for my room (posters and such) _____

    Books, magazines and library fines _____

    Software _____

    Electronic equipment _____

    CDs, records and tapes _____

    Video and computer games _____

    Videotapes _____

    Movies _____

    Concerts _____

    Other outings _____

    Prom (or other party expenses) _____

    Vacations, other special trips _____

    Odds and ends

Total Expenses $ _____

Total Income $ _____

Minus Total Expenses   - _____

Money Left Over (Total Cash Flow or
Discretionary Income) $ _____

- **Run down the list with them and attach a realistic price tag to each item.** Writing down the numbers will make them seem more real to your kids and will give you room to maneuver. If there's $300 in your clothing budget and the kids insist on new jeans, they'll have to forgo the jacket (or pay for it themselves). If you're willing to spend $100 on shoes, they'll have to decide on five pairs at $20 each or two pairs for $50.

Esther Berger, a first vice-president of Paine Webber in Beverly Hills, recalls that when her oldest son approached driving age, he assumed that being a child in residence at 90210 automatically entitled him to a car. "I'm from Cleveland," says Berger. "I told him he needed transportation, but whether he got a new car, a used car or a skateboard depended on how much he saved, which his father and I would match." Michael saved $5,000 on his own and bought a brand new Ford Escort.

Expanding the Allowance

Once children reach 13, they get more of their money from jobs than from allowances, and the gap continues to widen as they get older. In the High

---

Discretion Advised

. . . .

Q. *Dear Dr. Tightwad: I finally gave my teenage daughter a clothing allowance and let her shop on her own. She came home with the ugliest clothes ever. Now what should I do?*

A. Don't give her the lecture about how you should have known you couldn't trust her with that much money. Don't criticize or make her return the clothes just because *you* don't like them. You made this deal, and basically you're going to have to grin-and-bear-it.

But you needn't suffer in total silence, and you can change your terms for next time. If some of the clothes don't mesh with your family's values—because they're see-through or too tight, for example—it's appropriate for you to go with your daughter to return them. The same is true if she has spent too much on glamorous outerwear but has neglected to replace basics like underwear and socks (though you could make her darn the old ones).

Discuss how to make clothing dollars go farther by buying classic pieces that will last or buying on sale. Set down rules about what her budget needs to cover—are you going to spring for a winter coat and shoes, for example? If you really think she needs more experience, make her responsible for less of her budget. Then give it another try.

School Financial Awareness Survey, about 60% of the respondents said they work, while fewer than half receive allowances. The median weekly allowance was $11.

But some parents take a different tack. When Joan Boucher of Denver was housebound with her infant daughter, she read about an allowance scheme for teens that intrigued her. For years Boucher bided her time. Then, when her daughter reached 13, she sprung it. Instead of a token allowance, she and her husband offered their daughter the opportunity to manage a sum large enough to cover all her expenses, such as savings, lunches, clothes, gifts and dancing lessons (with the exception of medical care and any parties she might have, which mom wanted to keep under her control). Her daughter was "dazed and delighted," recalls Boucher. With mom and dad to help, she spent an entire summer monitoring her expenses. "It gives the parent and child something genuine and valid to talk about, instead of why aren't you combing your hair differently," says Boucher.

They eventually settled on an allowance of $50 a month, a princely sum at the time, which they reevaluated every summer and adjusted upward or downward depending on anticipated expenses for the coming year. After that, the plan "took off and flew," says Boucher. "We had zero problems with the rest of the teenage years." The arrangement stayed in effect till her daughter reached 18 and left for college. It was the object of much envy on the part of little brother, who couldn't wait till he was 13 and got the same privilege.

A system like this is a hands-on lesson in distinguishing between the fixed expenses that can't be avoided—lunch money, bus fare, basic clothing—and the discretionary ones that may have to wait for another day. One blessed side-effect: It can also snuff out many a potentially explosive parent-teen confrontation. Mom and dad can't be expected to pay for those rock-concert tickets if money for that kind of entertainment is already built into the allowance. "The child

Mom and dad can't be expected to pay for those rock-concert tickets if money for that kind of entertainment is already built into the allowance.

knows the rules because they've been discussed ahead of time, so it erases parent-child tensions," says Boucher.

Wouldn't a teenager be tempted to squander the money? Sure—but not often. "You just have to stiffen your spine," says Boucher. "Of course they made mistakes and ran out of money in a few weeks. But they went without and they learned their lesson."

The Commandments of Credit

One way to teach teens about credit and to make sure they write the first chapter of their credit history under your supervision is to get them a credit card of their own, with you as co-signer, when they're 16 or 17 and still living at home, or get them a card for your own account. They'll be responsible for paying the bills, but you'll get a copy and can monitor their spending, and paying, habits. Kathleen Hennessey's children got their own cards, with $100 limits, when they were 16. When they went off to college, they were expected to cover their credit card bills out of their allowance. If they couldn't, Hennessey paid the difference but docked their allowance the following month.

Don't feel obliged to hand your 16-year-old a credit card. Robert McKinley of Frederick, Md., who publishes *CardTrak,* a credit card newsletter, passed up that opportunity when his son Derek was in high school. But when Derek went to college, McKinley liked the idea of having him apply for a secured credit card, which required that Derek deposit money in a savings account with the issuing bank and limited his credit line to the amount of the deposit. Not only did the secured card offer a lower rate and a lower annual fee than unsecured cards available to teenagers, but it also "introduced a psychological factor that this is real money," says McKinley. Holders of secured cards can usually qualify for unsecured cards and higher credit limits once they've shown a satisfactory payment record. As a result, young people get the idea that credit isn't an entitlement but a privilege to be earned.

Of course, if you don't like the idea of a teenager having a credit card of any kind, stick with cash. That will force your kids to be more disciplined and less inclined to spend. What's really important is that they learn some key commandments about credit:

- **Keep all receipts and check off each purchase when the bill comes.**

- **Don't charge anything you can't pay for that month, except in emergencies,** when you might allow yourself three months to repay.

- **Don't get into the habit of making only the minimum payment each month.**

- **Don't charge pizzas and other perishable items** that will be used up before you even get the bill.

- **Don't charge to the max.** Some cardholders assume that if an issuer gives them a limit of $1,000, they must be capable of repaying it. What counts is your cash flow, not the bank's high opinion of you.

- **Remember that a credit report can come back to haunt you, even if your parents bail you out.** Prospective employers sometimes consult credit reports, and a record of delinquent payments can be read as irresponsible behavior—and cost you a job.

- **Don't drag your parents down with you.** If your parents have co-signed for a credit card or loan and you welsh on the deal, they're left holding the bag. (Not realizing the potential consequences of their own irresponsible behavior, kids often assume that their parents will guarantee their debts and are shocked when mom and dad are reluctant to take on the risk.)

Preparing to Cut the Purse Strings

Q. *Dear Dr. Tightwad: Our son is going away to college, and it will be the first time he's in charge of so much of his*

For Real

To impress your kids that a credit report is an open book, write away for your own and examine it with your children. To request a copy of your credit record, write to:

- *Equifax, P.O. Box 105873, Atlanta, GA 30348;*

- *TRW, P.O. Box 2350, Chatsworth, CA 91313-2350;*

- *Trans Union, P.O. Box 390, Springfield, PA 19064.*

own spending money. How can we keep things from getting out of control?

A. Before he goes, tell him the facts of life—how much it costs to wash a load of clothes, for example.

That's what Lynda and John McConnell did each time they sent off one of their three children to Wake Forest University. "We literally took things item by item," says Lynda, down to figuring out the price of a haircut and allocating contributions to charity. Then they put the kids on a monthly budget. If they ran out of money, they had to dip into summer earnings, which were otherwise saved or tithed.

The McConnells laid the groundwork ahead of time by helping their children open checking accounts when they were high school seniors. They got the names of prospective roommates and contacted them ahead of time to decide who would bring such essentials as the popcorn popper, refrigerator and stereo. Once school started, the McConnells began making monthly deposits into each child's checking account. They kept the children on the family health- and auto-insurance policies and gave each child a calling card for phone calls home.

Still, there were glitches along the way. Daughter Beth ran over budget a number of times, mostly because of long-distance telephone calls to friends. Son Johnny discovered that while his hometown bank charged a low monthly fee for his checking account, it charged a lot for ATM transactions. Had he gone with the on-campus bank, he figures he could have saved about $60 over four years.

Those kinds of problems are easily resolved. If you don't think your son is up to the challenge yet, you may be able to keep tabs on his spending from afar. A growing number of colleges have an arrangement similar to the University of Maryland's "Terrapin Express." Parents of students deposit a sum of money with the university and students, using their ID cards as debit cards, draw on the account to buy meals and books and make other on-campus purchases. That means fewer checks to write, less cash to carry and more control over where money is spent.

To help keep long-distance phone bills in check, MCI's personal 800 service, for example, lets you set up your own 800 number for calls home. If your child is living off-campus, AT&T's free Call Manager service will separate your child's calls from his roommates' on each bill, according to separate dial-in codes, so there's no question of who called whom.

What you won't be able to control is your son's use of credit cards. If he's never had experience using credit before, he needs to know what he'll be getting into. For the McConnell kids, credit cards weren't a problem; they never had any.

Credit and College

When you send your kids to college, they'll be on their own in one way you might never have considered. As soon as they register for their first class, they'll be fair game for credit

"Besides my allowance, can I have an expense account?"

card issuers. And as long as they're at least 18, they can get a card on their own without having you as a co-signer.

To attract students, issuers will sweeten the deal with an assortment of perks: travel coupons for free airfare, discounts on long-distance calls, coupons for free video rentals, trip giveaways. So successful are the strategies that about 50% of college students have credit cards.

To get a card, all college students usually have to do is prove that they're registered at a four-year school

Student credit cards carry low credit limits— $500 to $1,000—but interest rates and annual fees are high.

and don't have a bad credit history. If they have no credit history, which is highly likely, it won't count against them. Some cards stipulate that students have minimal income, but that requirement can generally be satisfied if the kids have a savings account, participate in a work-study program or get an allowance from home.

Student cards carry low credit limits—$500 to $1,000—but interest rates and annual fees are high. Students don't have the long, spotless credit records that low-cost card issuers usually demand. Because credit limits are low, issuers have relatively low loss exposure. In return, they get a golden opportunity to attract new customers who will stay on with them as adults. For American Express, which has been soliciting college students for a dozen years, students "have become some of our best and most loyal customers," says a company spokesperson. They are also among the best credit risks. College students have a better-than-average payment record, possibly because they're responsible users of credit, possibly because credit limits are low—and possibly because mom and dad are willing to bail them out if necessary. "If a card issuer threatens to cause problems for a child, parents will sell the farm to come up with the money to pay off the bill," says Kathleen Hennessey of Texas Tech.

Credit messes

For students, a credit card of their own can be a golden opportunity to get a head start on establishing a credit history, or it can be a disaster in the making. At Bryant College in Smithfield, R.I., Judy Clare, assistant director of career services, runs a program for seniors in which she invites recent grads back to talk about problems they had in making the transition to the real world. Credit overload ranks high on the list. One student told how he ran up a $10,000 debt by going out on the town with friends, putting the tab on his credit card, collecting his buddies' share in cash and then spending the money. When he hit the limit on one card, he'd get another.

Kenneth Wilson [a pseudonym] knows the cycle. When he was a college student in California, and working as a part-time waiter, he applied for, and got, ten credit cards. He paid his American Express bill in full each month but usually made only the minimum monthly payment on the revolving accounts. Then he started using one card to pay off another. "It became so easy that I kind of lost the idea of the true value of a dollar," says Wilson. "I was just in my own little world."

When his debts hit $20,000 and he began to miss payments, he applied for a debt-consolidation loan from one of his card issuers but was turned down. Then he was laid off and his house of cards collapsed. Faced with the prospect of coming up with more than $600 a month for three years just to pay off the principal, Wilson filed for bankruptcy at the age of 23. That's hardly an easy way out because a bankruptcy stays on your record for 10 years and can affect your ability to get a job or to buy a car or a house. If he had it to do over, Wilson would have stopped with two cards and never would have charged anything he couldn't pay off within two months. "People don't understand that 19% adds up really quick," he says. Wilson's case may be extreme, but it isn't unusual for college students to charge to the max and then make minimum payments with little hope of digging themselves out of the hole. If you owe $1,000 on a credit card charging 19.8% interest and you make the minimum monthly payment, it will take you 8½ years to pay off the debt.

Light at the End of the Tunnel

When your children reach their teen years, they—and you—will bear the full brunt of peer pressure. And they will want to buy things because their possessions will help them define who they'd like to be—a car for the man- or woman-about-town or a closetful of clothes for the glamour queen or hip king. Your job in meeting this irresistible force is to be, in a sense, the immovable object—not simply because

Getting involved will not only keep your kids busy, but it will also expose them to a broader group of kids for whom money may not matter as much.

you say no but because you give your children a reason to say no.

It can be tough to resist when your kids are trying to fit in. Remember, though, that being part of a group doesn't have to mean spending a lot of money. Depending on their interests, encourage your kids to play sports, try out for the school play, work on the school newspaper or join a service organization or church youth group.

Getting involved will not only keep them busy, but it will also expose them to a broader group of kids for whom money may not matter as much. In addition, they'll learn to shine in their own right instead of merely being a reflection of their friends.

Finding a comfortable niche can be tough for teens, but it's not impossible. One twentysomething woman, the daughter of a teacher, recalls that when she was in high school she couldn't keep up with fellow students whose parents were wealthier. How did she cope? By throwing herself into music lessons. She performed a piano solo at her high school graduation, which conferred a status that money couldn't buy.

Don't sell your kids short. In a recent survey by the American Board of Family Practice, a healthy majority of teens said they would be willing to get jobs, buy fewer clothes and give up some allowance to help their families through a financial crunch. And even the worst shall pass. In its surveys of the youth market, The Zandl Group of New York City finds that by the time kids reach age 18 or 19, they have grown rather sober about money. Asked what they would do with a million dollars, boys talk about investing it and girls say they'd buy a house.

How to Make Your Child a Millionaire

Q. *Dear Dr. Tightwad: I've been saving for my kids in custodial accounts, but I don't want them to take the cash when they're 18 and blow it on a car. Is there any way I can keep them from getting the money?*

A. Sorry, but you're out of luck. Once you give your kids a gift via a custodial arrangement, the money belongs to them. They can get it when they reach legal age, which is 18 or 21 in most states, and spend it any way they choose.

Children probably can't grasp an abstract idea like saving until they're around 4 to 5 years old. And at that age you can't reasonably expect them to set their sights on anything other than a small, short-term goal, such as an inexpensive toy. By the time they enter their teen years, they can start saving for longer-term goals such as college, which will begin to seem more real. At that age, they're even capable of moving beyond savings accounts and investing in the stock market.

But don't wait that long to start saving and investing on your children's behalf. The sooner you begin, the longer they'll benefit from the miracle of compounding, and the richer they'll be. In fact, just as many of today's grandparents were the first in their families to go to college, their grandkids may be the first to become millionaires. Here are three ways they could hit the million-dollar jackpot at age 65: Make 41 deposits of $2,000 a year starting at age 24. Make seven deposits of $2,000 a year starting at age 17. Or make one deposit of $2,000 at birth. These examples assume annual compounding of 10%.

Depending on how much you save and the rate of interest you earn, the numbers can become even more eye-popping. Let's assume, for example, that you give your 3-year-old daughter a gift of $10,000. If she doesn't spend any of the money and it earns an average of 7.71% a year, it will grow to a cool $1 million by the time she's 65. If her money compounds for 62 years at an annual rate of 10.4%—the average return since 1926 for the Standard & Poor's 500-stock index— she'll get to crack a nest egg worth $4,614,053. And for the *coup de gráce,* imagine that her money grows at a rate equal to the average annual return of stock mutual funds during the 1980s, which was 15.5%. In that event, she'd be able to retire with a staggering $75,872,260.

It's unlikely, of course, that her money would grow at that torrid a pace for that length of time, but you get the picture. Once compounding gets rolling, it becomes a snowball that can build even modest amounts of money into formidable sums.

A Newborn Citizen

• •

Q. *Dear Dr. Tightwad: We're expecting a baby soon, and I read that even newborns need social security numbers. It sounds silly to me, but if it's true how do you get one?*

A. You're half right. Children age 1 and over must have a social security number at the end of the year for which you're filing a return in order to be claimed as a dependent on your tax return. The easiest way to get one is to check a box on birth-record forms you have to fill out before your newborn leaves the hospital. If you don't, you'll have to show up later at your local social security office with proof of your child's age, identity and citizenship, such as an original birth or baptismal certificate, plus a second proof of identity, such as a vaccination record for infants.

The point is to prevent taxpayers from claiming tax breaks for dependents they don't have. In the interval between the last year that kiddie social security numbers weren't required and the first year they were, seven million dependents vanished from tax returns.

You say you don't have $10,000 to set aside? Not to worry. Suppose you celebrate the birth of your first child by investing just $1,000 at 10%. You know that in the first year the earnings will amount to $100. With $1,100 invested the second year, you earn $110. By year ten, annual earnings hit $235; in year 25, they're up to $985. In year 50, earnings alone add $10,672 to the investment. Finally, in the 65th year, 10% growth delivers $44,579.

Over the 65 years, your $1,000 grows to almost half a million dollars. (To hit a round $1 million in 65 years at 10%, you need to start with $2,039.27.)

What If Your Kids Can't Wait 'Til 65?

Now let's come back down to earth. That first thud you hear is taxes hitting you in the pocketbook. If your children owe tax on interest or dividend distributions and money has to be withdrawn from their stash to pay the bill, there's less to compound and the growth rate will be significantly retarded. That second thud is reality mugging you. Your children may need to tap their cash well before retirement, to pay for college, buy a house or start a business, so their dream of becoming million-dollar babies may prove elusive.

But don't let those considerations discourage you. You can finesse the tax issue by investing in stocks or stock mutual funds that generate the bulk of their return as appreciation in share price, which is generally not taxable until the shares are sold. In that case, it's likely that little or no tax would be due in the early years. When taxes are due, you should consider paying the bill from cash on hand. That keeps the nest egg compounding at full speed. And that's a good lesson for your children to learn before they take over.

Even if your kids have to tap their funds well before retirement, their returns can be impressive. Let's look again at that $1,000 gift compounding at 10%. In 18 years it would total $5,560—money that

"When we were first married, my wife and I promised we'd save 50 cents out of every dollar we earned. It wasn't easy but it was fun, and we did it for 15 years. It built up wonderfully well. I'd recommend that other newly marrieds do the same thing."
John Templeton,
mutual fund pioneer

How Much Will a Dollar Buy in 65 Years?

Okay, you're probably thinking, suppose my kids do retire with a million bucks. At the rate the dollar is shrinking, that'll probably be enough to keep them in groceries for about a month.

Your skepticism is understandable but probably exaggerated. Yes, by the middle of the next century a dollar is likely to be worth a fraction of what it is now. But if you can get a decent return on your investment, and the probability is high that you can, you'll still be ahead.

Assume that inflation averages 3.1% for the next 65 years—the same pace as over the past 65 years. In 2058, $1 will have the purchasing power of 14 cents today. Put another way, it will take $7.27 to buy what $1 buys now.

But you'll have a lot more dollars to spend. If your investments can produce a 6% after-tax return, each of today's dollars will produce $44 by 2058. Although the compounding rate is less than double the inflation rate, you wind up with six times more purchasing power. If you manage to earn an 8% after-tax return, you'll have 20 times the buying power.

What Your Kids Can Look Forward To

• •

	Today's Price	After 65 Years of 3.1% Inflation
McDonald's Big Mac	$1.79	$13
Blood pressure medicine (100 pills)	$4 to $84	$29 to $611
Movie ticket	$6.50	$47
Toy metal fire truck	$34	$247
Night at the Plaza Hotel (weekend)	$225	$1,637
Set of golf clubs	$550	$4,000
Medigap policy	$900	$6,547
One-week Caribbean cruise	$1,200	$8,730
Honda Accord	$17,160	$124,833
Median-price home	$103,100	$750,018

One great thing about compounding is that each year you beat the inflation rate, you widen the gap in your favor. So it makes a lot of sense to invest these long-long-long-term dollars as aggressively as you can without disturbing your sleep at night. Day-to-day ups and downs in the market are of little consequence when your time horizon is measured in decades.

If you still need a push to get you started on saving for the future, take a look at how much havoc even a relatively modest 3.1% annual inflation rate can wreak on prices.

won't have to come out of your income to pay for college expenses (for much more on saving for college, see Chapter 14). In 30 years it would grow to $17,450—a tidy contribution toward a down payment on a house. If you could afford to present your newborn with a gift of $10,000, he or she would have $55,560 in 18 years and, hold onto your hats, $174,450 in 30 years—68% of the cost of a median-priced home, considering future inflation (see the accompanying box).

Your Best Investment Strategies

If very-long-term growth is your goal, you can choose certain investments that encourage it.

Annuities

If the money goes into an annuity, for example, your children would generally have to pay a tax penalty to get at the cash before age 59½. Annuities and universal life insurance policies also have a key tax advantage. Earnings are tax-deferred, so there's no annual reporting to the Internal Revenue Service. And you don't slow down the compounding express by having to use part of each year's earnings to pay taxes.

To see the impact, consider $10,000 invested over 65 years at 10%. In a tax-deferred investment, the $10,000 grows to almost $5 million. In a taxable investment, with a modest 15% of each year's return withdrawn to pay taxes, the pot grows to just over $2 million. Sure, taxes must be paid on the tax-deferred investment when funds are withdrawn, but you're still far ahead.

These advantages don't come without a stiff price, however. Annuities generally carry significantly higher annual expenses than mutual funds. And with life insurance, in the early years at least, you're paying for insurance the child doesn't need. You'll have to weigh such costs against the benefits.

Savings Bonds

Another investment alternative is series EE U.S. savings bonds, on which federal tax is deferred until the bonds are redeemed. This option, however, has a couple of drawbacks for super-long-term savings. First, the bonds stop paying interest after 30 years, so you would have to either cash them in, pay the tax and reinvest what's left or roll your investment into series HH bonds, which pay out taxable interest semiannually. Another problem: The return on bonds is likely to lag significantly behind the return on stocks over the long haul.

Who Best to Own the Bonds?

• •

Q. *Dear Dr. Tightwad: I have been buying series EE savings bonds for my grandchildren, with myself as co-owner. I'd like to continue buying bonds, but I'm wondering if one of the children's parents should be listed as co-owner. What's the best strategy?*

A. It depends on what you're trying to do. If you want to give the bonds to your grandchildren and have the interest taxed to them, register them in the children's name only. If you want to be sure the bonds qualify for the tax break on U.S. savings bonds that are used to pay college expenses, register them in the parents' name only.

Since you are both purchaser and co-owner of the bonds you've already bought, they're considered your property for tax purposes and don't qualify for the college tax break; you—not the child—will be taxed on the interest. Unfortunately, you can't do much about that. Changes in registration on outstanding bonds are permitted only in rare circumstances.

Remember, too, as long as your grandkids are old enough to understand what they're doing and sign their own name, a bank will allow them to cash in bonds held in their name even if they're minors.

Growth Stocks and Mutual Funds

All in all, your best bet for long-term investing is growth stocks or growth-stock mutual funds. First, they're likely to stay ahead of inflation. Since 1926, common stocks have generated more than twice the average return of Treasury bills and have outpaced inflation by almost three and a half times, according to figures compiled by Ibbotson Associates Inc. in Chicago. Second, as we saw earlier, they're likely to offer you some tax protection, at least during the early years, because most of their return will come in the form of price appreciation rather than income, such as interest and dividends.

Taxing Considerations

Making a financial gift to your children (or grandchildren) is one good deed that probably will go unpunished, at least by the tax man. You can give any number of people up to $10,000 a year each without triggering the federal gift tax. If you and your spouse join in the gift, $20,000 a year per child is gift-tax free.

And you'll save on income taxes as well, up to a point. In most cases gifts to children are held in custodial accounts, with the child as owner and you, or another adult you name, as custodian. In fact, if you're giving stocks or mutual fund shares, they'll have to be held in a custodial arrangement. But the money actually belongs to the children, and earnings are taxed at the child's rate. On 1993 returns, the first $600 of investment income each year is tax-free. The next $600 is taxed at the child's 15% rate. So the tax bill on the first $1,200 of investment income would be $90. If that $1,200 was your income and was taxed in the 28% bracket, the tab would be $336.

Funds for the Long Haul

Here's a sample portfolio of no-load equity mutual funds for investors who won't need the money for at least ten to 15 years and can withstand any short-term losses. None of the funds requires a minimum initial investment of more than $2,500.

Fund	% of Portfolio	800 Number
Royce OTC	10% to 20%	221-4268
Janus Growth & Income	10% to 20%	525-8983
Meridian	10% to 20%	446-6662
Selected American Shares	10% to 20%	243-1575
Twentieth Century Ultra	10% to 20%	345-2021
Warburg Pincus Intl.	20% to 30%	888-6878

The $246 savings is where the tax benefit tops out in 1993 for children under 14. That's because a child's investment income over $1,200 is hit by the so-called kiddie tax, which means it's taxed at the parents' top rate. (That $1,200 maximum will increase in the future to keep up with inflation.)

When considering how much you can put in a child's name before colliding with the kiddie tax, remember that price appreciation of growth stocks and mutual fund shares is not taxable until the shares are sold. However, you may owe taxes on fund distributions if your mutual fund sells stock it owns and distributes the profits to fund shareholders.

The kiddie tax ends when a child turns 14. At that age, your children would simply pay tax at their own rate. That opens the door to another tax-saving opportunity: You could give assets that have already appreciated in value. As long as they're sold after the child turns 14, the gain—including any that built up while you owned the assets—will be taxed at the child's rate.

The Gift Tax Explained

Q. *Dear Dr. Tightwad: I often read references to the fact that I can give each of my children up to $10,000 a year without triggering the federal gift tax. But what is the federal gift tax, anyway, and what happens if my gift exceeds $10,000?*

A. This is one tax you'll probably never have to worry about. It's true that if you give any one person a gift of more than $10,000 a year, you (not the recipient of the gift) are technically responsible for paying federal gift taxes. (If you're married and your spouse joins in the gift, the annual tax-free amount is $20,000.)

If a gift exceeds the limit, you have to file Form 709, *United States Gift Tax Return,* and figure the amount of tax due. Special tax rates apply, ranging from 18% to 55%. However, you wouldn't really have to pay any tax unless taxable gifts during your lifetime exceed $600,000. Everyone has a credit that offsets the tax bill on the first $600,000 worth of gifts. Any part of the credit not used up during your life can be used to offset estate taxes after you die.

Can You Trust Your Kids?

But wait. Those tax benefits aren't without their price. Once you give your kids a gift via a custodial arrangement, the money belongs to them. You can't get it back, but they can get it out generally at the age of 18 or 21 depending on the law in your state. Using the money to pay for college is one thing, but how can you be sure your impatient 18-year-old, for whom retirement is eons away, won't blow the money on a Porsche or a trip to Europe?

Some parents figure they'll get around this simply by not telling their children about the money. But the kids will find out as soon as they start filing their own tax returns because income from the accounts will have to be reported. Besides, it might be to your advantage to let your kids know about their nest egg to see how they react. If they're going to blow the money, it's best that you find out as soon as possible so that you can hold off on giving them any more until they're more adept at managing it.

If you're set on making your kids wait till retirement to reap their rewards, you may want to forget about custodial accounts and swallow the expense of setting up a trust. That way, you can direct when and how the money is to be distributed. Legal fees for establishing a trust run anywhere from $200 to $1,500, depending on its complexity. But it could be worth the price if you anticipate that the assets will grow to a substantial sum by the time the kids are 18—say, more than $50,000. (For more on this, see Chapter 16.)

How to Keep Control in Your Hands

One of the least expensive, and most attractive, ways to save for your kids' long-term future is through a unique mutual fund called the Twentieth Century Giftrust. It's designed specifically to let donors exercise some control over their gifts, so that the investments enjoy the benefits of long-term compounding.

Here's how it works: You make a gift (the minimum is $250) to a trust account, name a beneficiary (anyone but yourself or your spouse) and set the date at least ten years in the future when that person will get

If they're going to blow the money, it's best that you find out as soon as possible so that you can hold off on giving them any more until they're more adept at managing it.

James and Virginia Stowers celebrated the birth of each of their three grand-children by setting up four $250 trusts for each child that will come due when the kids turn 25, 40, 50 and 60.

the money. You can pick any maturity date. Many accounts are set to come due when the beneficiary is 18, presumably to pay for college bills, around age 30, perhaps to make the down payment on a home, or at retirement age. The gift is irrevocable and once you open the account, neither the beneficiary nor the maturity date—nor where the money is invested—can be changed.

It sounded like a great idea to James and Virginia Stowers, who celebrated the birth of each of their three grandchildren by setting up four $250 trusts for each child that will come due when the kids turn 25, 40, 50 and 60. Stowers is founder and president of the Twentieth Century family of mutual funds, in Kansas City. Giftrust, with $125 million in assets, is one of Twentieth Century's smallest, most aggressive and most volatile funds. Shares increased in value by 50% in 1989, lost 17% in 1990 and gained 21.8% in 1992. Since its creation in 1983, the fund has generated an average annual return of 20.36%. (For a prospectus, call 800-345-2021.)

If the fund could maintain that torrid pace for 60 years, the Stowers grandkids would each get almost $17 million from their last accounts on their 60th birthdays. If the accounts compound at a more reasonable 10%, the kids' 60th-birthday presents would be around $76,000. That may seem puny next to $17 million, but remember that it's based on an original investment of $250.

What Can You Expect?

It's impossible to predict the future value of a Giftrust account, and not just because of the vagaries of the stock market. Taxes are another monkey wrench. The first $100 of trust income is tax-free each year. But after that, returns must be filed and taxes paid. The fund handles all the paperwork, but shares are redeemed to cover the tax owed. That leaves less in the account to compound. Look on the bright side, however. On a $250 investment, years would pass before income from dividends and capital gains distributions (all of which are reinvested) would be high enough to trigger the tax.

Assuming a 10% compounding rate, here's how a $250 gift would grow:

- 25 years: $2,709;
- 50 years: $29,348;
- 65 years: $122,593.

One more catch: The federal gift-tax exemption on gifts of up to $10,000 doesn't apply to Giftrust accounts. If you open one, you must report the gift, no matter how small it is, to the IRS on Form 709, *United States Gift Tax Return.*

Stowers calls Giftrust Twentieth Century's "sexy" fund. "The most motivating factor of the Giftrust is trying to be remembered," he says of folks who open accounts. To that end, the account statements that are sent to beneficiaries each year include a message from the donor, which serves as an annual reminder of the gift.

Back in 1970, Stowers's mother, Laura S. Stowers, opened $250 trust accounts for seven grandchildren. The accounts work the same as Giftrust but, because that fund had not yet been created, they're invested in Twentieth Century Growth fund. Each of those accounts is worth almost $8,000 now, and if they continue to grow at the same pace until maturity in 2015, they'll hold about a quarter of a million dollars.

And what will happen when the beneficiaries get their checks? Stowers will make a prediction: "They're going to put a picture of their grandmother on the mantel and thank her for putting that $250 away."

If the fund could maintain that torrid pace for 60 years, the Stowers grandkids would each get almost $17 million from their last accounts on their 60th birthdays.

Get Your Kids Started in an IRA

When her daughter Jennifer earned $5,000 at a summer job following her college graduation, financial planner Dee Lee of Harvard, Mass., thought it was time to give her a lesson in saving big time, and urged

If your children have income from a job, or from self-employment such as delivering newspapers or babysitting, they're eligible to open an IRA, regardless of age.

Jennifer to open an individual retirement account. But Jennifer was worried that she couldn't afford to give up $2,000 of her income. So Lee struck a deal: She'd match her daughter's contribution dollar for dollar, up to $1,000. That was an offer Jennifer couldn't refuse. And when her 17-year-old brother Bryan got wind of it, he wanted in on the action, too.

Lee agreed to match IRA contributions for both of her children for five years, until each had $10,000 in the account. At 8% a year, that would grow to well over $600,000 by the time they reached age 65. Now three years into the plan, Lee is convinced her $5,000 investment will give each of her children "a lesson beyond anything I ever could have dreamed of," and one they'll practice on their own once five years is up. "I should have made Jennifer the offer when she was five years younger, but it never dawned on me," says Lee.

How It Works

If your children have income from a job, or from self-employment such as delivering newspapers or babysitting, they're eligible to open an IRA, regardless of age. And they don't even need to use their own hard-earned money to do it. You can give them cash equal to what they earn to fund the IRA, up to the $2,000 annual limit.

That's how Paul Fain III of Knoxville, Tenn., came to start saving for his retirement when he was still in college and working at summer jobs, such as gofer at a local golf club and co-host of a televised sports show. Fain's father gave him gifts to get the IRA going, and by the time he was 30 he had deposited about $3,000 in the account. And, even if he never puts in another dime, he should get a handsome payoff.

Fain expects the account to hold almost $200,000 when he's 65. That assumes the current balance, which is split between fixed-income and stock investments in a variable annuity, grows at an average annual rate of 10%. If the IRA compounds at 12%, it will be worth more than $350,000 when Fain is ready to retire.

If your children earn any income (investment income doesn't count), using gifts to start an IRA may be the easiest way to set them on the path toward retiring as millionaires. And you don't even have to give your children $2,000 to get them going. Let's say you have a 14-year-old daughter who makes $200 a year babysitting. Then let's assume you give her money to make $200 IRA deposits for three consecutive years. Even if no other contributions are made, the account will hold more than $70,000 when your daughter turns 65, assuming 10% annual compounding.

A key advantage of the IRA is that earnings are tax-deferred, so you don't have to worry about reporting them to the IRS or letting taxes diminish the power of compounding. Since there's a 10% tax penalty if the funds are touched before age 59 ½, you have the government's blessing in encouraging your child to go for long-term growth. And you can give your kids a lesson in investing by helping them decide what to do with the money.

"I christen thee '070-28-9271'."

From the Wall Street Journal—Permission, Cartoon Features Syndicate

For Paul Fain, the IRA begun while he was in college got him into the saving habit. Although he no longer contributes to the account (his income is too high to allow him to deduct contributions any more), he saves through a retirement plan at work.

Some paperwork is involved in an IRA. Contributions have to be reported to the IRS, either on the child's tax return or, if he or she doesn't have enough income to require a return, on Form 8606, *Nondeductible IRA Contributions, IRA Basis, and Nontaxable IRA Distributions.* And be warned that some IRA spon-

sors won't allow a minor to open an account. The
Fidelity and Twentieth Century fund families say no,
for example. But don't be discouraged. Other sponsors,
including the Vanguard funds and Merrill Lynch, are
happy to take the accounts, though Merrill Lynch
requires that a guardian signs the contract. Merrill
Lynch even opened one for a six-month-old infant. The
baby girl worked as a model.

Yes, You Can Pay for College —But Start Saving Now

Q. *Dear Dr. Tightwad: Our first child is only a year old and we're already panicking about how we're ever going to be able to afford his college education. Are all the horror stories about college costs true?*

A. Yes, but don't let them paralyze you with fear. You should be getting a move on to start saving. Even small amounts set aside when your child is young can make a big difference when you get that first tuition bill.

When it comes to kids and money, parents ask lots of questions (many of which we've tried to answer in this book). How much allowance should they give? Should they pay their kids for doing chores? How much should they tell their children about the family's finances? How should they go about teaching values, as well as the value of money?

And always on their minds is the biggest puzzler of all: How are they going to pay for their kids' college education? So great is their concern that they pass it on to their children. Even when teens understand little

Here's a quick primer on how to lop nearly 75% off the amount you have to set aside for college each month.

else about money, they're well aware that college is a looming financial burden.

And the worries aren't exaggerated. For students who entered college in 1993, the four-year cost, including tuition, room and board, books and other expenses, will average $80,891 at a private university. At some elite institutions the tab has already cracked the $100,000 mark. Look at the accompanying work sheet and you'll see that if you assume 7% annual inflation in college costs, the average bill at a private school will balloon to $273,406 for the freshman class of 2011 (those kids who were born in 1993).

If your child will be in that class and you haven't started saving yet, swallow hard. If you could earn 10% a year on your money (that's the historical total return on Standard & Poor's 500-stock index), you would have to put away $455.25 every month to pay the full freight at a private school (the accompanying work sheet will take you through the calculations). And that's not accounting for taxes.

Bring Your Savings Goal in Line With Your Budget

So much for the worst-case scenario. It can only get better and, in fact, it does. Here's a quick primer on how to lop nearly 75% off the amount you have to set aside for college each month:

Send Your Children to a Public University

For students entering in 1993, the total four-year cost at a public university will average $38,343. Applying the 7% annual inflation rate, that would rise to $129,597 for the class of 2011. Again assuming that you're starting from scratch and can earn a 10% annual return (disregarding taxes), you'd only have to put aside $215.79 per month.

Choosing a public school (or even a low-cost private school) doesn't mean you're consigning your child to a second-rate education. Currently about 5.9 million college students are enrolled in public schools, and any number of directories will help you choose a good one.

Don't Try to Save the Entire Amount

While that's an admirable goal, it may be so ambitious that you'll become discouraged if you can't meet it. Besides, you may not have to meet it; when the time comes you may have other sources of college funding.

For example, you could pay some of the bills out of your income at the time, or by taking out a home-equity loan or borrowing against your employer-sponsored 401(k) or 403(b) tax-deferred retirement plan. And your child might qualify for scholarships or other financial aid. The College Board estimates that about 45% to 50% of all undergraduates receive some sort of aid, including grants, loans and work-study programs. Then there's the possibility that an angel (in the form of generous grandparents, perhaps?) will come to your assistance.

In any event, "if you have anywhere from 60% to 75% of the total cost accounted for when your child shows up for freshman orientation, you're in great shape," says Philip Johnson of Clifton Park, N.Y., a former college administrator who's now a financial planner specializing in college planning. Even saving 50% or 25% of the total cost will mean you have to come up with that much less from other sources when the first tuition bills come due.

Saving 60% of the projected four-year cost of attending a public university for the freshman class of 2011 would cut your monthly contribution down to $129.48 (again assuming a 10% annual return and not including taxes).

Have Your Kids Do Their Part

In most states parents have no legal obligation to pay for their children's college education. A few states specifically include the cost of college as a requirement

If you have anywhere from 60% to 75% of the total cost accounted for when your child shows up for freshman orientation, you're in great shape.

continued on page 208

How Much Do You Need to Save?

Use this work sheet and the accompanying table to calculate how much you'll need for your children's college education and to determine whether you're on track. The table projects total four-year college costs (tuition, room and board, books and other expenses), assuming a 7% annual increase (current costs are based on the College Board Annual Survey of Colleges, 1992-93 edition). The *potential*

Tuition Cost Estimate

1. Year your child begins college   _____

2. Total college cost (see table at right) $ _____

Total Amount Saved

3. Amount already set aside $ _____

4. Potential growth multiplier corresponding to the year your child will enter college (see table)   _____

5. Estimated tuition savings (multiply line 3 by line 4) $ _____

6. Additional money needed, not including college loans, financial aid and other sources of funds (subtract line 5 from line 2) $ _____

Amount Set Aside Each Month

7. Monthly investment divisor corresponding to the year your child will enter college (see table)   _____

8. Amount you'll need to save each month (divide the amount on line 6 by the number on line 7) $ _____

growth multiplier shows how much your current investments will grow, assuming that you earn 10% a year before taxes—the historic (but not guaranteed) return on large-company stocks—and that you reinvest all your earnings. The *monthly investment divisor* helps you calculate how much to save each month to reach your goal.

College Cost Projections

Year Student Enters College	Cost of Public College	Cost of Private College	Potential Growth Multiplier	Monthly Investment Divisor
1993	$38,343	$80,891	1.10	12.67
1994	41,027	86,553	1.21	26.67
1995	43,899	92,612	1.33	42.13
1996	46,972	99,095	1.46	59.21
1997	50,260	106,032	1.61	78.08
1998	53,778	113,454	1.77	98.93
1999	57,543	121,396	1.95	121.96
2000	61,570	129,893	2.14	147.40
2001	65,880	138,988	2.36	175.50
2002	70,492	148,715	2.59	206.55
2003	75,426	159,125	2.85	240.84
2004	80,706	170,264	3.14	278.73
2005	86,356	182,182	3.45	320.59
2006	92,401	194,935	3.80	366.83
2007	98,869	208,580	4.18	417.91
2008	105,790	223,181	4.59	474.33
2009	113,195	238,803	5.05	536.67
2010	121,118	255,520	5.56	605.53
2011	129,597	273,406	6.12	681.60
2012	138,669	292,545	6.73	765.64
2013	148,375	313,023	7.40	858.48
2014	158,762	334,934	8.14	961.03
2015	169,875	358,380	8.95	1,074.32

Source: Neuberger & Berman Management Inc.

of child support, but they're in the minority. Of course, most parents would probably consider it a moral obligation, if not a legal one, to do their bit to help pay for college. But that doesn't mean you have to do it *all*. Getting your kids to save their own money takes some of the pressure off you and can also ease the burden of student loans on them if it means they have to borrow less. Bonnie Hepburn, a financial planner in Acton, Mass., who specializes in college aid, points out that a debt of more than $20,000 is probably too much for any college graduate to owe.

It isn't realistic to expect young children to save all their pennies for college; the whole idea is too abstract and too far in the future. But it's appropriate to expect teenagers to save, especially when 33% of them are working regularly and have income of $88 billion a year, most of it discretionary (see Chapters 1 and 10). Instead of just complaining about the high cost of college, spell it out for your teens in dollars and cents. Take this opportunity to introduce them to family finances by showing them your household income and expenses, and brainstorming ways in which you can add college bills to the mix with as little pain as possible.

How much should you expect your children to contribute? There are probably as many answers as there are families.

- **When family psychologist John Rosemond and his wife, Willie,** were mapping out college plans for their two children, they decided that all they were willing to pay for was a public university. If the kids wanted to go to a private school, they'd have to get a scholarship or find some other way to finance it.

- **Victoria Felton-Collins and her husband, David,** were willing to foot the bill for their children's undergraduate education at the school of their choice, but that's where they drew the line; graduate or professional school was the kids' responsibility.

- **Pat and Jenny Nugent** gave their three daughters a choice of schools—any Jesuit college in the Midwest or East except pricey Boston College or Georgetown. "Once we found you could get a good education for a moderate price at a school like Marquette, we didn't want to spend any more," says Pat. He and Jenny provided tuition, room and board, and $100 a month in spending money, but the girls were expected to earn at least $1,500 over the summer to pay for books, clothes and transportation home for the holidays.

You shouldn't be so cowed by daunting projections of future costs that you do nothing. You can save for college and what's more, you should.

For the sake of our example, suppose you decided your kids should contribute $5,000 to their total college expenses—a not unreasonable expectation if they have after-school or summer jobs in high school and work during vacations while they're in college. That would further lower your own savings goal to $72,758, or $121.15 per month—73% less than the worst-case figure we started with and far more manageable for most families.

Of course, you'll want to adjust your own family's savings target depending on your goals and resources. You may have your sights set on a private school, or you may not want your children to feel forced into taking an after-school job to save money for college. The point here is that you shouldn't be so cowed by daunting projections of future costs that you do nothing. You *can* save for college and what's more, you *should*.

You Won't Be Penalized for Saving

Don't buy into the myth that having a tidy sum in savings will hurt your chances of getting financial aid. To determine your eligibility for financial aid, you'll have to fill out the *Free Application for Federal Student Aid,* and the government will apply a standard formula to the data. Your expected contribution to your child's education will be determined much more by your income than your assets. So if your income is relatively high, your expected contribution will be, too, regardless of your assets.

For example, a two-income family of four with an income of $40,000 a year after taxes and $50,000 in assets, excluding home equity, could be expected to contribute $6,230 a year from income and nothing from assets (see the accompanying work sheet).

Parental assets enjoy favored status in other ways as well. An asset-protection allowance will shelter a certain portion of your assets. The amount sheltered varies with the number of parents in the household and the age of the older parent. To see how much protection you would qualify for, see the table with the accompanying work sheet. (Federal rules exclude assets entirely if your family's adjusted gross income is less than $50,000 and you file a 1040A or 1040EZ tax form.)

What's more, parents are expected to use only 5.6% of their assets to pay for college, after allowances, while kids will be nicked for 35% of their assets. What really hits parents in the pocketbook is having to come up with their expected contribution out of current income, or borrow the money and incur interest costs. In either case, a savings cushion is your best defense against tuition shock.

It Isn't Going to Get Any Easier

Often the biggest obstacle to saving isn't the $50,000 or $100,000 you need at the end but the $25

continued on page 214

How Much Will College Really Cost?

Use this work sheet to figure your "estimated family contribution," the amount your family will be expected to pay toward college costs before receiving financial aid. The work sheet reflects the federal need-analysis formula—private schools may deviate from this formula when giving out their own aid. Calculations are designed for families with dependent students; calculations for independent students and families that own small businesses and farms are excluded.

Parents' Income

1. **Parents' income:** wages, including payments made this year to IRA, Keogh and 401(k) plans; social security benefits; interest and investment income; tax-exempt interest income; and housing or other living allowances. $_____

2. **Federal, state and social security taxes**   _____

3. **Income-protection allowance:** $10,520 for a family of two; $13,100 for three; $16,180 for four; $19,090 for five, $22,330 for six. Subtract $1,790 for each additional child if you have more than one in college.   _____

4. **Employment expense allowance** of $2,500 or 35% of the smaller income, whichever is less, if both parents work or if you're a single parent who works.   _____

5. Add lines 2, 3 and 4.   _____

6. **Parents' available income:** Subtract line 5 from line 1. $_____

How Much Will College Really Cost? (cont'd.)

Parents' Assets

7. **Total assets:** cash, bank accounts, stock, bonds, real estate (other than a first home), trust funds, commodities, precious metals $_____

8. **Asset-protection allowance** (from Table A, following) _____

9. **Parents' available assets:** Subtract line 8 from line 7. _____

10. Multiply line 9 by 0.12. If negative, enter zero. _____

11. **Adjusted available income and assets:** Add lines 6 and 10. _____

12. **Parents' contribution:** Using figure from line 11, see table B, on following page. _____

13. If more than one child is in college, divide line 12 by the number of students in college. The result is the contribution for each student. $_____

Student's Income

14. **Student's income:** wages, interest and investment income $_____

15. **Federal, state and social security taxes** _____

16. **Income-protection allowance** _____ $1,750

17. Add lines 15 and 16. _____

18. **Student's available income:** Subtract line 17 from line 14. _____

19. **Student contribution from income:** Multiply line 18 by 0.5. $_____

Student's Assets

20. **Assets in student's name:** cash, savings, trusts, investments, and so on. $_____

21. **Student contribution from assets:** Multiply line 20 by 0.35. $_____

Estimated Family Contribution

22. If one student is in college, add lines 12, 19 and 21. $_____

23. If you have two or more kids in college, add lines 13, 19 and 21 for each student. $_____

Table A: Asset Protection Allowance

Age of Older Parent	One-Parent Family	Two-Parent Family
40-44	$24,700	$34,100
45-49	27,600	38,800
50-54	31,100	44,300
55-59	35,200	51,300
60-64	40,300	60,300
65 plus	44,000	66,800

Table B: Parents' Contribution

Available Funds From Line 11	Parent Contribution
Less than -$3,409	-$750
-$3,409 to $9,400	22% of line 11
$9,401 to $11,800	$2,068 plus 25% of amount over $9,400
$11,801 to $14,200	$2,668 plus 29% of amount over $11,800
$14,201 to $16,600	$3,364 plus 34% of amount over $14,200
$16,601 to $19,000	$4,180 plus 40% of amount over $16,600
$19,001 or more	$5,140 plus 47% of amount over $19,000

Adapted from Don't Miss Out, *by Anna and Robert Leider (Octameron Associates)*

*Celebrate the birth
of a newborn by
opening a mutual
fund account on his
or her behalf, then
tell relatives.*

you need to get started. Yet we saw in the preceding chapter how, over time, even small amounts of money can pile up. "For someone who hasn't saved at all, even putting aside $25 a month is a powerful behavioral shift that can accomplish so much," says Anne Lieberman, a financial planner in Larkspur, Cal. Once you get into the habit, you can increase the amount as your income goes up. Or you can kick in a little extra if you come into a windfall—a bonus at work, for example, or a lottery prize.

For new parents who are often struggling financially, saving for college sometimes plays second or even third fiddle to other financial demands, such as funding a retirement plan or buying insurance. One solution is to get the rest of your extended family in on the act. Celebrate the birth of a newborn by opening a mutual fund account on his or her behalf, then tell relatives that as birthday and holiday gifts they can add money to the account. Especially when they're young, the kids won't miss another toy.

Young parents often make the mistake of thinking they'll start to save later, when they're older and more flush with cash. Nowadays, however, middle-agers in their prime earning years are often faced with the triple whammy of saving for college and retirement, as well as providing financial support to their own parents. Says Lieberman, "People get the idea that saving money will get easier later because they'll be making more, but it doesn't get easier. The ante just goes up."

Investment Strategies for College Savings

Now that we've convinced you to start saving, where should you put the money? That depends on how old your children are. You should be prepared to alter your investment strategy as your children grow.

Birth Through Age 10 to 12: Go for Growth

At this age, you can afford to take some risks. In fact, "safe" investments such as bank certificates of deposit or series EE savings bonds can turn out to be sure losers because it's likely that the return you earn won't keep up with inflation in college costs, which has been running about 7% a year.

As we saw in the preceding chapter, the best investments for parents of young children are growth stocks or mutual funds that specialize in growth stocks—

> ## Funding Mutual Funds
>
> •
>
> To find appropriate mutual funds for college saving, you can consult any of the publications cited in Chapter Seven that track fund performance: *Kiplinger's Personal Finance Magazine, Money, Forbes,* or *Barron's,* for example.

companies that don't pay much in the way of dividends but whose share prices stand to increase over time. They will outperform all other assets over the long haul, which in this case is five to ten years. If it will be at least that long before your children start school, you have time to ride out the ups and downs of market cycles and can afford to keep the bulk of your money in stocks.

Not only do mutual funds give you an opportunity to stay ahead of college-cost inflation, but they also make it easy for you. A number of funds with historically impressive track records require a minimum initial investment of $1,000 or less. And some even waive that requirement if you sign up to have money automatically transferred to the fund from your checking account every month (three that do are the Janus Fund, 800-525-8983; Gabelli Asset, 800-422-3554; and Strong Opportunity, 800-368-1030). This kind of automatic transfer is the simplest and least painful way to get into the discipline of regular saving.

Fidelity reduces its typical $2,500 minimum to $1,000 for college saving in its Asset Manager, Growth and Income, Puritan, and Blue-Chip Growth funds (800-544-

8888). If you don't have the $1,000, you can place as little as $100 in its Cash Reserves money-market fund, add to your investment $100 at a time, and transfer the $1,000 minimum when you've accumulated it.

Age 11 to 13 Until Tuition Day: Protect Your Investment

While stocks traditionally deliver the best return in the long run, they can plummet overnight and cost you much of what you have gained. It can take several years to recoup your losses, but if you need the money for college you might not be able to wait that long. That's why, once your child reaches age 11 to 13 or so, you should start easing your money out of stocks and into investments that pay a fixed rate of interest.

You could, for example, sell off some of your growth-stock funds and move the money into bond funds. Or you could gradually shift assets from growth funds to funds that own both stocks and bonds. A few funds that fit that category and are worth considering are Linder Dividend (314-727-5305), Vanguard Wellington (800-635-1511), and

Mutual Funds for College Saving

Once you have accumulated several thousand dollars in one fund, you can, if you choose, diversify into others to spread your risk. Here's a sample portfolio of no-load mutual funds for investors with an eight-to-ten-year horizon, such as parents with children of elementary-school age. None of the funds requires a minimum initial investment of more than $2,500.

Fund	% of Portfolio	800 Number
Fidelity	10% to 20%	544-8888
Harbor Bond	15% to 25%	442-1050
Janus	10% to 20%	525-8983
Neuberger & Berman Guardian	10% to 20%	877-9700
Royce Premier	5% to 15%	221-4268
Strong Opportunity	5% to 15%	368-1030
Warburg Pincus Intl.	10% to 20%	888-6878

Scudder Short-Term Bond (800-225-2470).

By the time your child reaches age 14 or 15, you should begin shifting out of stocks with a vengeance. One plan, the Twentieth Century College Investment Program, will do all the work for you. You invest initially in Twentieth Century Select, a growth-stock fund, then, as T-Day approaches, your assets are automatically moved to a money-market fund (see below) over four, five or six years, whichever you choose.

You can achieve the same result on your own, by transferring your money in regular installments. Your goal is to have all your college savings in bond funds, certificates of deposit, or other short-term, relatively low-risk investments that pay a fixed rate of interest, such as money-market funds, within two years of the first tuition bill.

Remember that you won't need all of your money at once, so you might want to time when your investments come due so that a portion of the total matures just before you have to make each tuition payment.

Here's a look at a few of your saving options:

EE savings bonds

They aren't the best way to keep up with college costs over the long haul, but as a short-term strategy for protecting your assets they're tops. Bonds pay a competitive market rate (about 4.75% at press time), but if you hold the bonds five years or longer, they'll pay no less than a minimum of 4% interest.

Another bonus: If you buy series EE bonds in your name and use them to pay your kids' college tuition, some or all of the earnings may be tax-free. The tax break starts to be phased out when adjusted gross income plus interest on the bonds exceeds $45,500 for single parents and $68,250 for married couples in 1993. It disappears entirely at $60,500 for single parents and $98,250 for couples.

But those figures are indexed to inflation. So by 1996, for example, assuming prices rise 4% annually, joint incomes as high as $77,445 may be able to reap

Your goal is to have all your college savings in short-term, relatively low-risk investments that pay a fixed rate of interest, within two years of the first tuition bill.

Zero-coupon bonds, like savings bonds, can be just the ticket in the short run if your goal is to get out of the market and preserve your capital.

the full benefit of the tuition tax break. And there's a move afoot in Congress to remove all income restrictions. For parents in the 28% federal bracket who qualify now for the full exemption, a yield of around 5% is equivalent to a taxable yield of 6.94%.

Zero-coupon bonds

Like savings bonds, zero-coupon bonds pay no current interest; instead, they are sold at substantially less than face value, and when they mature they pay off at face value. Like savings bonds, they are too conservative for long-term saving.

But like savings bonds, they can be just the ticket in the short run if your goal is to get out of the market and preserve your capital—especially if you're a high-income taxpayer who doesn't qualify for the tax break on EE bonds. Interest on municipal zeros, which are issued by state and local governments, is exempt from federal taxes. And you'll usually escape state taxes, too, if you buy a muni issued in your state.

You can also buy zero-coupon Treasury bonds issued by the U.S. Treasury, but you have to pay taxes each year on the income your investment is assumed to have earned. Interest is exempt from state and local taxes, however, so zero-coupon Treasuries can be an attractive option for parents who live in high-tax states and won't qualify for the federal tax exemption on EE bonds.

Money-market funds, bank certificates of deposit

These traditional vehicles for short-term cash reserves are appropriate for college savings that you'll need within a couple of years. Compare their after-tax return with other savings options to see what's best for you.

Over the last couple of years, investors accustomed to higher yields on money-market funds and CDs were shocked to see interest rates plummet to the 3%-to-4% range or even lower. In that situation, one attractive alternative is *short-term bond funds*. These funds have longer maturities than money-market funds—sometimes as long as five years—so they pay a higher yield. But their longer maturity also increases their risk.

CollegeSure certificate of deposit

Sold by the College Savings Bank, in Princeton, N.J. (800-888-2723), these CDs are federally insured, come in maturities of one to 25 years and generally require a $1,000 minimum deposit. But they also sock you with a stiff penalty if you withdraw the money early, and they're fairly complex instruments.

For example, on balances of less than $10,000, they pay a variable interest rate equal to 1.5 points less than an index of college-cost inflation. The rate is adjusted each July 31 and applied retroactively to CDs held during the preceding year. The CollegeSure CD would be most attractive if college costs were to skyrocket while other prices, and interest rates, remained relatively stable.

Whose Money Is It?

Once you've started saving for your kids' college education, you'll have to decide whose name the account should be in, yours or your children's.

At first, the answer appears to be obvious. It's their education, right? So the money should be in their name. Besides, as we saw in the preceding chapter, saving in your child's name entitles you to a tax break: In 1993 the first $600 of annual investment income is tax-free, and the next $600 is taxed at the child's 15% rate. So, for example, the tax bill on the first $1,200 of interest, dividends or capital-gains distributions would be $90, compared with $336 if that income were yours and you were in the 28% bracket. (Remember, however, that there's a limit to the government's generosity. For children under 14, investment income over $1,200 is taxed at the parents' top rate. This "kiddie tax" no longer applies once a child turns 14.)

But a tax savings of a couple of hundred dollars a year may not be enough to compensate for the three things you could lose by saving in your child's name:

Even if you're the custodian of money saved in your children's names, your children own it and can spend it as they wish once they reach the legal age, and sometimes even before.

The Money

You may intend that the funds be used to pay for college, but you'll have to trust your child not to fritter them away somewhere between the bank and the bursar's office. Even if you're the custodian of the money, your children own it and can spend it as they wish once they reach the legal age, and sometimes even before. For example, banks will allow minors to cash in U.S. savings bonds held in their own name as long as the kids are old enough to understand the transaction and sign their name.

In most families that won't be a problem (especially if you've been following the advice in this book), because children will know where their responsibility lies. But there are plenty of horror stories about plans gone awry. One lawyer tells of a panic-stricken client whose 18-year-old daughter had run off to follow a guru, and then mailed a certified letter from the commune asking mom and dad to send all the money they had been saving in her name for college. "The parents were horrified," says their attorney. "They saw all that money being squandered on a passing fad."

The Financial Aid

As noted earlier, financial-aid formulas require that 35% of a student's assets be used toward the family contribution while parents contribute only 5.6% of theirs, after allowances. Philosophically, that makes sense. After all, it's the children's education and they should be willing to invest their own money in it. Practically, however, the formula could cost you financial aid.

Assume, for example, that your daughter holds $10,000 in her own name. Under the standard financial-aid formula, she'd be required to come up with 35% of that, or $3,500, as part of the family contribution to college costs. If that same $10,000 were held in your name, however, you'd only have to contribute $560, possibly making you eligible for more financial aid.

What's tough about this is that you'll have to decide years in advance which is more valuable to you: the certainty of qualifying for a tax break by saving in your child's name today, versus the possibility of qualifying for more aid in the future. If your income is so high that you don't need assistance and probably won't get it, the tax break is more attractive. (Remember, though, that if saving on taxes is one of your goals, there may be other ways to achieve it—by investing in tax-free municipal bonds, for example.)

On the other hand, the more certain you are that you'll qualify for aid, the more attractive it is to save in your own name. Families who would end up qualifying for significant aid, particularly grants, lose out by having saved in the child's name, even after tax benefits are taken into account.

Remember, too, that in order to qualify for the tax break on U.S. savings bonds used to pay for college, you have to hold the bonds in your name.

Nowadays, however, a big portion of student aid is in the form of loans, so a further complicating factor is that by saving in your name you'd be giving up cash in hand, the tax break, for the "opportunity" to take on more debt.

The Control

Once you give your children money or other assets via a custodial arrangement, you can't get it back. That means you lose the ability to redirect the assets to other purposes should the need arise. Financial planner Philip Johnson tells of one client who decided to keep college savings for his four children in his own name and was glad he did: One child attended the U.S. Naval Academy and another joined a convent. Since the client ended up paying for only two college educations, he was able to redirect the rest of the money for other purposes.

Of all the arguments for keeping the money in your own name, control is the most compelling. Saving

It's your choice: the certainty of qualifying for a tax break by saving in your child's name today, versus the possibility of qualifying for more aid in the future.

in your child's name may make sense if the amount is relatively small, certainly no more than the amount it would take to max out on the tax break. But if you have any doubts about putting a substantial amount of money into your kids' hot little hands, you might as well keep it in yours.

How to Win at the College Aid Game

Earlier we saw that one of the great myths about saving for college is that you'll be penalized for your thrift. The truth is that having any college savings, no matter what the amount, is better than having none.

Another great myth about paying for college is that if you're an average middle-class family, and certainly if you're above average, you won't qualify for any financial aid. While it's true that your "expected family contribution" is determined to a great extent by your income (see the work sheet beginning on page 211), the amount of aid you're actually entitled to is determined by other factors as well, such as the cost of the school your child is attending and the number of kids you have in school at the same time.

For example, if your total expected family contribution is, say, $10,000 a year ($8,000 from you, $2,000 from your child), that may cover all the costs, and then some, at State U. But if your child has her eye on a pricey Ivy League school that costs $20,000 a year, that still leaves a $10,000 gap that the school may be willing to fill with a combination of grants, loans and work-study programs. If you have two children at that pricey Ivy League school and assuming the second child contributes as much as the first, your expected family contribution would increase to $12,000, but the gap grows to $28,000 and it's even more likely that you'll qualify for some aid. "Families with incomes under $40,000 do very well," says financial planner Hepburn. But her clients with family income of $70,000 or more have also qualified for substantial aid.

How do they do it? Take a lesson from a master. Phyllis Wordhouse of Plymouth, Mich., put four children through college on more than $80,000 in grants, work-study earnings and student loans. When the eldest of her four children graduated from high school, "we were living from paycheck to paycheck and were caught short like the typical American family," says Wordhouse.

But over the ten-plus years she and her husband, Jerry, have had children in school, Wordhouse has used aggressive aid-boosting strategies. When her oldest, Heidi, was in college, Wordhouse went back for her own master's degree. Having two family members in college halved the family contribution for each. Later, having two and in some years three children in college boosted aid. Starting a financial-planning business allowed Wordhouse to deduct business losses and expenses from income, which also increased aid.

Wonder, Wonder Who? •

Q. *Dear Dr. Tightwad: I'm a divorced parent with custody of my two children. The eldest will be a senior in high school this year, so I'll have to apply for student aid. I have remarried, and I'd like to know whose income is going to count on the financial statement—mine, my new spouse's or my former spouse's?*

A. Possibly all three. The federal financial-aid form that's used by most public universities and colleges requests income and asset information on the custodial parents—you and your new spouse.

However, some private institutions may also seek information on the finances of absent parents. If the ex-spouse doesn't come through with financial assistance, that puts pressure on the custodial parents and the student to ante up more money.

But you do have some recourse. Decisions about financial aid are often subjective, so if you can prove that the other biological parent is out of the picture, a school may waive the requirement.

Twice she refinanced the family home, borrowing against the equity, and rolled the money into her business. That reduced the family's assets that could be tapped for college bills because there's an allowance for small-business assets. Today Wordhouse teaches courses in how to qualify for college aid.

You might as well spend the student's savings early so you'll qualify for more aid in later years.

Strategies for Increasing Your Eligibility

You can expect to file the critical financial-aid forms—the *Free Application for Federal Student Aid* and others, if required by prospective schools—after January 1 of your child's senior year in high school. But you have to start preparing for them a year in advance because the forms ask about your finances for the calendar year starting in January of a typical student's junior year in high school. Even without a business or several kids in school, you can increase aid eligibility.

Consult a financial planner or books such as *Don't Miss Out,* by Anna and Robert Leider (Octameron Associates; P.O. Box 2748, Alexandria, VA 22301) and *The Student Access Guide to Paying for College,* by Kalman Chany with Geoff Martz (Princeton Review). They offer an arsenal of strategies for reducing your estimated contribution. Some examples:

Spend your children's savings first.

We've already noted that 35% of your children's assets will be figured into your family contribution each year. So you might as well spend the student's savings early so you'll qualify for more aid in later years. If you anticipate significant aid, put last-minute savings in your own name.

Defer income.

After the student's assets and income, your income takes the next-largest hit. Realizing large capital gains before January of the student's junior year in high school or postponing them until after his or her junior year in college will keep that income out of the financial-aid picture. The same goes for bonuses and other lump sums if you have control over when you will receive them.

Shift assets.

The federal aid formula doesn't take certain assets into account, such as tax-deferred retirement plans, annuities, cash-value life insurance and (under new rules that take effect in 1993) home and farm equity. Moving savings into those "hidden" assets can boost federal aid.

But remember that parents' assets are the least heavily assessed by the federal formula, so asset-shifting strategies have the smallest payoff. Even more important, you should make such moves only if they make sense regardless of whether you'll get more aid. Annuities and other insurance products, for example, hit you with big up-front fees as well as penalties if you withdraw your money early. If you try to use them as a way of sheltering assets, you could end up worse off, because you've locked away money that you're going to need to pay the college bills.

How Much of Your Need Will Each School Meet?

Trying to hide assets on the federal financial-aid form can be futile anyway. Many schools, especially private ones, have their own forms that routinely ask about life insurance cash values, pension plans and other assets that the federal formula doesn't take into account. Ivy League schools tend to factor in your retirement assets, for example, and most private schools are likely to add in home and farm equity as a way of reducing the aid they're expected to give.

Some schools will meet 100% of your need (remember, that's the gap between your expected contribution and the total cost of the school), typically with a mixture of student loans and work-study programs first and then with grants, which don't have to be repaid. If your child has won an outside scholarship, the school will incorporate it into the package and probably substitute this money for grants, or perhaps for loans.

You should make asset-shifting moves only if they make sense regardless of whether you'll get more aid.

But as aid money becomes tight, fewer schools are making a 100% guarantee. A school's aid policy can affect your final cost as much as the federal formulas do. So when you're touring college campuses, make it a point to meet with financial-aid officers to get an idea of how one school's aid package might compare with others. Here's a brief list of questions to ask, as suggested by financial planner Bonnie Hepburn and authors Anna and Robert Leider (for a more complete list, see the box on page 229):

- **Do you meet 100% of financial need?** Schools that do will offer better aid packages than schools that leave a gap. As more students clamor for a limited pot of student aid, fewer schools are making a 100% guarantee.

- **What's included in the cost of attendance?** Some schools include books, commuting and transportation expenses, and even spending money in the total cost, so the aid package increases accordingly. Stanford University, for instance, includes cross-country commuting expenses for East Coast students.

- **What's your expected student contribution?** Regardless of the federal need analysis, some schools expect students to contribute a minimum amount toward costs, which you'll have to pay if your child can't.

- **How do you treat outside scholarships?** Some schools use them to reduce dollar-for-dollar any grants they would have offered, so you end up having to pay as much as you would have if your son or daughter hadn't received the scholarship. But a few schools, such as Georgetown and Middlebury, offer a better deal by allowing you to use them to reduce the required family contribution, at least in part. It's also smart to seek scholarships if you won't qualify for any aid or if you'll qualify only for loans.

Schools with large endowments have more money to give away than schools with less, so they can offer more generous grants. Harvard, Yale, Princeton, Stanford and the University of Texas are among the richest, with more than $2 billion each in endowments. You also may be offered a "preferential" aid package—one that replaces loans with grants, for example—if your child is especially desirable to the school, because of top academic performance or a special talent in music, science or athletics, for example. Consider applying to at least one school where your child is in the top 10% to 25% of the applicant pool.

In fact, as aid becomes tight some schools are giving a nod in admissions to students who require less aid, or none at all—yet another argument for starting a savings plan early.

Scouts for Scholarships

Is it smart to use a computerized service to help you find scholarships? Not always. You'll pay anywhere from $40 to $200 and you may end up with a list of awards with narrow eligibility or ones that your child has only a remote chance of winning. One search service that keeps its data current and its cost low is **College Aid Sources for Higher Education,** run by National College Services, in Gaithersburg, Md. (301-258-0717). The service, which normally costs $30, is available for $16 to anyone who purchases a helpful aid guide, *Need A Lift?* ($3 from the American Legion, P.O. Box 1050, Indianapolis, IN 46206).

To do it yourself, consult *The A's and B's of Academic Scholarships* (edited by Daphne A. Philos, Octameron Associates).

Don't Be Afraid to Bargain

Even after a school has told you in writing what kind of aid package you qualify for, don't accept it as the last word. Often you can bargain to get a better deal. "Once you have been accepted by two or three schools and received their financial-aid offers, negotiate with them," advises Johnson. "It's a competitive marketplace." He tells of one client whose son's first-choice school was Carnegie-Mellon, but who received an aid offer from Cornell that was $2,500 richer. When the father explained to a Carnegie-Mellon financial-aid officer that the extra money might be the deciding factor, Carnegie-Mellon matched it. Another client persuaded Brandeis to add $4,000 to a financial-aid package to match one that is offered by Amherst.

If you try this tactic, keep in mind that it works best when the two schools are almost equally matched in reputation and admission standards. You also have a better shot if your child is desirable to the school. Negotiate before you've accepted an offer of admission; you won't have much leverage afterward. If you're asked to accept an aid package or to send a deposit early, you can often get an extension, says Hepburn.

Your attempts to bargain won't always fall on receptive ears. But you can always ask an aid officer to reconsider your aid package if you feel there are extraordinary circumstances that the school hasn't taken into account. For example, federal formulas no longer reduce your contribution if you have high medical bills or if you send younger children to private elementary or secondary schools. But financial-aid officers can take those things into account at their discretion.

Creative Financing

• •

To ease the burden of college costs, many schools have come up with creative ways to pay the bill:

- **At Washington University** in St. Louis, you can choose to prepay four years of tuition and living expenses at the freshman rate, borrow from the university for ten years at a low, fixed interest rate or pay the tuition in monthly installments.

- **At St. Norbert College** in DePere, Wis., you can pay an extra $2,000 at the beginning of your child's freshman year to "buy" a guarantee that tuition and fees, currently around $11,000, will stay fixed for four years.

- **At Hartwick College** at Oneonta, N.Y., students who earn a B- or better average each year can convert part of a loan from the college to a grant.

- **At Antioch College** in Yellow Springs, Ohio, students who receive loans under a special middle-income family assistance program can have their debt forgiven if they stay to graduate from the school.

When You Need to Borrow: The Best Deals

Face it: Regardless of whether you qualify for aid, you're most likely going to have to come up with a chunk of cash to pay for college. And despite your noble intentions and best efforts, your savings may not measure up. If you end up having to borrow money, don't worry about finding lenders; you'll have plenty of opportunities to go hip-deep in debt.

The best deals are federal Perkins and Stafford loans. Your child's school of choice will determine whether you qualify and for how much. You generally arrange a Perkins loan through the school and a Stafford loan through a bank. Perkins loans currently carry a fixed rate of 5%; Stafford rates are variable, currently around 6.22%, but they have a 9% cap. In the case of a Perkins loan or a subsidized Stafford loan, your

Other Questions to Ask Financial-Aid Officers

Financial planner Bonnie Hepburn of Acton, Mass., and financial-aid authors Anna and Robert Leider recommend that you ask any prospective school's financial aid officer the following:

- **Does your admissions policy overlook the need for financial aid** or is the school more likely to accept a student whose parents can pay the entire bill?

- **What forms do you require** (*Financial Aid Form, Family Financial Statement,* etc.)?

- **Do you require that students apply for aid as freshmen to be considered for aid as upper-classmen?**

- **Do you set limits on how much you expect students to borrow each year?** Do the limits increase in the upperclass years?

- **Do you expect parents to borrow as part of the financial-aid package?** If so, do you offer low-cost loans?

- **Can we expect the same type of package each year,** assuming our child's academic performance is acceptable?

- **What if we have two kids in school at the same time for several years?** Will you halve the contribution you expect from us for each student?

- **Does your office help students find work-study jobs on campus** or do you expect students to line up their own employment?

- **Who can qualify for aid as an independent student,** for example, someone who is age 24 or older, a veteran, a ward of the court, an orphan, or a person who is responsible for a dependent other than a spouse?

- **Do you make adjustments in midyear,** for example, if I lose my job?

Borrowing against the equity in your home may be a better deal than taking out an unsubsidized government loan.

child won't owe any interest while in school and doesn't have to begin repaying the loan until after graduation.

Even if financial-aid formulas show that you can afford to pay the whole bill, you can still get an unsubsidized Stafford loan. The interest rate is the same and you can defer repayment, but your children will owe interest for the time they're in school.

Under Stafford loan limits, you can borrow up to $2,625 annually for freshmen, which gradually increases to $5,500 a year for seniors. If you need more than that, you can borrow up to the full cost of college through the government's PLUS program (Parent Loans for Undergraduate Students). PLUS loans have a variable interest rate that's currently around 6.64%, with a 10% cap and a 5% origination fee. You must begin repaying immediately.

In a low-interest-rate market like the one we've enjoyed over the last couple of years, borrowing against the equity in your home may be a better deal than taking out an unsubsidized government loan. Interest rates on home equity lines of credit, which typically are tied to the prime rate, have been competitive; lenders often promote the loans with few, if any, origination fees; and interest payments on up to $100,000 of debt are tax-deductible. On the downside, you won't get the benefit of the attractive rate caps on government loans, and you'll be using your house as collateral.

Life Insurance: Looking Out for Your Kids

Q. *Dear Dr. Tightwad: We just got a mail solicitation offering life insurance coverage for our children and touting it as a way to save for college. Should we buy it or not?*

A. Not. That goes for both the policy and the logic. The purpose of insurance is to protect your family in case of economic catastrophe, which is unlikely in the event of a child's death. It's a roundabout way of saving for college, since some of your money will be diverted to paying for insurance you don't need. Better to use a more direct route with a regular saving or investing plan (for ideas see Chapters 6, 7 and 14).

Let's suppose you have taken to heart the advice in this book and have mapped out your strategy for raising kids who are both money-smart and money-wise. You take advantage of natural opportunities to discuss the financial facts of life with your children. You give your kids hands-on experience in managing money, either by giving them an allowance or paying them for work done around the house. You communicate clearly your own family values, even if it means just saying no. With your help your kids have opened their own bank accounts, and they even own a few shares of stock. For your part, you invest regularly in mutual funds to help

Americans hold 500 million life insurance policies—two for every U.S. resident—many of which are outdated, overpriced and just plain superfluous.

pay for their college education. In short, you've covered all the bases.

But what if suddenly you weren't around to coach your kids from the sidelines? With luck your spouse would be there to replace you, but would there be enough money to continue saving for college? And what would happen if both you and your spouse were to die before your kids were on their own? Who would take care of the children—and could you depend on them to pass along your own family's values?

Going into a lengthy discussion of insurance and estate planning is beyond the scope of this book. But we can give you some straightforward answers to questions that weigh on parents' minds, and, in the Dr. T tradition, leave you with practical ideas on how to buy peace of mind without breaking the bank.

And Baby Makes Three

There's nothing like the birth of a child to jolt you into facing your own mortality. Before you had kids, you probably didn't think much about life insurance, and may not have had any. When you were single, or even part of a two-income couple, chances are no one would have suffered a serious financial loss as a result of your death (unless you owned a house and depended on both incomes to pay the mortgage).

But then baby makes three, and that tiny bundle of joy is the three-thousand-pound gorilla that upsets your financial equilibrium. Suddenly you're faced with the prospect of saving for college, moving to bigger digs and buying life insurance. And if you resist bringing up the subject of insurance, rest assured that your brother-in-law the agent will do it for you. Because insurance is unpleasant to talk about and complicated to understand, there's a saying in the business that insurance is sold, not bought. So it's important to know when you're being sold a bill of goods.

The first thing to consider is how much coverage you need. It's an obvious question, but one that's obviously confusing to many Americans. Americans hold 500 million life insurance policies—two for every U.S. resident—many of which are outdated, overpriced and just plain superfluous. Yet the average insured household is covered for $130,000, which in many cases is inadequate. Every family's circumstances are unique, of course, but you can get a rough idea of how much you'd need by using one of several rules of thumb:

Replace your income.

By far the most conservative, this rule would have you buy that amount of life insurance which, when invested at a reasonable rate of return, would produce enough annual income to replace your salary. So, for example, if you make $30,000 a year and figure you can earn an investment yield of 5% a year fairly safely, you'd need $600,000 worth of insurance (and that's not even taking inflation into account).

But that's a worst-case estimate that probably overestimates how much you should buy. For one thing, there's nothing wrong with assuming that your heirs will dip into the principal, which would reduce the total coverage you need. Also, your spouse may have access to other income from a job, investments or social security survivors' benefits. (If a well-paid 45-year-old dies, a surviving widow or widower with two children under age 18 could collect as much as $2,162 a month from social security.)

Replace a portion of your income.

This rule assumes that you'd only have to replace your after-tax income, or anywhere from 50% to 75% of the total. Assuming you're shooting for two-thirds of your income, that would mean roughly $19,800 in the case of a $30,000 salary. At an interest rate of 5%, it would take $396,000 worth of insurance to produce $19,800 a year.

Buy insurance equal to around eight times your annual income.

You should include in the total any coverage you have through your employer. If you had group policies equal to twice your annual income, for example, you'd only have to buy insurance equal to six times your salary. Again using a $30,000 benchmark, the eight-times-income rule would mean $240,000 worth of insurance. (In the case of a two-earner couple, add both incomes together to figure total coverage, and then divide it proportionately between individual policies on each spouse. Even a stay-at-home parent needs coverage if the wage earner would have trouble paying for child care.)

In a more detailed version of this rule, the recommended amount of insurance varies with your income and age. Younger, less affluent families need proportionately more coverage, based on a multiple of their annual income, than older, more affluent

Roughing Out Your Life Insurance Needs

This table will help you estimate the coverage, expressed as multiples of annual salary, needed to replace 75% of your take-home pay until you (the insured) would have reached age 65. This doesn't take into account any income your survivors can expect from Social Security, investments, or other sources. Of course, more or less coverage may be needed, depending on individual family circumstances.

Annual Pay Before Taxes	Current Age of Person Insured						
	25	30	35	40	45	50	55
$20,000	14	13	12	10	9	7	6
30,000	14	13	12	10	9	7	5
40,000	13	12	11	10	9	7	5
60,000	12	12	11	9	8	6	5
80,000	12	11	10	9	8	6	4
100,000	11	10	9	8	7	5	4
150,000	10	10	9	8	7	5	4
200,000	9	9	8	7	6	5	5

Source: Principal Financial Group

parents. To see where you fit in, consult the accompanying table.

Keep in mind that your goal is to provide a fund that's large enough to pay off any death-related expenses and outstanding debts, as well as generate enough income for your family's daily living expenses and a college savings fund. To get a detailed look at how much that would be in your case, take the time to fill out the following work sheet.

Go With Term Insurance

Each of these rules of thumb comes up with a slightly different amount of coverage, but no matter how you figure it, it adds up to big bucks. So big, in fact, that when you get down to considering what kind of insurance to buy the answer may be obvious. In order to afford the amount of coverage you need, young families with children under 18 will have to go with low-cost term insurance.

Term insurance is pure insurance: You buy it for a certain period, or term, which is often one year but can also be five, 10 or 15 years. The policy doesn't build any cash value. At the end of the term, coverage expires and you have to renew the policy. With annual-renewable term (ART) you get the right to renew every year without a medical exam, but the rate will rise with your age.

With a five- or 10-year level-premium term policy, your premiums stay the same for the length of the policy, and although they start out higher than premiums for annual-renewable term, you'd actually end up paying less than you would for an ART policy over the entire period.

The catch is that to renew a level-premium policy you normally have to qualify all over again; if you're not in good health, you'll pay high rates as a "substandard" risk. So if you feel you'll need coverage for a long time, it's best to go with a longer-term level policy or keep an ART policy that's renewable to age 65 and beyond.

It's also a plus if the policy is convertible, meaning

In order to afford the amount of coverage you need, young families with children under 18 will have to go with low-cost term insurance.

continued on page 238

Looking at Your Needs in Detail

1. Annual family expenses $_____

2. Expenses avoided after your death
   (typically 20% to 30% of line 1)   _____

3. **After-tax income needed**
   (subtract line 2 from line 1)   _____

4. Spouse's after-tax income   _____

5. Social security benefits   _____

6. Other income available to survivors   _____

7. **After-tax income available**
   (add lines 4 through 6)   _____

8. **Survivors' income shortfall**
   (subtract line 7 from line 3)   _____

9. Multiplier from table at right   _____

10. **Capital needed to provide income**
    (multiply line 8 by line 9)   _____

11. Education fund (optional)   _____

12. Payoff of home mortgage and other
    debts (optional)   _____

13. Other cash needs   _____

14. **Total capital needed by survivors**
    (add lines 10 through 13)   _____

15. Your investments   _____

16. Other insurance on your life   _____

17. Other available assets   _____

18. **Total capital available**
    (add lines 15 through 17)   _____

19. **Insurance needed**
    (subtract line 18 from line 14) $_____

Factoring In Nest Egg Earnings

The amount of cash needed at the outset to meet your survivors' income needs depends on how the money will be invested and how long it needs to last. Invested conservatively, in certificates of deposit, for example, a nest egg might lose ground after taxes and inflation. That means your survivors will need more to start with. If you assume more aggressive investments, your insurance needs decline. The numbers in this table are based on what your survivors would keep—after taxes and inflation—assuming investment returns of 5% (conservative), 8% (moderate) and 10% (aggressive). When choosing a multiplier for line 9 of the work sheet, consider how the money is likely to be invested and how long it needs to last.

| Years Income Needed | Multiplier Based on Projected Investment Returns | | |
	Conservative	Moderate	Aggressive
10	10	10	9
20	22	18	17
30	35	26	23
40	48	33	28

Adapted from a work sheet developed by David Bohl, a senior tax manager at Arthur Andersen & Co. in Milwaukee. The accounting firm publishes two helpful booklets on buying life insurance, Life Insurance in Your Personal Financial Plan *and* Life Insurance: Answers to Questions You Should Ask. *Both are distributed free by Mass Mutual (800-872-2050).*

Besides being the most affordable insurance, term is also the simplest to understand and the easiest to shop for, by comparing the cost per $1,000 of coverage.

that it can be exchanged for a cash-value insurance policy without the need for a new medical exam if you decide you need or want permanent coverage (see the discussion on cash-value insurance below).

It's easy to get snookered when you're buying a complicated product such as life insurance, so simplicity is a virtue. And besides being the most affordable insurance, term is also the simplest to understand and the easiest to shop for, by comparing the cost per $1,000 of coverage. Assuming a cost of $1.08 per $1,000 of coverage for a 35-year-old male nonsmoker (not including a $60 policy fee—a competitive rate used as a benchmark by the National Insurance Consumer Organization) you'd have to pay $259 for $240,000 of coverage. For a nonsmoking woman of the same age the cost would be $1.02 per $1,000, or a total of $245.

But such a policy isn't very lucrative for the agent, so it's not the kind of coverage your brother-in-law the agent is likely to sell you. Chances are he'll push higher-cost, higher-commission cash-value insurance, such as whole life—so called because, unlike term, it remains in effect for your whole life with no increase in premiums. It builds up a cash value, based on how much you contribute and on dividends declared by the insurance company. Other variations of cash-value life insurance include universal life, which ties cash values to short-term market interest rates, and variable life, which offers you a choice of investments, including mutual funds.

Refuting the Arguments for Whole Life

Your brother-in-law will probably tell you that whole life is preferable to term because: (1) premiums remain the same from year to year; (2) the insurance stays in force until you die; (3) it's a form of forced savings, since you're not likely to forget to pay your premium; and (4) you get the benefit of tax deferral on the savings component of the policy. Each of these arguments can be true, but none is compelling. Let's look at them one by one.

Premiums remain the same from year to year.

True, but that means that in the early years of the policy you're paying a far higher premium than if you were buying term insurance. The excess goes toward building up the policy's cash value, but the premium can be so high that you simply can't afford the amount of coverage you need. For example, while that 35-year-old nonsmoking male could buy $240,000 worth of term coverage for $259 a year, a whole-life policy with the same death benefit could cost $2,775.

The insurance stays in force until you die.

True, but you may not need insurance for your whole life. The whole idea of insurance is to protect your family from financial disaster in case of your premature death. As your children get older the amount of coverage you need will diminish, and once they're on their own it could disappear entirely.

If you wanted to maintain a small amount of coverage, you could continue to qualify for annual renewable term insurance until around age 65 or sometimes 70. Premiums would rise with your age, of course, but since you'd be buying less coverage, you could hold down the cost. At $1.08 per $1,000, a $240,000 policy at age 35 would cost $259 for a nonsmoking male. At age 55, with a rate of $3.42 per $1,000, a $100,000 policy would cost $342. At age 65, a $50,000 policy would cost about $428. (Comparable rates for a woman would be $1.02 per $1,000 at age 35, $2.85 at age 55 and $7.08 for a $50,000 policy at age 65.)

It's a form of forced saving.

True, but it's a costly one. If you really need that kind of discipline, you can always arrange for your bank to automatically transfer money from your checking to your savings account each month, or to make automatic monthly contributions to a mutual fund. Insurance policies often carry such high up-front commissions and expenses (not to mention additional fees if you surrender—that is, cash in—the policy early) that it can

As your children get older the amount of coverage you need will diminish, and once they're on their own it could disappear entirely.

take at least ten years, and more likely 20 years, for your policy to start building any significant cash value. Yet half of all people who buy life insurance policies surrender or change them within ten years, and only 10% of all policyholders keep the same policy for 20 years.

Shopping by Phone

• •

If we've convinced you that term insurance is the way to go, you can get price quotes on policies over the phone from several services that offer competitive rates:

- **InsuranceQuote** (800-972-1104) and **SelectQuote** (800-343-1985) sell policies by mail and offer free, no-obligation quotes.

- **Quotesmith** (800-556-9393) gives free quotes from its data base of policies sold by independent agents.

- **Insurance Information Inc.** (800-472-5800) charges $50 to find you the lowest-cost policies but refunds the fee if it can't save at least $50 on a current policy.

Savings build-up is tax-deferred.

True, you won't have to pay tax on interest or dividends that you earn unless you cash in the policy. But you can get an even better tax break on other savings vehicles, such as a tax-deductible IRA or a 401(k) or 403(b) retirement plan, because your contributions are deductible from income as well.

If you are eligible for any of those plans, you should fund them to the max before you load up on insurance, and not just because of the tax benefits. As important as insurance coverage is, it's just one of many obligations competing for your dollars; retirement saving is another. The odds are that you won't die before you retire, so it makes no sense to provide for lots of life insurance if by doing so you won't have enough to live on in retirement.

If Cash Value Still Has Appeal

After due consideration, you may still find that, for one reason or another, you prefer some form of cash-value policy or a combination of term and cash-value. Maybe you aren't eligible for a tax-deductible IRA or don't have access to a 401(k) plan. Maybe you feel you need permanent coverage that will last till your death, and the cost of term insurance is becoming too steep. Maybe you want the option of cashing in the policy while you live. Or maybe you're convinced that the discipline of paying premiums is the only thing that will get you to save.

All this assumes that you can afford cash-value insurance and are knowledgeable about what you're buying—a big assumption given the complexities of these policies. You'll first have to decide whether you want to go with whole or universal life—in which case the insurance company decides how to invest your savings, usually in conservative investments like bonds and real estate—or take a chance with variable life, which lets you call the shots, usually from a group of mutual funds. Then you have to choose an insurer based on its financial soundness, its investing track record and the cost of the policy.

The odds are that you won't die before you retire, so it makes no sense to provide for lots of life insurance if by doing so you won't have enough to live on in retirement.

Smart Ways to Shop

Figuring all this out just by looking at a policy illustration is just about impossible:

Look at safety.
To get information on a company's financial health, you should look up its ratings with at least two agencies that rate insurers for safety (see the following box).

Look at results.
To check on a company's investment performance, you can go to a couple of sources:

- *Best's Review* conducts an annual survey comparing how insurers' projected whole-life dividends compared with actual performance over time. Your agent should be able to provide copies of these studies, or check a local library for copies of *Best's Review*.

- *Morningstar's Variable Annuity/Life Performance Report* tracks the performance of variable-life policies' underlying mutual funds. It's also available at libraries or from Morningstar (800-876-5005) for $15.

Keep your costs down.

If you're still set on a cash-value policy, chances are that buying it from your brother-in-law won't be the best deal. To ensure the quickest build-up of cash value, you want a policy with low up-front commissions and other costs.

- **Your best bet may be to buy a policy from a direct marketer,** such as USAA (800-531-8000) and Ameritas (800-552-3553). With either company you won't pay a commission or a consulting fee, but you'll have to know what kind of policy and how much coverage you want because you won't get much guidance.

- **Another option is to buy a so-called low-load policy,** which is sold through fee-only financial planners and

The Insurance Ratings Maze

How much stock can you put in insurance-company safety ratings if the same firm is rated A++ by one agency and B- by another? The key to your peace of mind is knowing the scoring systems used by the various agencies when assessing the financial health of insurers. Here's the range of scores handed out by each rating company to its top-ranked insurers. You should check at least two agency ratings. They're available from agents or directly from the rating agencies at the phone numbers listed.

Company	Top Ratings	Phone Number
A.M. Best	A++, A+	900-555-2378, $2.95 per minute*
Duff & Phelps	AAA, AA+	312-629-3833
Moody's	Aaa, Aal, Aa2	212-553-0377
Standard & Poor's	AAA, AA+	212-208-1527
Weiss Research	A+, A, A-, B+, B, B-	800-289-9222, $15 per rating

*First call 908-439-2200, ext. 5742, for the insurer's ID number.

insurance advisers (see the following box). These policies build cash value faster because nearly all of your premium starts working for you immediately. To see the difference, let's look at high-load and low-load universal life policies sold by John Alden Life. Assume a 40-year-old man buys $250,000 of coverage and pays $3,200 a year in premiums. Assuming a 7% interest rate, the high-load policy has a surrender value of zero after the first year and $10,482 after the fifth, while the low-load policy's first-year surrender value is $2,487 and its fifth-year value is $16,681.

Shop around.

If after all this you're still inclined to listen to your brother-in-law's sales pitch, at least listen to a couple of other agents as well. Maybe even ask them to evaluate each other's product. "You'll know in the first 15 minutes whether you like the person," says Stephan Leimberg, a lawyer and professor of taxation and estate planning at the American College in Bryn Mawr, Pa. "If the agent starts telling you what policy you should have, cross that person off your list. If the agent spends time asking you questions, keep listening."

Remember your purpose.

We can't repeat often enough that the main purpose of life insurance is to provide adequate protection for your family if either spouse isn't there. If you only have a limited amount of dollars to spend—and who doesn't—buy the most coverage you can afford to fit your needs. Don't decrease the amount of coverage and jeopardize your family's financial security just to buy a fancier policy that's more expensive.

Insurance You Don't Need

When you're parceling out your insurance dollars, there's no point in spending any on coverage for your kids. Unless your child is a budding Macaulay

If you're still inclined to listen to your brother-in-law's sales pitch, at least listen to a couple of other agents as well.

Culkin, your family probably won't suffer financially in the unlikely event of a child's death. If such a tragedy did occur, it's better to plan on paying for any final expenses out of your emergency fund or other savings.

It isn't necessary to buy life insurance for your children just to make sure they will be insurable as adults. Most child-size policies are too small for grown-ups, and when your children need the coverage, chances are they'll qualify on their own.

Student Accident Insurance

Your kids probably bring home the form every year when school starts. The coverage isn't very expensive, but it's not very valuable, either. You don't need it as long as you already have a comprehensive family health insurance policy.

Most student policies only cover accidents that occur while your children are at school, and many kick in only after your family coverage has paid for a claim. If your family plan has a large deductible or large co-payments, you could recover some of your out-of-pocket expenses. But student plans often have strict limits on how much they'll pay for each service.

Some student plans do offer primary coverage, meaning they'll pay regardless of your other insurance. But payment limits can be as low as $100 per claim—

Advice for a Fee

• •

Nine insurers sell low-load products through **Fee-for-Service** (800-874-5662), a network of fee-only insurance advisers. You pay a consulting fee of $125 to $150 per hour for an adviser to evaluate your insurance needs and shop the market for you.

Another group of fee-only advisers is the **Life Insurance Advisers Association** (800-521-4578).

Among the highly rated, low-load life insurance companies that you might consider are the following:

- **Ameritas** Life Insurance Corp. (800-552-3553).
- **Commonwealth** Life Insurance Co. (owned by Capital Holding; 502-587-7371).
- **People's Security** Life Insurance Co. (owned by Capital Holding; 800-444-5431).
- **Great West Life and Annuity** (800-688-4952).
- **John Alden** Life Insurance Co. (800-327-7771).
- **Lincoln Benefit** Life Co. (800-525-9287).
- **Security Benefit** Life Insurance Co. (800-888-2461).
- **Southland** Life Insurance Co. (404-980-5100).
- **USAA** Life Insurance Co. (800-531-8000).

not much if you're paying a premium of $65. And your family policy will reduce its benefits accordingly, so you'll never collect more than your actual expenses. Further, the $25,000 payment ceiling on most student policies is too low to cover the cost of catastrophic injuries to athletes.

For some parents, any kind of insurance brings peace of mind. "If one of my children were to die, the money could help me get through a time when I might not be emotionally capable of working," says one. It's true that the cost isn't high and there are worse ways to spend your money. But there are better ways, too—notably, insuring the family bread-winners in the event of their death or disability.

Give It the Once-Over

Before you plunk down your money on any policy, the **National Insurance Consumer Organization** will evaluate the proposal for you. The service costs $40 for the first policy, plus $30 for each additional policy sent in at the same time. Send copies of the projection sheet and a self-addressed stamped envelope to NICO, P.O. Box 15492, Alexandria, VA 22309.

Insurance You Probably Need More Of

In a Gallup poll, Americans estimated they had a 16% chance of being disabled for three months or more during their working lives. In fact, the chances are 43% for men and 54% for women, according to Unum Corp., the insurance firm. Between the ages of 35 and 65, your chances of becoming disabled are about equal to your chances of dying. Yet far fewer people have disability insurance than life insurance, and many of those who do are underinsured.

Don't assume that you have disability insurance through your employer. Fewer than half of all large employers and less than 20% of small employers provide long-term disability insurance, and to save money many employers are cutting back on the length of coverage. A policy might pay benefits to age 65 if you're disabled by an accident, but pay for only three years if you're the victim of an illness.

And don't assume that you'll get disability benefits from social security. Eligibility requirements are strict, and even if you qualify, government benefits may offset private benefits to limit total coverage.

To protect yourself and your family adequately, you should have enough coverage to replace about two-thirds of your income in case of disability (you won't have to replace that part of your salary that goes to taxes and work-related expenses). Check with your employer to find out the extent of your coverage.

Remember that benefits you receive from a policy that is paid for by your employer or that you purchase with pretax dollars through a "cafeteria" plan are fully taxable. So if your employer's policy will replace 65% of your income, you'll actually get less than that after taxes. But if you buy a policy yourself, the benefits are tax-free. You're effectively boosting your income-replacement level: 65% of income replaced tax-free may actually equal 90% of taxable income.

Disability coverage doesn't come cheap. A policy can easily cost $1,500 or more a year. One way to cut costs is to extend the waiting period before benefits begin. A 30-day elimination period is very expensive; a 90-day waiting period is a better buy, but you'll save even more if you go 180 days or longer. As an example, consider an individual policy for a 45-year-old non-smoking professional man with a $3,000-a-month benefit to age 65 and a 90-day waiting period. Such a policy from one insurance company would cost about $2,060 a year; an identical policy with a 180-day period would cost about $1,690, or $370 less.

Other Important Questions

Deciding how much coverage you need and choosing a policy is only the beginning. Setting up the policy and keeping tabs on it afterward are just as critical.

Most parents, for example, would be inclined to name their spouse and children as beneficiaries (or, in the case of a single parent, the children alone). But insurance companies won't pay large amounts of money directly to minor children. At your kids' expense, the court would have to appoint a custodian to handle the money on their behalf until they reached 18 or 21, when they'd get the money.

A better alternative would be to set up a trust for your children in your will, and name that as the beneficiary of your insurance (for more on wills and trusts, see Chapter 16). A trust would also give you more control over when your children would get access to the money and how it should be spent in the meantime.

If you bought insurance when your first child was born, did you remember to add subsequent children to the policy as beneficiaries? If your spouse was named as the primary beneficiary and you're now divorced, did you remember to change the policy in favor of your children? Because it's easy to forget little things like these, Stephan Leimberg recommends that you check your policies at least every three years to make sure that they're in order and that the beneficiaries you named are still appropriate.

While you're at it, consider whether you want your life insurance proceeds to go equally to all your children. If one of them has special needs, for example, or if younger ones still have college ahead while the oldest are out on their own, you may want to divide the proceeds less equally, but more equitably.

More Money Trivia

- What movie did Clint Eastwood star in as a gunfighter caught between two feuding Mexican families?

- What was the name of the Rodney Dangerfield movie in which his mother-in-law was willing to leave him money to straighten out his life?

- What famous female singer sang "Money Changes Everything"?

- Who sang "Baby Hold On"?

Answers

In order: *The Color of Money;* the Beatles; *How to Marry a Millionaire; Miss Moneypenny; The Six Million Dollar Man; Other People's Money; Cabaret; A Fistful of Dollars; Easy Money;* Cyndi Lauper; Eddie Money.

Making a Will: Taking Care If You're Not There

Q. *Dear Dr. Tightwad: My wife's sister has agreed to take care of our children in case my wife and I die. We've named the kids as beneficiaries of our life insurance policies, and they'll inherit everything else we have. Do we still need to go to the trouble and expense of making a will?*

A. You bet your life. Without one, you can't count on any of your other arrangements actually being carried out. Your sister may not be named as guardian. Though your children will get the insurance proceeds or inherit your other property, the process may be more complicated than you would have wished. And you won't have any control over how they spend their inheritance. Get thee to a lawyer as soon as possible (or get thee a do-it-yourself willmaking guide).

Many families apparently feel that estate planning is the province of the wealthy; three in four adults under age 45 don't even have a will. But if you have children, that's wealth enough to justify specifying how your family's finances should be handled in your absence.

Finances aside and even more important, the court will decide who is going to take over as guardian of your kids if you, as a single parent, or if both you and your spouse die before your children are grown. Any wishes that you've expressed informally to friends or family members may be taken into consideration, but there's no guarantee.

As we saw in the previous chapter, naming your kids as beneficiaries can backfire if they were to inherit while they were still minors. Without a will, you're setting up your children for court intervention in the handling of the property that could result in depleted assets. They deserve better, and it only takes a little planning to give it to them.

The biggest disaster is a court-supervised guardianship.

The Guardianship Issue

Suppose you feel that your sister would be the ideal guardian for your children, but your husband's brother thinks he'd be an even better one. In the absence of a will naming one or the other, both could make a claim and a nasty court fight could ensue. The cost of the battle would come out of your estate—that is, your kids' pockets.

Whoever won would probably have to remain under the court's supervision, a cumbersome procedure under which the guardian has to report how he or she is managing your children's property. Then, when the kids reached the age of majority, they'd be entitled to their inheritance outright, regardless of whether they were capable of handling it. "The biggest disaster is a court-supervised guardianship," says Rodney Owens, an estate-planning lawyer in Dallas.

What to Do

Avoid the hassles by naming a guardian in your will. You should choose as the so-called "guardian of the person" someone who shares your family values and your philosophy of child-rearing, as well as your religion, if it's important to you that your children be raised in the same faith. Because a minor can't own much property without supervision—not more than $5,000 in some states—you should also name a "guardian of the property," who would manage your children's assets. Often this may be the same person you chose as the guardian of the person, although you can choose someone else with more financial acumen. A divorced parent is sometimes more inclined to choose a separate property guardian because the ex-spouse typically gets custody.

In addition to your will, don't be shy about leaving a letter or tape on which you give detailed instructions about how you want your children to be reared. One mother and father whose children would be financially well off in the event of their death have nevertheless left a letter telling the guardian they'd like their kids to get summer jobs when they're teenagers and save half the money they earn for college.

In their letter these parents have also stipulated that their children's money can be shared with the guardian's children for something like a big family trip to Europe, "so as not to set up an 'us and them' situation with the rich orphans moving in." Instructions left in letters or tapes usually aren't legally binding, but they can be an invaluable guide to the guardian and give you a lasting voice in your children's upbringing.

Before you choose any guardians, discuss with the candidates whether they'd be willing to fill the role. And name a back-up, or even two back-ups, recommends Stephan Leimberg, professor of estate planning and taxation at the American College in Bryn Mawr, Pa. If your children are old enough, ask them for their opinion on your choices. "Some of my clients have 7- and 8-year-olds with some keen observations," says Don Silver, a Los Angeles lawyer and author of *A Parent's Guide to Wills & Trusts* (Adams-Hall Publishing). "Don't overlook the valuable resource of your children's wisdom."

Don't make the mistake of thinking that trusts are only for rich people.

Put Your Faith in Trusts

Naming guardians of the person and property is a great beginning, but if your minor children inherit assets outright, even the property guardian will still be subject to court supervision until the kids reach 18 or 21.

In many states the guardian must report to the court each year how every penny of income was spent and must get the court's permission to spend principal. Some states require that money left to children be invested only in government-insured bank accounts, which may not be the best selections for a college fund. Other states require a guardian to post bond.

What to Do

Avoid *these* hassles by setting up a trust to be the beneficiary of any property you leave to your kids, including the proceeds of life insurance policies. Don't make the mistake of thinking that trusts are only for rich people (defined as someone other than yourself). If you have only $100,000 in life insurance, and we saw in the last chapter that you probably need a lot more than that, your kids could come into quite a chunk of money—enough to justify paying anywhere from $200 to $1,500 to execute a will with a trust (the more complicated the trust the higher the fee).

The simplest and least expensive option, and one

You can choose the trustee and leave detailed instructions about how you want him or her to invest, spend and eventually distribute the money to your children.

that's appropriate for small estates, is probably a testamentary trust—one that's set up within your will and takes effect only after your death.

Another option is a revocable living trust, which you manage while you're alive. You can easily name such a trust as the beneficiary of your life insurance policy to avoid the problem of minors as contingent beneficiaries. (Some insurance companies may resist naming a testamentary trust as beneficiary because it can lead to problems if the will is challenged.) In addition, the insurance proceeds will be kept out of your estate for probate purposes.

If your estate is large enough that estate taxes may be due—over $600,000 on the federal level (although this may change with the new tax law)—an irrevocable life insurance trust can keep the insurance proceeds out of your taxable estate as well.

Calling the Shots

Whatever its form, a trust can help you accomplish several goals. It can specify:

How you want the money spent

A trust avoids court supervision and lets you call the shots. You can choose the trustee (who may also be the guardian) and leave detailed instructions about how you want him or her to invest, spend and eventually distribute the money to your children. Or you could give the trustee discretion to spend the money as needed to provide for the health, education and support of your kids. You could divide the money into equal shares, or create what's called a "family pot" trust, in which all the money is pooled together so that the trustee can provide for a child with special needs or make sure that each child finishes college.

It's possible that, because of their inheritance, your children could be wealthier than the guardian's own family. If that's the case, you can head off any resentment by stipulating that some of the money could be used for the guardian's own children—for education or travel, for example. It's often recommended that you allow the guardian to use a portion of the money to add an extra room, if necessary, or cover some other special need.

When and how you want the remaining money distributed

Instead of giving your children a lump sum at age 18, you could direct that they get their inheritance in installments. One common arrangement is to begin giving the child income from the trust at age 21 and then distribute the principal in three installments: one-third at age 25, one-third at age 30 and one-third at 35. "The idea is that he won't get so much that he'll squander his life away in anticipation of it," says Martin Shenkman, a lawyer in Teaneck, N.J., and author of *The Estate Planning Guide* (John Wiley and Sons).

If you were kindly disposed, you could let your children have access to their money at any time for educational expenses or to buy a house or start a business. On the other hand, you could tie lots of strings to it. One mother and father, who had little faith in the thriftiness of their grown children, arranged their trust as a retirement plan: The money was to grow untouched until the children reached age 60, when they would start receiving 10% a year. With a trust you're practically limited only by your imagination.

You can also make sure that your kids eventually get the money they have coming to them by setting up a trust for your spouse. That way, if you died and your spouse inherited, the property would remain in the trust, and in the family, instead of passing out of your control if your spouse were to remarry.

Provide tax advantages if you need them

Once your estate passes the $600,000 mark, federal estate taxes figure into the equation. That may sound

You could let your children have access to their money at any time for educational expenses or to buy a house or start a business.

Some parents are tempted to avoid the bother and expense of setting up a trust by leaving their money directly to a trusted relative. That strategy is fraught with risk.

like a lot, but once you add up insurance proceeds, home equity, pension plans and other assets, it can be within shouting distance. If young parents think their net worth will increase to this level, they should use trusts, perhaps an irrevocable life insurance trust that would keep insurance proceeds out of their taxable estate.

The "Poor Man's Trust"

If your estate will be a small one and you don't want to go to the expense of setting up a trust, you could instead set up a custodial account under the Uniform Transfers to Minors Act (UTMA), which applies in 42 states. It's a simple procedure that lets you name the custodian (who holds the property for your children) as the beneficiary or contingent beneficiary of life insurance or a pension. Under UTMA, you can also name a custodian of other property you leave to your children in your will.

Remember, though, that even under UTMA your kids are entitled to their property when they reach the age designated by your state's UTMA for the end of the custodianship, generally either 18 or 21 (and, in some cases, up to 25 in California). A UTMA strategy makes sense for small estates—under $25,000 or so in states that require children to inherit at age 18, or up to the anticipated cost of your children's college education in states that allow custodianships to last until age 21 or 25.

Appropriate Caution

In non-UTMA states, setting up a trust is still a better option. Otherwise, your property guardian could be tangled in court-supervisory red tape.

It may not be perfect, but even a custodial arrangement under UTMA is better than a Rube Goldberg approach to estate planning. Some parents are tempted to avoid the bother and expense of setting up a trust by leaving their money directly to a trusted relative, usually the guardian, with instructions to use it to care for the children and give them what's left over when they reach a certain age. That strategy is fraught with risk.

If you're lucky, it could work out all right if there's no more in the estate than the guardian is likely to need in raising the children. But it could also backfire, especially if college funds are involved. That money legally belongs to the guardian, and someone else could lay claim to those assets if the guardian were sued, went into debt, got divorced or died. And if a large amount is left to distribute to your children as adults, the guardian could get hit with gift taxes (or his or her heirs with estate taxes) because, technically, the guardian is giving away his or her money.

Don't take chances. Follow the strategies outlined in this chapter.

Special Issues for Single Parents

In cases of divorce, it's likely that the court would name your ex-spouse as guardian of the children. So if you prefer that someone else be the guardian, you need to name that person in your will.

In a letter or affidavit that should accompany your will and be given to your chosen guardian, you must make a strong case for why your ex-spouse is unfit. Even so, the court's inclination will be to give custody to the surviving parent, so you should state in your will that, if necessary, assets from your estate can be used to challenge the court's decision. It also becomes more important for you to choose a property guardian if you prefer that your ex-spouse not fill that role.

Single parents who remarry face another ticklish problem: Who should inherit their estate? They may want to take care of both their new spouse and their children from the prior marriage. Many parents face this issue even before an estate exists by distributing their assets to adult children while they, the parents, are

If you prefer that someone else besides your ex-spouse be the guardian, you need to name that person in your will.

QTIP trusts are an attractive way to ensure that children from a previous marriage or other beneficiaries will receive a portion of the estate.

alive. Others write prenuptial agreements and set up accompanying trusts outlining how their assets should be distributed after their death.

Trusty Solutions

With the help of a lawyer, you can set up a trust that can equitably and creatively provide for surviving spouses and children from each marriage.

- **For example, with a so-called QTIP trust** (short for qualified terminable interest property), income from the trust and even a portion of the principal go to the surviving spouse. Upon his or her death, the assets are distributed to whomever the maker of the trust, designates—possibly children from a previous marriage.

- **You can also set up a life-insurance trust** as a way of channeling assets to specific individuals. For example, you might set up a life-insurance trust for a child from a previous marriage and, through the trust, pay the premiums as a gift. Proceeds from the policy would be the child's legacy, and you could leave the rest of your estate to your current spouse or other beneficiaries.

A Final Checklist

Whatever arrangements you make in your will, make sure they're in sync with the beneficiary designations on your life insurance and pension. Presuming you've taken the trouble to set up a trust, take care to name the trust as the beneficiary. That sounds obvious, yet "people don't remember how they hold title to property or make beneficiary designations," says Don Silver, and those designations generally override a will or trust. If you set up a trust in your will but neglect to name it as beneficiary, you'd end up with both a court-supervised guardianship and a trust, each with its own expenses.

Also take care to name an appropriate executor—one who has the time, inclination, competence and trustworthiness to take on the job. (In keeping with Leimberg's rule of two, name two back-up executors and trustees.) Watch out for conflicts of interest. If, for example, you were to name your business partner as your executor, she would be legally obliged to dispose of your assets, including your share of the business, and to get the best (highest) price for them. At the same time, as your business partner, she would want to buy up your share of the business at the lowest possible price.

Review your will each time you have a child. Review your will if you divorce, remarry or move to a new state. Review your will in the event that someone named in it (whether beneficiary, trustee or executor) dies, divorces or remarries.

In fact, Leimberg recommends an annual "financial fire drill," in which you sit down with your spouse and review what would happen if either or both of you were to die or become disabled. Is your insurance adequate? Are you satisfied with your will? Does each of you (and your executor) know where all the pertinent

Do It Yourself?

Don't let fear of high legal fees keep you from looking out for your children's welfare. A do-it-yourself book or software program may be an inexpensive alternative. To help you set up wills, Nolo Press publishes *Nolo's Simple Will Book* and *WillMaker 5.0* software for IBM-compatible and Macintosh computers.

Don't expect these to handle anything complicated, however. With *Nolo's Simple Will Book,* for instance, you can create a testamentary trust that splits your assets evenly among your children, but you can't set up a pooled trust that allows the trustee to allocate as much money as needed to a child with medical problems or other special needs.

Other resources for planning your estate include:

- *Getting It All Together* software (IBM compatibles only; $79.95, plus $5 for shipping; ChetTrax Data Systems, 125 East Roland Road, Brookhaven, PA 19015; 215-874-7648), which will organize your important papers including mortgage, insurance and beneficiary information.

- *How to Settle an Estate,* by Charles K. Plotnick and Stephan R. Leimberg ($18.95; Consumer Reports Books; 914-378-2000), a manual for executors and trustees.

papers are? Leimberg suggests that they be kept in a safe-deposit box rather than with your attorney, so that your executor doesn't have to pay a visit to the lawyer and perhaps feel obligated to use him or her.

Most important, though, is to get the will made as soon as possible after your child is born (and you're getting enough sleep to think straight), or perhaps even during pregnancy if you're not superstitious.

They're Back!

Just When You Thought It Was Safe to Relax

Q. *Dear Dr. Tightwad: We thought we were finished worrying about kids and money when our children graduated from college. But now one is in grad school and one is looking for a job, and they're both back home eating our food, talking on our telephone and watching our cable TV. Should we charge them rent or toss them out?*

A. Charge them rent, *then* toss them out. But read this chapter first, and you'll feel better about doing both.

It's a scene that every parent anticipates with either exhilaration or dread: the day you bid a tearful farewell to your last child as he or she starts college. While you return to an empty nest, the kids are spreading their wings.

But what happens if, after graduation, your offspring get grounded by a soft job market and land back on your doorstep?

Your chances of finding yourself with one or more "boomerang kids" on your hands are better than you think. About 40% of young adults who leave home return at least once. All told, 51% of never-married adults between the ages of 20 and 29 live with their parents. That means a lot of newly decorated guest rooms are being converted *back* into full-time bedrooms. Martha Farnsworth Riche, a demographer who has studied trends among young adults, says parents shouldn't expect to have an empty nest when their last

> *"Your parents want you out of the house. They really want you out of the house. They are worried about you, they love you, but, God, they want you out of the house."*
>
> Bill Cosby

child turns 18; age 24 is more like it.

A lot of young adults boomerang after college while waiting for a job to come through or attending graduate school. Some come back to regroup after a change in their lives—getting a divorce or losing a job, for example. A smaller number come back home to help care for an ailing parent. Many, however, come back because they feel they just aren't ready, or think they can't afford, to be on their own. If you follow the advice in this book, your young adults shouldn't feel shaky when they're standing on their own two feet. If you don't, and they do, it's time for a crash course in Life 101.

Where Does All the Money Go?

What really throws new grads a financial curve is the security deposit. And the homeowners insurance premium. And the cost of a professional wardrobe. And the dry-cleaning bill. And the price of a tube of toothpaste. When alumni are invited back to Bryant College in Smithfield, R.I., to give students a seminar in "The First Year on the Job," one hot topic is "Living on a Shoestring Budget." Even $25,000 a year may not be enough to cover rent and other expenses of living in an apartment in a big city.

For young adults savoring their independence, the first postgraduate assignment is to get a handle on their new expenses. As a rule of thumb, they should figure on spending 30% of their take-home pay for housing and 20% for food. Debt service on a car loan, credit card balances and student loans should consume no more than 20% to 30%, so there's room to put 5% to 10% in savings. That leaves 15% or so for insurance and miscellaneous cash expenses for such things as public transportation, gasoline and entertainment.

To get a more accurate picture of where their money is going, they should keep a written record of every expense, no matter how small, for at least a month or two (see the income and outgo work sheet on page 178). That's the kind of attention to detail that got Rick

Johnson back on track. Johnson worked his way through Portland State University, in Oregon, as a salesclerk. When he graduated and landed a full-time job paying $23,000 a year with a chain of drugstores, he thought his ship had come in. But the rent on his apartment, a block from the ocean in Laguna Beach, Cal., nearly sank him.

Johnson managed to get himself back on an even keel when his company transferred him to its Denver office, where he found the cost of living more manageable. He began a savings account earmarked for buying a house and started investing in stocks and contributing to his employer's 401(k) tax-deferred retirement plan. But the key to getting a grip on his cash flow was keeping a ledger listing his bills and when he paid them. Once he had that under control, he was able to keep a mental record of his ongoing expenditures and rarely exceeded his budget.

How to Deal With Banks and Credit

Automatic transfers are ideal for new grads who haven't gotten into the saving habit. All they have to do is ask their bank or credit union to make monthly transfers from their checking account to a savings account or money-market fund. Their first goal should be building an emergency fund that would cover their expenses for three to six months, so they should keep the money where they can get at it quickly. Money-market funds (explained in Chapter 7) usually pay a higher yield than bank money-market accounts or savings accounts, but they don't have the benefit of deposit insurance.

Checking Accounts

If your kids are starting a new job in a new town, opening a checking account can be tricky. Even if they're depositing a payroll check from a local employer, they'll probably have to wait several days before getting access to their money. To tide them over, they

If your children have federal loans that add up to $5,000 or more, they can ask their lender about consolidating them.

should come with cash in hand—a cashier's check, for example, or an automated teller machine card that gives them access to their account back home.

They can get a checking account that pays interest, but rates are so paltry that they're better off with an account that has low monthly fees and low minimum-balance requirements instead. For customers who don't write more than ten checks or so a month, a category your children are likely to fall into, most banks offer a "no-frills" account with a monthly fee of around $3 and no required minimum balance. (Note: Checks that come with carbon copies can make life easier for your kids at budget- and checkbook-balancing time.)

Credit

New grads probably have at least one credit card, so they should concentrate on paying off any balances before charging additional purchases. When Steve Grupe graduated from the University of Denver, he already owed $1,800 on his Visa card. By the time he got a job in the computer industry several months later, the balance had reached $2,100. Grupe decided that was "unmanageable" and began paying several hundred dollars a month to whittle it down.

For many recent grads, their biggest single debt is student loans. If your children have federal loans totaling $5,000 or more, they can ask their lender about consolidating them. That would lower their payments, either by increasing the length of time they have to repay or by keeping the same time schedule but letting them pay less at first and gradually increasing their payments. Either way, they'll pay a lot more in interest over the term of the loans, so your children should pursue this option only if they're really strapped.

Making a Home Sweet Home

In most big cities rental costs will be astronomical by your kids' standards, so they probably won't be rid of roommates just yet. When Ashley Tappan left Indiana University for a job at the Philadelphia Zoo, she couldn't afford to pay $500 a month for her own apartment. Instead, she paid $300 plus one-third of the utility costs to share a three-bedroom apartment in Cherry Hill, N.J., outside Philadelphia. Living with a well-chosen group has other advantages, as well. It can help your kids meet people in a new city, provide them with a measure of security, reduce what they might otherwise need to spend or accumulate to set up housekeeping, and give them access to such amenities as a swimming pool.

Your kids may also want to consider living in a group house, if that's an option in the areas they're considering. A group house combines economy with the advantages of living in a real house, including more space and such homey features as a porch or deck, yard, driveway, garden and pets. Group houses benefit if at least one housemate has some do-it-yourself ability, and it helps if everyone is willing to lend a hand with household projects and yard care.

Make sure the names of all roommates appear on the lease and on any other documents that have to be signed so that no one will be left holding the bag if there is a dispute. Divvying up the long-distance telephone bill each month can be a pain, but some long-distance carriers have come up with services that simplify the process. AT&T, for example, will give each roomie a two-digit code to punch in when dialing. Then calls will be tallied separately, and charges on the bill will be organized according to code (call 800-222-0400 to register; there is no fee for the service).

Leases

A one- or two-year lease is probably most economical; the shorter the period, the higher the rent for apartments and houses. In recent years, many big cities have been bulging with empty units, so there are deals to be had. Also check the newspaper classifieds; renting a few rooms in someone's house can be a real bargain.

A group house combines economy with the advantages of living in a real house.

Employer-matched savings plans are the easiest money your kids will ever make.

Insurance

Premiums for renters insurance will vary depending on the value of your kids' possessions and the location of their apartment. Expect a minimum policy that protects $4,000 worth of property and provides $100,000 in liability insurance to cost at least $100 a year. A policy that reimburses for the replacement cost of possessions instead of their current value is more expensive.

A Smart Start on the Job

Taxes

Chances are your new grads will be starting a job midyear or later. When they fill out their W-4 tax withholding form, they should ask their employer to use a special part-year method that computes tax based on actual earnings instead of a full year's wages. If their employer is willing to go along, it means more money in your kids' pockets.

Retirement or Savings Plans

It's never too soon to take advantage of these, especially since employer-matched savings plans are the easiest money your kids will ever make. They'll contribute a portion of their salary and their employer will match it, often 50 cents on the dollar but sometimes dollar for dollar. Even contributing as little as 1% of their pay is worth doing because of their employer's "free" money and the power of compounding. If they could manage a contribution of $1,250 a year (including the employer match) to a 401(k) or 403(b) tax-deferred retirement plan from age 21 to age 25, it would grow to almost $350,000 by the time they're 65, assuming an average annual return of 10%.

Health Insurance

One thing your children have going for them is their youth and good health, so it's sensible for them to get the least expensive insurance coverage their employer offers. Having an annual deductible as high as $1,000 or even $2,000—meaning they would have to pay that much themselves before their insurance kicked in—would lower monthly premiums considerably.

Coverage through a parent's health insurance policy generally ends when a child's dependency does—when he or she graduates or reaches the age stated in the policy, usually between 21 and 25. Under federal law, kids may be able to extend coverage under their parents' plan for up to 36 months. Once they have a job, they can probably pick up employer-sponsored group coverage.

If there's a gap between the time the parental policy lapses and their employer's coverage kicks in, your kids shouldn't tempt fate by going without any insurance. Some companies offer short-term policies aimed at people in their situation. Premiums for short-term major medical coverage range from $20 to $35 a month for a policy lasting 30 days and from $50 to $60 for 60-day plans. Coverage can usually be renewed for up to a year.

Life Insurance

Employers may provide some coverage as a benefit, but your kids shouldn't waste their money buying more. Unless a spouse, a child or a parent is dependent on their income, they don't need life insurance.

Don't Go Overboard on a Car

After four years of coaxing a clunker around campus, your kids may be tempted to make the car dealer one of their first postgraduation stops. Encourage them not to. They may have to ante up as much as 20% for a down payment, money they probably don't have. If the

Your kids shouldn't tempt fate by going without any health insurance.

clunker is really dying, at least encourage them to consider buying a used car instead.

Price Breaks

If they must go the new-car route, they should ask about price breaks and other incentives for recent college grads. In general, soon-to-be employed grads who can afford a car payment (as a certain percentage of their income) may be eligible for interest-rate reductions and special financing plans. Encourage them to shop smart using any of the car buying guides, such as *Consumer Reports* and *Kiplinger's New Car Buyer's Guide,* which appears annually. And when they shop for financing, steer them first to a bank or credit union to see what kind of loan terms they can work out. Then they can compare that deal with the car dealer's terms.

Unless your kids can make a strong case for themselves—in the form of a 50% down payment, for example—you'll probably be required to co-sign the loan. Remind your children that that doesn't take the heat off them. Co-signers often have their largess noted on their credit report, so if your kids stiff the lender it's a black mark against you.

"Son, you're all grown up now. You owe me two hundred and fourteen thousand dollars."

Car Insurance

As with health insurance, coverage on a parental auto-insurance policy ends when a child is no longer a dependent. Have your kids start with your agent when they shop around for their own policy. Premiums vary widely, depending on the driver's sex, the car's make and model, and the geographical area. As an example, a 23-year-old woman who drives a three-year-old Ford Taurus and lives and works in a suburb might pay $900 to $1,000 a year for $100,000 worth of liability coverage in Atlanta; men can expect to pay 30% to 50% more.

What If They Land on Your Doorstep?

In spite of your, and their, best efforts, your children may still end up back home. That isn't necessarily bad for either one of you. Young people today have many choices to investigate before settling into adult life, and their parents' house becomes a sort of home base. But parents often have more trouble adjusting to the homecoming than their children do. In their children's absence, they have gotten used to more freedom and less commotion. Studies show that half of all boomerangers stay for only six months or less, but for parents it can seem like a *long* six months.

What really appears to bother parents is the added financial responsibility. And nothing is as bothersome as the subject of room and board. For her book *Hey, Mom, I'm Home Again!* (Marlor Press), Monica Lauen O'Kane surveyed over 125 families with at least one adult child living at home. What surprised the parents was that their children didn't automatically offer to pay room and board. Of the children who were working full-time, about two-thirds were paying rent. And of that number, only about one-third were paying what it would cost to live in a comparable setting outside the home. The average contribution was $125 a month, with a range of $75 to $300.

Several fathers were particularly bitter about the situation. Said one, "Not asking for room and board was the biggest single mistake I have made with my five grown children, who freely move in and out" and also

Studies show that half of all boomerangers stay for only six months or less, but for parents it can seem like a long six months.

Problems of the past come home to roost with the child. Kids who had everything handed to them see no reason to pay room and board.

feel free to ask him for extra money when they run short of cash. Another dad resented that his children took him, and his money, for granted. "It's as if they feel they have a God-given right to my support," he said. A third father complained that his son didn't even acknowledge the financial support he had received, much less express gratitude for it. This dad suggested that parents save all receipts and canceled checks for education and other expenses so that they can prove how much financial assistance they have given.

It seems that problems of the past come home to roost with the child. Kids who had everything handed to them see no reason to pay room and board. Kids who never heard their parents discuss household expenses have no concept of mortgage payments or utility bills. O'Kane found that parents who are well off financially and don't need the money are least likely to ask for room and board, yet it's their children who most need to pay it. Otherwise, they get used to living a lifestyle that they can't afford.

How Much Should Your Kids Be Paying You?

Parents have come up with lots of creative ways to charge their kids for room and board:

The Token Amount

Ruth and Jim Santos of Larchmont, N.Y., at one point had both of their postgraduate children living at home while they were between jobs. They didn't charge the kids rent while they were looking for work but decided that once they were employed they'd have to make a nominal contribution for room and board of around 10% of their salaries.

You're not necessarily letting the kids off easy by not charging them a market rate. If they have come home because they're having trouble making ends meet, they probably can't afford it anyway. The money they pay is not so much rent as reimbursement for their share of the food and utility bills. Rather than a landlord-tenant relationship, it's more of a cost-sharing relationship among roommates. (FYI: The Internal Revenue Service doesn't require you to report such payments as rental income.)

The Sliding Scale

O'Kane herself has eight children, and anywhere from one to four of them at a time have lived at home as adults. When her first boomeranger came home, O'Kane agonized about the rent question and finally decided to charge her daughter $20 a week. When she broached the subject, her daughter was reluctant. "She was a file clerk at the time, and said she was barely making enough to buy gasoline and cigarettes," recalls O'Kane. But O'Kane persisted, then gradually increased the rent to $25 and kept on going. "When it got high enough," says O'Kane, "she figured she might as well move out and rent her own place."

Payment-in-Kind

When Pete Lombardo graduated from Indiana University, he decided to live at home in Libertyville, Ill., while he completed a management-training program. His mom agreed and immediately told him she'd expect him to pay rent. They settled on $150 a month. But Pete was also expected to treat his mom to an occasional dinner out, pick up extra groceries and help out around the house with heavy-duty chores such as painting and putting up storm windows (his mom did the laundry).

If you don't really need the money your children are contributing, O'Kane suggests that you save it and make a gift of it to them when they finally move out. Her survey showed that over half of the young adults living at home were already saving money on their own. In fact, if your kids are trying to save enough to rent their own apartment or buy a house, that would be one

One mother gradually increased the rent to $25 and kept on going until her daughter figured she might as well move out and rent her own place.

Adding an extra driver to the family policy more than likely won't affect your rates, but adding an extra vehicle will.

case in which you might consider not charging them for room and board (but there's still no reason why they couldn't lend a hand with household jobs).

Other Financial Matters

Health Insurance

As noted earlier, coverage under a parent's policy usually ends when the young adult stops being a full-time student or reaches the age stipulated in the policy. These conditions apply even if the child is living at home. So if your kids are unemployed, they'll need some kind of temporary coverage. Ruth and Jim Santos were willing to pay for their kids' health insurance premiums, on the theory that "if something tragic happens, we're the ones who would be footing the bill anyway."

Car Insurance

Unless your son or daughter already owns a car and has an insurance policy, it will probably be cheaper to add your child to the family policy than to arrange for separate coverage. Adding an extra driver to the family policy more than likely won't affect your rates, but adding an extra vehicle will.

Say your 25-year-old daughter, who has never had a ticket or an accident, bought a 1991 Ford Escort to commute to work. Putting her car on the family's State Farm policy would cost over $600 a year if you lived in Seattle and over $1,500 if you lived in Atlanta. If she didn't buy her own car and you simply added her to your policy, your premium wouldn't change.

Debts

What if your son or daughter lands on your doorstep with a pile of credit card debts? Resist the temptation to pay them off. Instead, parents should help their children come up with a practical solution, such as seeking credit counseling or legal assistance or developing a budget and sticking to it.

When it comes to parents giving money to their children, both parties must understand whether the money is a loan or a gift. If it's a loan, make it a business deal with a signed agreement. Softies like Dr. Tightwad might cut their kids a break on the interest rate. But always keep in mind the first rule of lending money to your children: Don't give them anything you can't afford not to get back.

Always keep in mind the first rule of lending money to your children: Don't give them anything you can't afford not to get back.

If your children have been laid off or are job-hunting, they may be able to defer payments on school loans. Borrowers can request deferments of up to one year for Stafford student loans if they are unemployed but actively searching for a job. Requests for deferments are more likely to be granted if the borrower hasn't fallen behind on the payments. Your kids should contact their lender for more information.

Telephone

Feel free to ask a talkative child to install and pay for a separate phone line. Nancy and Joseph Re of Springfield, Va., came up with a different solution. With two boomerangers and two teenagers living at home, "one of the hassles was figuring out who called California on August 30 for 45 minutes," says Joseph. They ended up giving each of the children a calling card billed to a separate account and made them responsible for paying their own phone bills.

Taxes

If your boomerang child has a job, it's unlikely that you can claim him or her as a dependent on your tax return. Although you may pay more than half of the child's support, another requirement for getting this tax break is that the child earn $2,300 or less during the year. (This figure can rise slightly each year to

If kids want to march to the beat of their own drummer, so do parents.

account for inflation.) An exception lets you claim someone under age 24 as a dependent, no matter how much he or she earns, if that person was a full-time student for at least five months of the year.

Setting the House Rules

Even if your children pay room and board, you're still paying the mortgage. And you have the right to set the rules (within reason). Sit down and discuss them with your children before they move in so that they can decide whether the arrangement is one they're willing to live with.

Lay Down the Law

Establish your own policy on whether smoking or overnight guests will be allowed. If the boomeranger is a single parent, everyone should be clear from the start about how the grandchildren will be disciplined and how much babysitting the grandparents will do.

Don't overlook minor irritants, such as loud music or crumbs on the kitchen counter. Floyd Brown, the father of two former boomerangers who are both now married, points out that if kids want to march to the beat of their own drummer, so do parents. "When you have them out of the house," says Brown, "you're used to having things cleaned and straightened."

Still, you have to recognize that your children are adults and there are limits to how far you can go in dictating their behavior. Phyllis Jackson Stegall, a Seattle psychotherapist and author of *Boomerang Kids: How to Live with Adult Children Who Return Home* (the book is out of print, but try your library), notes that at this point in all your lives "who the child's friends are or how he or she dresses is generally not the parent's concern." At the O'Kane household, for example, curfews were never a problem for boomerang children because the O'Kanes didn't impose any. If you're a chronic worrier who can't get to sleep until all the children are safe at home, one compromise might be to ask your kids to call when they're going to be late. Either that, says O'Kane, or "get a good book."

Giving your adult children advice is another ticklish area. The very fact that they've come home again could indicate that they need (and perhaps would even welcome) guidance from you about whether to go back to school, where to look for a job or how to save enough money to make it on their own. But while you have a right, and even a duty, to speak up, they don't have to listen. Instead of telling them what to do, offer them advice. Or, better still, give them several options (and keep your fingers crossed that they choose the right one).

Spell Out Responsibilities

It's important for young adults to understand what their role in the household will be. Are they expected to show up for dinner every night? Will they have to do their own laundry? What chores will be shared?

"Son, your mother and I have decided to let the free market take care of you."

When the Res had a total of six people living under their roof, each one, including the high-schooler, was assigned a night of the week on which to plan and cook dinner and to clean up afterward. "It turned into a fun thing," says Joseph Re. "The kids were very creative."

Make Sure It's Temporary

There is one area in which you're perfectly justified in issuing an ultimatum, and that's in setting a time limit on how long your children are allowed to stay. For

Hanging around too long isn't good for young adults either, because it simply postpones the inevitable day when they have to leave for good.

a young person out of work, the deadline might be three months with an option to renew; for a graduate student, a year or two might make more sense.

Not being firm enough on this point is one of the biggest mistakes parents can make. If your children's stay turns out to be open-ended, you're more likely to resent the drain on your financial resources or the interference with your plans. And hanging around too long isn't good for young adults either, because it simply postpones the inevitable day when they have to leave for good.

If you feel the job hunt is dragging on too long, or if your child seems to be settling back in the nest too comfortably, you may have to force the issue. The late Lee Salk, who was a clinical psychologist and author of many books on family-related issues, advised that if children aren't gone by the agreed-upon deadline, parents should "help them find a place to live, even if it's at a 'Y' and even if you have to pay for the room yourself. You have to make it sufficiently uncomfortable to motivate them to do something, without being cruel."

A Parting Word

With luck, you'll never have to resort to such drastic action. One reason you've taken the trouble to read this book is to make sure you don't. Giving your kids an allowance when they're 8 years old is no guarantee that they'll grow into mature, self-reliant adults. But money is such a powerful symbol that being able to manage it is seen as a good indication of being able to manage life.

That's probably because both require self-discipline, something that's tough to teach your kids in today's world of instant gratification. Yet money offers teaching opportunities that are unique and concrete— not just managing an allowance, but also distinguishing between needs and wants, saving for future purchases, juggling work with other responsibilities, resisting the temptations of TV advertising. In mastering these skills your kids are mastering life, which is, after all, an exercise in setting priorities, working toward goals and striking a balance.

No, money doesn't grow on trees. But if early on you can plant the seeds of good money management and watch your children blossom into responsible adults, you'll have reaped a priceless harvest.

KIPLINGER BOOKS

To order any Kiplinger product, call toll free, 1-800-727-7015 between 9:00 A.M. and 9:00 P.M. Eastern Time, or send your check to: Kiplinger Books and Tapes, P.O. Box 85193, Richmond, VA 23285-5193.

Please send me:

Books	Price		Quantity	Total
Kiplinger's Survive & Profit From A Mid-Career Change (paper)	$12.95	D		
Kiplinger's Buying and Selling a Home (paper)	$13.95	T		
Kiplinger's Facing 40 (hardcover)	$19.95	R		
Kiplinger's Taming the Paper Tiger (paper)	$11.95	M		
Kiplinger's Make Your Money Grow (paper)	$14.95	S		
Kiplinger's Invest Your Way to Wealth (hardcover)	$23.95	G		
Kiplinger's Working for Yourself (paper)	$14.95	N		
Kiplinger's 12 Steps to a Worry-Free Retirement (paper)	$14.95	U		
Kiplinger's Career Starter (paper)	$10.95	V		
Video Guides				
Money-Smart Women	$29.95	W		
Small Business Growth	$29.95	P		
Retirement Security	$29.95	I		
Personal Finance	$29.95	L		
Family Finances	$29.95	J		
Estate Planning	$29.95	Z		
			Subtotal	
			*Sales Tax	
			Shipping	$3.00
			Total	

DC, FL, MD and VA residents, please add sales tax.

For information on bulk rates or to order in bulk, call Dianne Olsufka at 202-887-6431.

❑ My check payable to Kiplinger Books is enclosed for $_____.

❑ Charge my: ❑ VISA ❑ MasterCard ❑ American Express ❑ Discover

Card No. ❑❑❑❑❑❑❑❑❑❑❑❑❑❑❑❑

Signature _____

Exp. Date _____ Daytime Phone (_____) _____

Name _____

Company _____

Address _____ Apt. No. _____

City _____ State _____ Zip _____